262/15.9.10

K

e Quan

Markets

Rose Quan

Outward Investment from Emerging Markets

Experiences of Chinese SME Managers

Lambert Academic Publishing

Impressum/Imprint (nur für Deutschland/ only for Germany)
Bibliografische Information der Deutschen Nationalbibliothek: Die Deutsche Nationalbibliothek
verzeichnet diese Publikation in der Deutschen Nationalbibliografie; detaillierte bibliografische
Daten sind im Internet über http://dnb.d-nb.de abrufbar.
Alle in diesem Buch genannten Marken und Produktnamen unterliegen warenzeichen-, marken-
oder patentrechtlichem Schutz bzw. sind Warenzeichen oder eingetragene Warenzeichen der
jeweiligen Inhaber. Die Wiedergabe von Marken, Produktnamen, Gebrauchsnamen,
Handelsnamen, Warenbezeichnungen u.s.w. in diesem Werk berechtigt auch ohne besondere
Kennzeichnung nicht zu der Annahme, dass solche Namen im Sinne der Warenzeichen- und
Markenschutzgesetzgebung als frei zu betrachten wären und daher von jedermann benutzt
werden dürften.

Verlag: Lambert Academic Publishing AG & Co. KG
Dudweiler Landstr. 99, 66123 Saarbrücken, Deutschland
Telefon +49 681 3720-310, Telefax +49 681 3720-3109, Email: info@lap-publishing.com

Herstellung in Deutschland:
Schaltungsdienst Lange o.H.G., Berlin
Books on Demand GmbH, Norderstedt
Reha GmbH, Saarbrücken
Amazon Distribution GmbH, Leipzig
ISBN: 978-3-8383-4014-2

Imprint (only for USA, GB)
Bibliographic information published by the Deutsche Nationalbibliothek: The Deutsche
Nationalbibliothek lists this publication in the Deutsche Nationalbibliografie; detailed
bibliographic data are available in the Internet at http://dnb.d-nb.de.
Any brand names and product names mentioned in this book are subject to trademark, brand
or patent protection and are trademarks or registered trademarks of their respective holders.
The use of brand names, product names, common names, trade names, product descriptions
etc. even without a particular marking in this works is in no way to be construed to mean that
such names may be regarded as unrestricted in respect of trademark and brand protection
legislation and could thus be used by anyone.

Publisher:
Lambert Academic Publishing AG & Co. KG
Dudweiler Landstr. 99, 66123 Saarbrücken, Germany
Phone +49 681 3720-310, Fax +49 681 3720-3109, Email: info@lap-publishing.com

Printed in the U.S.A.
Printed in the U.K. by (see last page)
ISBN: 978-3-8383-4014-2

CONTENTS

CHAPTER FOUR FINDINGS AND DIACUSSIONS

CHAPTER FIVE CONCLUSIONS AND IMPLICATIONS

CHAPTER SIX CONTRIBUTIONS TO PRACTICE AND REFLECTIONS

LIST OF TABLES

LIST OF FIGURES

ABBREVIATIONS

MNEs ----- Multi-National Enterprises

SMEs ------ Small Medium-Sized Enterprises

CSMEs ---- Chinese Small Medium-Sized Enterprises

OLI -------- Ownership Advantages (O)

Location Advantages (L)

Internalisation Advantages (I)

CHAPTER ONE

INTRODUCTION

1.1 Introduction

The purpose of this opening chapter is to provide an overview of how this research has been conducted as a whole process in answering the question of 'How do Chinese Small Medium-Sized Enterprise (CSME) Managers Make their Strategic Market Entry Choices when Entering the UK?' It first introduces readers to the research background. This covers a review of the existing research on strategic market entry choices and then leads to the research questions and aims. Research methodology and methods adopted in this study are briefly described afterwards. In moving from the research questions to data collection and analysis the logical structure of this projectis outlined at the end of this chapter to provide readers with a full picture of this study and guide them through the rest of the research journey.

1.2 Background to the Research

For over twenty years internationalisation has been undertaken as an important strategy for companies that intend to expand their businesses from one nation to another (Bennett, 1999). Historically foreign investors from Western developed countries have played major roles in international business development. However, with fundamental changes of world economic structure, the forms of internationalisation and geographical distributions of international investments have been changed increasingly (Treasury, 2004). Due to the difficulties experienced by large corporations during 1970s and early 1980s, Western multinational enterprises (MNEs) lost their grip

on world trade (Carter and Jones-Evans, 2006). Internationalisation is not exclusive only for MNEs

from Western developed countries but is now available to small and medium-sized enterprises (SMEs)

from developing countries. For instance, compared with other European countries, the UK has been

the most popular destination in Europe for both large and small overseas investors (Child, Faulkner

and Pitkethly, 2000). Between 1994 and 1997, the North of Englandattracted the highest proportion of

foreign direct investment (FDI) in the UK. These overseas investors are not only Western companies

such as those from the US but also East Asian companies (Garrahan and Ritchie, 1999). According to

the One North East (a regional development agency in the UK) database (2004) The North of

Englandis becoming an attractive FDI destination for SMEs from mainland China. Driven largely by

remarkable external and internal changes CSMEs have increasingly embraced the international

growth path as a way of leveraging their competitive advantage. However, SME internationalisation

is largely ignored by governments, policy makers and international researchers (Carter and

Jones-Evans, 2006).

As a key issue, a firm's internationalisation has been studied from different perspectives in the

international business research (Buckley and Ghauri, 1999). The choice of market entry mode as a

frontier issue (Anderson and Gatignon, 1986) has been recognised as a critical decision when a firm

decides to expand their business internationally since this strategic decision has great impact on the

success of a firm's international expanding performance (Choo and Mazzarol, 2001). To gain a

comprehensive understanding of this important issue, extensive empirical research and theory

development have been carried out by many international business researchers (e.g. Anderson and

Gatignon, 1986; Buckley, 1998; Dunning, 1988; Erramilli and Rao, 1995; Hill; Hwang and Kim,

1990; Rogers, Ghauri and George, 2005; Root, 1987 etc.). The dominant international theories and models of market entry choice have been focused on MNEs from Western developed countries. However, it is noticed with the increasing internationalisation of SMEs from both Western and Eastern countries, some scholars (e.g. Burgel and Murray, 2000; Jones, 1999; Zacharakis, 1977) have attempted to investigate whether the mainstream theories and models of internationalisation based on MNEs are applicable for SMEs. Others (Sim and Pandian, 2003; Lalls, 1983; Turner, 1973; Wells, 1983) showed interest in exploring whether findings established on Western developed countries are adequate to explain Asian firms' foreign market entry mode choices from developing countries.

Indeed, limited research into SME internationalisation has confirmed that theories of entry mode choice built upon MNEs fail to explain SME managers' entry mode choices (Burgel and Murray, 2000; Jones, 1999; Nakos, Brouthers and Moussetis, 2002). Particularly, very little has been investigated to explain the activities of SMEs from developing countries (Baran, Pan and Kaynak, 1996; Shi, Ho and Siu, 2001). Much remains to be explored with regards to SME strategic market entry choices, especially SMEs from developing countries in the case of entering Western developed countries.

Moreover, reviewing the existing research concerning firms' entry mode choices, debates exist between theoretical literature and practical options. Early attempts at the choice of entry mode were largely based on a single theory: product life circle, market imperfection, transaction cost which emphasises one aspect but ignored others. However, the foreign market entry choice is a very complicated social process. It involves a variety of individuals and organisations rather than just economic factors (Aharoni, 1966). Such a complicated phenomenon can not be satisfactorily

3

explained by a single theory (Dunning, 2001). Building upon on these assumptions, Dunning (1988) synthesised different factors and developed an eclectic framework by integrating these factors. However, the practical values of Dunning's (1988) eclectic framework have been criticized as too much 'paradigm' and too little 'model' for practitioners (Buckley and Casson, 1998; Decker and Zhao, 2004). In addition, the existing literature typically focuses on the factors and their impact upon a firm's entry mode choices and has neglected other aspects such as the entry decision making process decision makers adopt. Indeed, entry mode decision making is a very complicated social processes, including an intricate structure of attitudes and social relationships in and outside the organisation (Aharoni, 1966). Other elements such as motives and strategic approaches which decision makers adopt should be integrated into influencing factors as they may have impact on managers' strategic market entry mode choices. However, little empirical research has been conducted from this aspect. Arguments here have revealed that more practical-based models should be developed to give practitioners guidelines in making their entry mode decisions more effectively.

It is also noted that a number of influencing factors in relation to the choice of entry mode such as the firm's size, the firm's international experiences, and national culture differences, have been investigated intensively in the previous research. However, the results contrast each other (Erramilli, 1991; Anderson and Gatignon, 1986; Kogut and Singh, 1988; Chung and Winderwich, 2001). For instance, some empirical research confirms that firm size is positively correlated to high control entry mode choice whilst others indicate that firm size has no impact on entry mode choices. The contradiction confuses managers and hinders their ability to make optimal entry mode decisions from practical perspectives (Deck and Zhao, 2004). Reviewing existing studies in line with a firm's strategic market entry mode choices it is evident that research has been dominated by statistical

4

surveys. However, restricting research to the selected factors may easily lead to wrong or inconsistent conclusions. Additionally the results of sample-based surveys strongly depend on sample quality which is difficult to control (Zhao and Decker, 2004). Consequently, this issue encouraged the author to explore the managers' strategic entry mode choices from a qualitative perspective.

Moreover, the researcher was formerly an international business manager in both large and SME organisations, her international experiences sparked the initial concept of this research. Some practical issues the author encountered encouraged her to conduct further investigation in relation to CSME managers' entry mode choices. Theoretically, there are many factors which affect firms' foreign entry mode choices. However, no empirical research has been conducted to reveal what factors are taken into account by CSME managers when making entry mode choices. Why are some factors more important than others, and in which context? These issues stimulated the author to conducte the further investigation.

1.3 Research Question and Objectives

This project sets out to advance knowledge and practice in the area of internationalisation. It aims to make a contribution to business and management practice in relation to entry mode decision making of SME managers. The research question addressed in this study is:

How do Chinese SME Managers Make Their Strategic Market Entry Choices When Entering the UK?

To answer this question, the following questions are to be considered during this research:

- Why are CSME managers interested in entering the North of England markets?

5

- What market entry modes are adopted by CSME managers in the North of England?

- What factors affect CSME managers' entry mode choices? Why are these elements critical in determining their entry mode choices?

- In practice, which processes do CSME managers follow in making their entry mode decision?

1.4 Research Methodology

The philosophical stance of this research is based on social constructionism that focuses on uncovering the ways in which individuals and groups participate in the creation of their perceived reality through social processes (Crotty, 1998; Schwandt, 2000). As meaningful realities are socially constructed, people are inevitably viewing phenomena through lenses bestowed upon them by their own cultures (Crotty, 1998). This research is interested in looking at the ways of how CSME managers individually create their meanings in relation to their strategic market entry choices in the context of entering the UK markets. Moreover, as socially constructed reality is seen as an ongoing and dynamic process, it is believed that mainstream FDI theories based upon Western culture may be re-produced differently by CSME managers via their own culture lens. To understand CSME managers' socially constructed realities, meanings in their strategic market entry choices must be interpreted (Denzi and Lincoln, 2005; Crotty, 1998; Easterby-Smith *et al.*, 2002). This assumption leads to the choice of interpretivism as the theoretical perspective for this research.

Guided by the constructionism and interpretivism the qualitative approach is adopted as an appropriate research methodology for this study. Given the nature of qualitative research semi-structured interviews are conducted to obtain more detailed data to achieve the research objectives. 10 CSME managers, including 3 females and 7 males, were interviewed in the North of

6

England. The participants are derived from a wide range of industry sectors, such as jewellery industry, textile industry including garment and house soft decoration, food industry, computer industry including accessories and software design, Chinese medicine and consultant services. King's (2004) template approach is the main data analysis technique employed for this research. Additionally, to build confidence in the findings of this qualitative research, Strauss and Corbin's (1998) and Lincoln and Guba's (1985) evaluation framework of trustworthiness and Hammersley's (1992) relevance criterion are employed to evaluate this qualitative research.

1.5 Structure of Project

This projectis constructed into six chapters. **Chapter One** provides an introductory overview of the thesis. By presenting the background to the research and briefly reviewing the issues of the existing literature, it further addresses the research questions and objectives followed by the overview of the research methodology employed for this research. Finally, the structure of the projectis outlined in this chapter.

To build a theoretical foundation upon which this research is based, **Chapter Two** provides a detailed review of the relevant literature in the past research. By critically examining the existing theories of strategic market entry choices that have been mainly derived from MNEs and SMEs from Western developed countries, the research issues are highlighted and research gaps are identified.

Chapter Three describes the philosophical paradigm upon which the methodology was built for this study. As a starting point this chapter reviews epistemological and philosophical issues and arguments that determine the research methodology from a theoretical perspective. Justifications of

7

methodologies and methods used for data collection and analysis in this research are introduced. Moreover, limitations of the research methods and ethical considerations are provided at the end of this chapter.

To provide a context specific picture of CSME outward investments, **Chapter Four** begins with a brief historical review of East Asian foreign investment in the UK. After giving a brief description of the research portfolio, the findings of the study are presented in relation to CSME managers' choice of entry mode. Synprojectand discussions are provided by integrating the findings with the existing theories and modes that are discussed in literature review chapter.

Chapter Five, as a summary to the whole research, provides the full picture of the findings within the main body of knowledge in relation to CSME managers' strategic market entry choices. In this chapter conclusions are drawn on the basis of the findings and discussions provided in Chapter Four. Moreover, after presenting theoretical contributions and implementations, research evaluations of the study are provided.

The final **Chapter Six** begins by investigating the practical contributions of this research to both SME managers and Government SME policy makers in both home and host countries. Additionally, as an important part of a qualitative research processes, the author offers her epistemological reflexivity and methodological reflexivity in this chapter. The author's research role as a researcher during this research journey is also identified. To end this research story, the researcher discussed her personal and professional development throughout this intellectual journey.

1.6 Chapter Summary

This chapter has laid the foundation for this project to communicate how this research has been designed, developed and conducted. From introducing the background into how this research question has been identified, it has provided an overview of the contents of each chapter that gives a chance for the researcher to review this study as a whole process and gain better understanding of the topic. On basis of these foundations, a detailed description of the literature review is to be presented in the next Chapter.

CHAPTER TWO

LITERATURE REVIEW

2.1 Introduction

Beginning in the late 1960s and throughout the following decades the debate on the choice of foreign

market entry modes has been given high priority in previous research. However, amongst the vast

amount of studies, contradictions exist. It has been found that some influencing factors in relation to

entry mode choices, such as international experience and national culture, have caused completely

contradictive results in the past research. It is therefore argued that more empirical studies should be

conducted in this area (Zhao and Decker, 2004; Cannon, 1993). To clarify the research questions and

build up a theoretical foundation for this study, this chapter provides a literature review in more

details by concentrating on firms' strategic market entry mode choices with the focus of SMEs.

As definitions of SME differ from country to country, this chapter begins by providing a review of

what is meant by the term of SMEs under different contexts. Moreover, distinguishable

characteristics between SMEs and MNEs are discussed followed by relevant literature review of

motives of SMEs internationalisation. Adding to that, varieties of foreign market entry modes are

examine in general, and the strengths and weaknesses, patterns and formats of entry modes by firms

from different countries are explored. Furthermore, the influencing factors in relation to the choice of

market entry mode are presented. Finally, the multistages of the decision making process of entry

mode choices and the decision marker's role are highlighted and reviewed from different perspectives.

Overall, this chapter sets out to review the relevant concepts and theories to support the further analysis in the following chapters.

2.2 Main Features of SMEs

Research of firms' foreign investment began in the 1960s (Hymer, 1960; Vernon, 1966). Throughout the following decades intensive theoretical frameworks and empirical studies based on MNEs have been carried out (Johanson and Vahlne, 1977; Dunning, 1981; Anderson and Gatignon, 1986; Buckley, 1998; Buckley and Ghauri, 1999). However, critics suggest that some of the developed theories and frameworks based on MNEs are inadequate to explain SMEs' international activities due to SMEs' unique features. Research explicitly tailored for SMEs is therefore required (O'Goraman and McTiernan, 2000; Nakos, Brouthers and Moussetis, 2002, Zhao and Decker, 2004). To gain a comprehensive understanding of SMEs' foreign investment activities, it is crucial and necessary to acknowledge the differences between SMEs and MNEs, starting with the different definitions of SMEs.

2.2.1 Alternative Definitions of SMEs

There is no simple or single definition of what constitutes a SME. This is because no single measure such as turnover, invested capital, profitability is likely to fully account for the size of an enterprise (Carter and Jones-Evans, 2006; Harvie and Lee, 2005). A manufacturer may be considered as a small enterprise if it employees 300 workers. However, it is definitely considered to be large if it is an IT company. Many alternatives make it extremely difficult to give a uniform definition of SMEs.

There is no global consensus on the definition of a SME. It differs widely among different countries. In EU, an attempt to provide a more uniform definition of a SME has been provided. First introduced by EU in 1996 and updated in 2002, a SME is a firm having 'fewer than 250 employees' and turnover is less than € 50 million (The European Union, 2002). Although introduced by EU, individual European countries still have their own interpretations of what constitutes a SME. For example, the UK government defines their SMEs by only considering the number of employees. A small firm normally has 0-9 employees. A medium-sized firm employs 50-249 workers in the UK (Carter and Jones-Evans, 2006). Differently, in UAS and Canada, companies with 'fewer than 500 employees' are treated as SMEs (Karmel and Bryon, 2002).

Compared with Western nations, Asian countries also set their 'benchmarks' of SMEs differently. For example, in Malaysia companies employed 150 full time employees with a sales turnover that does not exceed RM25 million can be treated as SMEs. Firms with less than 200 employees and 20-100 million baht of fixed assets are identified as SMEs in Thailand (Hall, 1995). In China an alternative definition of a SME is provided. Interestingly, criteria differ largely among different industries in China. In some of the labour intense industries, such as automotive and steel industry, CSME are those companies that employ less than 2000 workers. However, updated in 2003, the Chinese Government use the employee number as the main criterion in defining CSMEs. It is decided that for most of the industries, companies with less than 500 employees can be treated as CSMEs.

Due to alternative definitions of SMEs between countries, researchers must consider this issue carefully in their SMEs' research design. Reviewing previous SME studies, Erramilli and Rao (1993) use sales revenue as benchmark of their definition of SMEs. Differently, Baird, Lyles and Orris (1994) consider both sales revenue and employment in constituting their definition of SMEs. Indeed, Buckley (1989: 99) argued that "definitions of SMEs vary according to author and context". It is "not

12

right or wrong, just more or less useful".

In the specific context of this study, the number of employees is to be used as the criterion in defining CSMEs. Chinese companies with less than 500 employees are treated as CSMEs in this research. There are 2 main reasons to use this decisive criterion to measure of a firm's size. First, information about employment is 'readily available' (Pratten, 1991: 1). According to Nakos, Brouther and Moussetis (2002), many SMEs are sometimes reluctant to disclose their financial performance data, which causes problems for researchers to define SMEs precisely on the basis of company's sales. Secondly, many leading SME researchers (e.g. Nakos, Brouther and Moussetis, 2002; Karmel and Bryon, 2002; Pratten, 1991) sampled their SMEs with less than 500 employees in their studies. Especially, in one of their current SME research of market entry mode choices, Shi, Ho and Siu (2001) sampled Hong Kong SMEs with less than 500 employees. In order to maintain the consistency with prior conducted SME studies in this area, the number of employee (less than 500) is the most appropriate and useful criterion to define a CSME for this research.

As previously noted in Chapter One, one purpose of this research is to explore whether mainstream Western MNEs based foreign investment theories are applicable in explaining SME international activities, especially CSMEs. To achieve this goal, different characteristics between SMEs and MNEs should be distinguished because a firm's own unique features determine its ownership advantages and disadvantages. According to Dunning, (1977, 1981, 1980, 1995, 1998), ownership advantages play an important role in a firm's entry mode choices.

2.2.2 SMEs versus MNEs

There is a debate about the matter of a firm's size. In the mid-1970s, the size of firm grew dramatically due to the biggest merger and acquisition wave of the century in 1990s. However, the trend is currently being reversed. Large firms have down-sized by reducing their workforce (Doole and Lowe, 2001). Many firms tend to get smaller through varieties of business process innovation (Karmel and Bryon, 2002), such as Business Process Outsourcing (BPO) which helps large companies to overcome barriers of heavy hierarchy by reducing its size. Of note, the rates of growth in the number of SMEs have been increasingly higher than before. For example, the number of SMEs in EU has increased dramatically in the later 1990s (European Fifth Annual Report for SMEs, 1997), and SMEs' contributions to Japanese economy are rising continuously in Japan (Fujita, 1998).

In order to have a better understanding of SMEs' management and performance, many SME researchers examine the differences between SMEs and MNEs by looking at 4 main aspects: organisation structure and process, financial situations, ownership and resources, as well as management style (Lu and Beamish, 2001; Carrier, 1994; Burns and Dewhurst, 1986; Pleitner, Brunner and Habersaat, 1998; Fujita, 1998). Table 2.1 below provides the overview of general characteristics of both SMEs and MNEs.

Table 2.1   Comparison of SMEs and MNEs

SMEs	MNEs
• Small size	• Large size
• Low market power	• Powerful market position
• Lack of resources (for example HR)	• Richness of various resources
• Financial constraints	• Strong assets power
• Lack of funds for future investment	• Access to financial supports with easy
• Less bureaucratic structure	• Hierarchy structure
• Fast responses to environment change	• Slow response to environment change
• Take the most risk of R&D	• Intensive R&D
• Owners and managers are often innovators	• Research technicians are often innovators
Management style -	**Management style -**
• *Flexible management style*	• Restrict management style
• *Lack of strategic planning*	• Elaborate strategic planning
• *Short cut in decision making*	• Top-down decision making
• *Limited managerial resources*	• Sufficient management expertise

Source: Adapted from Pleitner, Brunner and Habersaat 1998, Karmel and Bryon, 2002.

Reviewing the factors listed in the above table, it is clear that a firm's size not only leads to different organisation structures but also management styles. In general, SMEs are less powerful in the markets comparing with MNEs because of their limited resources and lack of external financial supports (Doole and Lowe, 2001). However, the small size benefits SMEs avoiding overpowering bureaucracy and enables them to respond to internal and external environment changes quickly (Karmel and Bryon, 2002; O'Gorman and McTiernan, 2000). For example, SMEs obtaining individualised products and services offer a flexible cost structure, and act quickly when market environments and customer needs changed due to its less hierarchal structures (Lu and Beamish, 2001; Carrier, 1994). Moreover, in one of his SME surveys, Fujita (1998) found that in Japan 52 per cent of SMEs' innovations was created by employers and 72 per cent of innovations in large companies were created by research technicians. As many SMEs are willing to take significant R&D risks, innovative activities tend to emerge more from SMEs than MNEs. This is because SME owners and managers adopt different management approaches compared with CEOs from MNEs (Burns and Dewhurst, 1986; Pleitner, Brunner and Habersaat, 1998). In contrast to MNEs, SMEs have the flexibility of decision making authority and short information structure. Moreover, rather than using a top-down hierarch decision making process, as Buckley (1998) argued, SMEs normally take short cut in their decision making mainly because of their shortages of skilled management and lack of strategic planning. More details of decision making characteristics links to SMEs' foreign market entry decision process are discussed in section 2.5.

It is argued that SMEs, compared with MNEs, are a less powerful force outside their home territory because expanding business internationally requires firms' great commitment of various competitive resources (Doole and Lowe, 2001). However, a SME's flexibility and agility can be relevant to success in its internationalisation. To gain more insights of SMEs' internationalisation, the roles that SMEs actually play in foreign investments have been examined by many international researchers.

2.2.3 Trends of SMEs' Internationalisation

The term 'internationalisation' commonly refers to the process of increasing involvement in international operations (Welch and Luostarinen, 1988; Bell, *et al.,* 2004). Similarly, Calof and Beamish (1995: 115) state that "internationalisation is the process of adapting exchange transaction modality to international markets". This process increases the flows of goods, capital, and services across national frontiers and decreases regulatory controls over those transactions (Zeweig, 2002). For over 20 years now internationalisation has been undertaken as an important strategy by MNEs that seek to expand their business from one nation to another (Johanson and Vahlne, 1990; Bennett,

1999; Griffin and Pustay, 2005; Rugman and Collinson, 2006). However, internationalisation nowadays is not exclusive to large companies. SMEs are playing an important role in international business (Bean, 2004; Bonaccorsi, 1992; Oviatt & MuDoungall, 1997; Nakos, Brouthers and Moussetis, 2002) and have the "potential to become considerably more important in the future global economy" (Doole and Lowe, 2001: 178). Over the last few years, research on the international activities of SMEs has been increasing.

Building upon discussions in section 2.2.2, a number of international researchers assert that SMEs' unique characteristics make them behave differently in the international markets (Nakos, Brouther and Moussetis, 2002). Compared with MNEs, SMEs have different ownership advantages that shape different forms of its investments, performance, and competitive advantages. One of the positive trends is that SMEs possess some degree of market power (niche market sectors) in foreign markets that accrues from its less hierarchal structure, flexible decision making process, fast responses to emergencies, and ability to take R&D risks (Karmel and Bryon, 2002; Fujita, 1998). However, there are also some problems related to the nature of SMEs that constrain their international activities. For example, insufficient managerial capacity and limited human resources are deemed big problems for SMEs (Hall and Naude, 1998). Moreover, insufficient financial strength, difficulties of raising capital, limited transfer capability, lack of information of target market, a weak position to negotiate to business partners, and the government in host countries, all of these elements constitute relative restrictions when SMEs consider operating abroad (Fujita, 1998; Coviello and Munro, 1998; Gelinas and Bigras, 2004).

Foreign investment by SMEs is a relatively recent phenomenon. In his survey, Fujita (1998) found that about two thirds of foreign investments were made after 1980. Furthermore, his research shows that major foreign investors in SME sector are from developed countries. The destinations of these SMEs' foreign investments were located in both developed and developing countries. In the late 1980s, Canadian and United States SMEs preferred investing in North America. Western European SMEs habitually invested in other European countries. In contrast, Australia and Japanese SMEs appeared to prefer developing countries such as South and East Asia (Fujita, 1998). With new members joining the EU, as a trend, many SMEs from Western developed countries target Central East European (CEE) countries as new destinations of their foreign investments.

Another trend of SMEs' internationalisation is that Asian SMEs from developing countries are playing certain roles in the international business. In one of his SME foreign investment studies, Buckley (1998) discovered that many foreign investors from less developed countries are SMEs. They are "largely small scale manufacturers, with high adaptability to local conditions and flexible users of capital equipment" (Buckley, 1998:109). However, there is as yet limited empirical research that investigates Asian SMEs' strategic market entry mode choices in the context of entering the Western developed countries.

2.3 Motives of SMEs' Internationalisation

Since the last decade, there is a growing body of literature that highlights SMEs' international operations, and a numbers of empirical studies have been conducted relatively (Buckley, 1998; Covielo and Munro, 1997; Antti and Donckels, 1998; Anderson, Boocock and Graham, 2001; O'Gorman and McTiernan, 2000; Alon, 2004). Due to the different characteristics it is proposed that motives of 'going global' might be different between SMEs and MNEs. Beginning with some reflections on the FDI theories, this section provides review of motives of SMEs' internationalisation

and explore the destination choices by SMEs from both developed and developing countries.

2.3.1 Motives Theories of Internationalisation

The internationalisation of a firm has been "a key issue in international business research right from

the outset" (Buckley and Ghauri, 1999: 1). Since 1960, a number of theories have been developed by

international researchers. Among them, the most well known and widely used are product life cycle

theory (Vernon, 1966), market imperfection and monopolistic advantage theories, (Kindleberger,

1969; Hymer, 1976) and Dunning's (1980, 1981, 1997, 1998, 2000) eclectic theory.

Product life cycle theory hypothesis (Vernon, 1966) asserts that a product has a 'life cycle'

comprising a series of stages, including birth, maturation, decline and eventually death. Once a

product has reached the end of its life cycle in one country it, however, may have a fresh lease of life

elsewhere. The life cycle theory is normally used to explain the motives and patterns of foreign direct

investment by large companies from Western developed countries operating in developing countries

(Bennett, 1999). According to market imperfection and monopolistic advantage theories

(Kindleberger, 1969; Hymer, 1976), large firms normally engage in international business to create

near monopoly conditions for their operations. These theories can be used to effectively explain why

international investments flow from developed countries to developing countries.

Building upon single theories, Dunning (1980, 1988) developed his eclectic theory that has been used

to explain not just where but why international activities take place (Erdener and Shapiro, 2005). The

use of the Dunning's (1980, 1997) eclectic theory enables a better understanding of why firms engage

19

in international investment from multiple aspects rather than a single theory. The eclectic theory asserts that successful MNEs often develop their competitive advantages at home (Organisational advantages), then transfer them to specific countries (Location advantages) through foreign direct investment (Internalization advantages). The further discussions of the eclectic mode in relation to firms' entry mode choices will be presented in section 2.5.

Debates exist over existing FDI theories. Critics suggest, for example, that the product life cycle theory can sufficiently explain firms' internationalisation from richer nations to less developed countries during the 1950s and early 1960s but not thereafter (Bennett, 1999). For example, many MNEs now could launch new products simultaneously in both developed and developing countries. Products do not face inevitable death within predetermined periods. Indeed, 'the death of the products' is very much a management decision. Moreover, as many FDI theories are developed based on MNEs' international activities, they could not explain SMEs' international business activities. Some SME researchers (Zimmerer and Scarborough, 2002; Fraser and Stonehouse, 2000) suggest that entrepreneurship theory should be given certain attention to explain SMEs' international management and performance. From an entrepreneurial behaviour theory perspective, entrepreneur's individual characteristics have a great impact on their behaviour. It has been identified that the risk-taking (Brochhaus, 1980); needs for achievements (McClelland, 1987; Delmar, 1996; Johnson, 1990), and desire for autonomy (Sexton and Bowman-Upton, 1985; Fagenson, 1993) determine an entrepreneur's management attitude. Attitude is one of the major concepts in motivation theory (Cater and Jones-Evans, 2006). For the purpose of this research, one of the important objectives is to investigate the motives of CSME managers entering the Western developed countries. However, it appears that no empirical studies have been conducted by interacting entrepreneurship theories into

Asian SMEs' foreign market entry mode choices.

Another FDI theory which is used to explain SMEs' motives of internationalisation is network theory (Carter and Jones-Evans, 2006; Hellman, 1996; Johanson and Vahlne, 1992). Network theory asserts that some SMEs entering new foreign markets are not driven by strategic decisions or market research but networks. These networks pull SMEs involving international business positively. Nevertheless, existing international business research based on the network theory mainly focuses upon SMEs' international process (Johanson and Vahlne, 1992; Melin, 1992; Coviello and Munro, 1997). Less attention has been given to the network influences on motives of SMEs' internationalization, especially, it is not explicitly explained how networks in the host country initially triggered Asian SMEs' international activities. Reviewing the main features of networks theory, a strong link can be between networks and Chinese 'Guanxi' culture (Beamer, 1998; Chen, 1994; Luo, 1997, 2002). According to Luo (2002), Guanxi is a network of relationships a person or a company cultivates through the exchange of favours to attain mutual benefits. It is a unique feature of Chinese business culture. Through connections with people, Chinese firms try to build Guanxi networks into their business webs.

Examing the empirical studies, it is found that motives of firms' internationalization can be very different in different circumstances. The general motives of a firm's internationalisation are to be considered next.

2.3.2 General Motives of Firm's Internationalisation

Theoretical literature and a vast amount of empirical studies (mostly derived from the experience of large firms) give a great deal of insight into the motives behind a firm's internationalisation. Externally, from macro-level, environmental changes and globalisation facilitate firms' international business activities. In the country-level, changes in the political and economic environment, such as market liberations, motivate firms to internationalise (Griffin and Pustay, 2005; Rugman and Collinson, 2006). However, it is important to realise that differing political systems influence firms' motivations to internationalise differently (Buckley, 1998; Nolan, 2001; Child and Tse, 2001). For example, over the past 2 decades, although the foundation of China's economic reform is to increase enterprise autonomy (Nolan, 2001), Chinese firms, whether MNEs or SMEs, still remain relatively controlled by the Chinese government. China's Communist political system and huge hierarchy play significant roles in influencing business activities of Chinese enterprise. This has become a distinctive feature to studies of Chinese business and management in many research areas (Child and Yan, 2001; Dunning, 1988; Buckley, 1998). Inevitably, the Chinese Government's role in determining CSME managers' strategic market entry choices must be taken into account in fulfilling the purpose of this research.

Considering international activities from the firm-level, according to Erdener and Shapiro (2005) and Lalls (1983), there are 3 main internal reasons why firms invest in the foreign markets including nature resource seeking, low-cost of products seeking, and new market seeking. Agreed by Griffin and Pustay (2005), most firms enter international markets to acquire resources of low cost raw materials and labour in host countries because they are either scarce or unavailable for certain products or services in home countries. Rugman and Collinson (2006) indicate that seeking new markets to generate high revenue and profit growth is a common motive for firms' international expansions when a firm's domestic market is mature. Arguably, in many Asian developing countries,

22

its markets are less developed but still many MNEs and SMEs are going international. Obviously, the motives discussed above can not be used to explain firms' international motivations for firms from developing to developed countries. Further investigation regarding this issue is needed.

Another important internal motive of firms' internationalisation is to leverage their competencies (Griffin and Pustay, 2005). Operating in the foreign markets is far more complex and risky comparing with doing business in domestic markets. It provides firms an opportunity to develop their competitive advantages and enables them to better compete with their rivals from all over the world. General motives of firms' internationalisation are summarised in table 2.2.

Table 2.2 General Motives of Firms' Internationalisation

	Motives
Macro - level	• Environment changes (e.g technology changes) • Globalisation
Country - level	• Political system changes and other powerful influences • Economic system changes • Market liberations • Declining home markets
Firm - level **(classic motives)**	• New market seeking • Raw material seeking • Low cost of production seeking • Leverage competences

Source: Adapted from Buckley (1998), Griffin and Pustay (2005), Rugman (2006),
Erdener and Shapiro (2005) and Lall (1983)

Table 2.2 explores the general motives of firms' internationalisation. Accordingly, it becomes apparent that motives at macro-level are universal. Factors from country-level may vary as it is more dependent on a firm's chosen markets and its cultural characteristics in both home and host countries

(Carter and Jones-Evans, 2006). Motives from the firm-level are commonly recognisable in many cases of MNEs' foreign direct investments, especially for those that are from Western developed countries entering emerging markets in developing countries.

Thus far, a general review regarding motives of firms' internationalization has been explicitly introduced into the discussion. Given their obvious differences in terms of resources (financial and managerial) and attitude to risk and control (Carter and Jones-Even, 2006), it is assumed that motives of internationalisation between SMEs and MNEs may be distinguishable.

2.3.3 Motives of SMEs' Internationalisation

As far as FDI theories are concerned, little empirical research has been conducted in relation to the motives of SMEs (Brush, 1995; Hall and Naude 1998; Karagozoglu and Lindell, 1998). A few studies (Brush, 1995; Karagozoglu and Lindell, 1998) examined SMEs' motives of internationalization and found some shared common motives between SMEs and MNEs. For example, Donckels and Aerts (1998) classify several reasons for SME and group them into 2 categories: Macroeconomic and microeconomic elements. They argue that both external (host and home countries conditions) and internal (company conditions) factors influence SME decisions of 'going or not going' international. Being consistent with Donckels and Aerts (1998) but more specifically, Buckley (1998) summarises 3 patterns of motives of SMEs' internationalisation theoretically: pull factors, push factors, and classic factors. He argues that favourable government FDI policies of a host country are important forces to pull SMEs into the international market. As push factors, competitions from foreign international companies in home markets, particularly MNEs, exceptionally push SMEs to seek new markets and low nature raw materials and labour cost of

24

efficiency. From a host country perspective, Rugman and Collinson (2006) argue that large size of market in host country is one important factor pulling many MNEs seeking markets growth. This suggestion has been supported by many international researchers (Griffin and Pustay, 2005; Child and Tse, 2001). Moreover, Erdener and Shapiro (2005) indicate that physical infrastructure, political environment, and effective governance at the political and economic levels are normally considerable factors that determine destinations of firms' foreign investments.

Motives of SMEs' internationalisation discussed above are similar with MNEs examined earlier. It is apparent that both SMEs and MNEs are pulled by favourable government policies in host country and pushed by market conditions in home country. These SMEs and MNEs from Western developed countries have the same classic motives of FDI with market-orientation and low-cost orientation. However, peculiar motives to SMEs exist and they have to be taken into account when researchers carry out ongoing SMEs' internationalisation research as these different motives may lead to distinguishable international patterns of SMEs. Buckley (1998:107) additionally argues that SMEs may "invest abroad as a result of entrepreneurial foresight (for achievement)" as SME owner-managers are greater risk takers than other types of decision makers. This suggestion has been empirically proved by Fujita (1998) whose SME survey findings indicate that entrepreneurial literature can be used to explain motives of internationalisation of SMEs. Moreover, by investigating SMEs from 18 developed countries, Fujita (1998) also finds that some SMEs' internationalisation can be regarded as failed investments based on inadequate evaluations (e.g. misinformation). More interestingly, building upon the network theory (Coviello and Munro, 1995; 1999; Hara and Kanai, 1994; Tjosvold and Weicker, 1993), it is found that SMEs may also be pulled into foreign markets by larger firms who are their business partners (Fujita, 1998). In summary, according to Buckley (1998)

25

and Fujita (1998), 3 more peculiar motives to SMEs' internationalisation emerged. They are entrepreneurship foresight, encouragement by large companies, and misevaluation.

International researchers have made great efforts to identify the general motives of internationalisation for all kinds of SMEs. However, debate arises regarding this. Scholars have devoted attention to concerns of distinguishable motives among different 'types' of SMEs (Hall and Naude, 1998; Gerhard, 2000; Shi, Ho and Siu, 2001; Chen, 2006). Critics suggest the overall factors are not sufficient to precisely explain the motives of SMEs internationalisation from different countries. As Buckley (1998: 107) argued "there are differences in predominant motives related to the nationality of SMEs". Building upon this debate, it is believed that the motives of SMEs' internationalisation differ from one country to another.

2.3.4 Motives of SMEs Entering Different Countries

Discussions of regional clusters on SME international growth have attracted many international researchers' interests (e.g. Hall and Naude 1998; Gerhard, 2000; Nakos, Brouthers and Moussetis, 2002; Anderson *et al*, 2003; Shi, Ho and Siu, 2001; Chen, 2006). The main body of the research on this theme suggests that motives of SMEs' internationalisation are distinguishable among SMEs from one nation to another.

SMEs from developed countries - SMEs from developed countries normally enter either developed countries or developing countries. Both groups of SME foreign investors share some common motives. However, differences exist. In the case of SMEs from developed countries entering other developed countries, Hall and Naude (1998) investigated British SMEs entering other Western

26

developed countries and found out the following main reasons why British SMEs involved in international business. These include:

- Small size of home market,

- Expectation of higher profit margins than domestic markets,

- Security of customer from domestic market along to diversifying into overseas markets,

- Belief in the attractiveness of products to foreign customer,

- Encouragement and support from third parties.

Differently, Gerhard (2000) carried out 4 case studies of Australia SMEs entering the US market. The findings of his empirical study show that Australia SMEs entered the US markets intend to:

- Tap into informal networks in host country,

- Be close to both distributors and customers,

- Develop a feeling for markets,

- Sourcing of local technology,

- Pure personal (owner-managers) preference of internationalisation.

Comparing the results of these 2 empirical studies, it can be recognised that British SMEs prioritise new markets on the top of other motives of their foreign investments to expect higher profit and growth due to its small size of the home markets. However, Australian SMEs seem to be more interested in building business networks to develop good relationship with foreign customers. Additionally, as most US companies obtain the most advanced technology in the world, sourcing of advanced local technology in the US markets obviously becomes one of the important motives for Australian SMEs. Of note, some motives of these 2 empirical studies correspond with the general motives of SMEs' internationalisation identified previously. However, both British and Australian SMEs are not motivated by raw materials and low cost of production seeking when entering Western developed countries. Moreover, some motives discovered in these 2 cases, such as sourcing of local technology and owner-manager's personal preference of internationalisation, add new insights to SMEs motives of entering other Western developed countries.

In the case of SMEs from *Western developed countries entering developing countries*, Fujita (1998) argues, in the early 1980s most SMEs from Western developed countries chose other Western developed countries as their destinations. In recent years, with globalisation, especially the evolution of the single European markets, some SMEs from Western developed countries benefit from diverting their foreign investments to both Asian and Central or East European developing countries (Meyer, 2001; Meyer and Estrin, 2001; Meyer and Skak, 2002). However, less attention has been given to this phenomenon. Two empirical studies based on European SMEs from developed countries entering CEEC markets (Kakos and Brouthers, 2002; Meyer and Skak, 2002) have claimed that the important motives of these SMEs' international business activities are mainly low cost of production seeking and market seeking. In either of the case, details of the motives of these SMEs' internationalisation were uninvestigated in-depth in these emerging markets.

SMEs from developing countries - Dynamic and fast environment changes and globalisation create more opportunities for SMEs involving international business. The structure of foreign investors has been changed over time. Internationalisation is not exclusive to SMEs from developed countries but is also common in developing countries. Fujita (1998:83) argues that "the evolution of the single European markets perhaps affects the pattern of SMEs' international activities continuously. Transitional countries may benefit from SMEs oriented towards servicing the Western European markets." Another strong indication shows that the twenty-first century will be characterized as the

Asian era of regional trading blocks (Dunning, 1997; Ohmae, 1985; Mohotra, Ulgado and Agarwal, 2003; Root and Ahmed, 1978, 1979; Hwang, 2000). The research interest of foreign investments from Asian countries is increasing (Garrahan and Ritchie, 1999). By extending the Western-based FDI theories to developing country scenarios, Wells (1977, 1978) and Lall (1983) studied MNEs from Asian developing countries and found that drivers and motives of Asian firms' internationalisation distinguish them from Western companies in certain aspects. For instance, Wells (1978) concludes that for Hong Kong companies, one of the reasons behind their overseas activities is to escape quotas restrictions. Moreover, Lall (1983) found that Hong Kong companies entering developed countries such as Canada, Britain, The United States, and Switzerland is often for the convenience of acquiring foreign technology. In one of their most recent studies, theoretically, Child and Rodrigues (2005) proposed that Chinese MNEs' motives of internationalisation include:

- To overcome the hazard of highly competitive domestic markets with low margins

- To look for opportunities

- To export based on domestic cost advantages

- To develop advanced technology and

- To gain entrepreneurial and managerial freedom

SMEs from developing countries have different motives when entering international markets (Yeung, 1994, 1997; Ulgado, Yu and Negandhi, 1994; Ting 1985; Wells, 1998; Lall, 1983; Sim and Pandian, 2003). Reviewing the existing literature, very few studies investigate outward investment of SMEs from developing countries. Shi, Ho and Siu (2001) conducted a survey by sampling Hong Kong SMEs investing in Mainland China. The findings of their research show that the motives of Hong Kong SMEs entering Mainland China are to seek new markets and low cost of production. Shi, Ho and Sui's study (2001) provides understanding and explanation of the market entry strategies of Asian

SMEs at the first place. However, Hong Kong, for the historical reasons is treated by Westerners as the most 'developed' of the developing region in Asian. Their research is by no means a complete explanation of SMEs, particularly Asian SMEs from developing countries. Further investigation is required in this research area.

In summary, from above discussions, it can be concluded that although SMEs and MNEs share some common motives of internationalisation, differences exist. Furthermore, motives of international activities vary among different SMEs groups from different nations. Synthesising and summarising motives of internationalisation explicitly discussed so far, peculiar motives of SMEs' internationalisation are presented in table 2.3 below.

Table 2.3 Motives of SMEs internationalisation

General factors	*From developed country to developed country*

• *Macro level - Globalisation*
• *Country level:*
   o *Economic system changes*
   o *Market liberation*
   o *Declining home markets*
• *Firm level*
   o *New market seeking*
   o *Raw material seeking*
   o *Low cost of production seeking*
   o *Leverage competences*
	• *Small home market size*
	• *High profits seeking*
	• *Security of customer overseas*
	• *Encouragement from third party*
	• *Building business networks*
	• *Gain direct market knowledge*
	• *Sourcing local technology*
	• *Personal preferences*
	• *Misevaluation*

From developed country to developing country	**SMEs from developing to developed countries**
• Liberation of host country • Seeking new markets • Seeking low cost of materials /labours **** less investigated****	**? ?**

Source: Adapted from Fujita (1998), Buckley (1998), Donckels and Aerts (1998),
Hall and Naude (1998), Gerhard (2000), Shi, Ho and Siu (2001)

SMEs' international activities are dynamic and complex (Carter and Jones-Evans, 2006). For such a complex issue one debate suggests that future international research should be more precise by investigating firms from a certain country at a certain area so that scholars can make theoretical

statements more concrete (Hoesel, 1999). This study attempts to contribute to this ongoing debate. By

reviewing the existing empirical studies no research has been conducted in the context of Asian

SMEs from developing countries entering Western developed countries. As a departure from

empirical research, this study is to explore the motives of CSMEs entering the North of England

markets because different motives might lead to different entry mode choices.

2.4 Selections of Foreign Market Entry Mode

A company which initially stands outside the foreign country must decide on its entry mode. The

determination of foreign entry mode choice is among the most crucial decisions that managers and

management teams have to make (Root, 1994; Cateora, Graham and Ghauri, 2000; Koch, 2001a;

2001b). With fundamental changes in technology, production and fast information flows, it is

important to recognize that there are different ways of going international (Chan and Hwagn, 1992;

Chang and Rosenzweig, 1998; Davis, 2000). By reviewing relevant theories and empirical studies

this section discusses foreign market entry modes utilized by both MNEs and SMEs.

2.4.1 General Entry Mode Choices

An entry mode is the institutional arrangement by which a firm gets its products, technologies, human

skills, or other resources into a market (Wild, J., Wild, L. and Han, 2000). There are numerous foreign

market entry modes that can be considered by firms to expand their businesses across borders.

Various attempts have been made to classify firms' entry modes by international researchers. In the

early literature on foreign entry mode choices Anderson and Gatignon (1986) claim that control is

essential for firms' success of foreign investments. Without control it is difficult for firms to carry out their strategies and pursue their own interests in the foreign markets. Furthermore, they argue that

control determines both risk and return. Considering the inter-dependent linkage among control,

return and risk, Anderson and Gatignon (1986) divide entry modes into 3 different levels: high

control entry mode that increases return and risk, medium control entry mode, low control model that

minimises resource commitment but often at the expense of returns. Underlying these 3 themes, 17

different entry modes are further defined. However, as Anderson and Gatignon's (1986) classification

of entry modes is grouped on the basis of both management and economic streams, some of their

classified entry modes, such as dominant shareholder, restrictive exclusive contract, nonexclusive

and non restrictive contracts, have not been widely cited by other international researchers. As this

research focuses upon management factors rather than economic elements, therefore, classification of

entry modes suggested by Anderson and Gatignon (1986) is not appropriate.

Focusing more on management issues, Root (1987) suggests alternative classifications of foreign

entry modes by identifying 6 different entry modes (see figure 2.1). As shown in figure 2.1, Root

(1987) classified entry of modes into 1) export entry modes including indirect export, direct export

through agents and distributors, branch and subsidiaries. 2) Licensing mode 3) Investment entry

modes including joint manufacturing venture and new manufacturing plants.

Figure 2.1 Types of entry modes

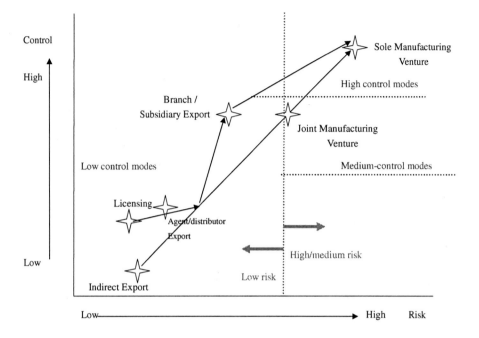

Root, R. F. (1994) *Revised and Expanded Entry Strategies for International Market*

According to Root (1998) indirect exporting is an entry mode used by firms to start exporting by using indirect channels such as agents and distributors. Companies adopting direct exporting entry mode normally set their own branches and subsidiaries in host country. By joint venture and sole manufacturing venture, as high control modes, companies involve manufacturing operations in the host country directly. Export and licensing entry modes can reduce risks but they are less controlled. In contrast, firms adopting investment entry modes are more construable to their international activities. However, risks increase as well. This can be recognised in figure 2.1 where the arrows indicate that from indirect export to direct exports (sales subsidiary export) and then to joint venture model and finally to the foreign investment module, both control and risk are gradually increased.

Drawing upon the viewpoints of Root (1987) and Anderson & Gatignon (1986), many other international researchers (e.g. Young *et al*, 1989; Stonehouse *et al*, 2000; Bradley, 2002; Pan and Tes, 2000; Mudambi R. and Mudambi S., 2002; Gorg, 2000; Kogut, 1988; Erramilli, 1990; Holger, 2000) have summarised 4 main groups of entry models that are commonly used in the previous international studies. They are exporting, licensing, joint ventures, and sole manufacturing venture. According to Doole and Lowe (2001) exporting includes indirect and direct exporting. Indirect exporting is the simplest and lowest cost method of entry that a company has its product sold by trading companies, or local distributors. Direct exporting, in contrast, is a market entry method whereby a company becomes directly involving in the process of exporting (Stonehouse, *et al*, 2000). Licensing is a form of a management contract in which a licenser authorises a licensee the right to uses their trademark, patent etc.

Joint venture and foreign manufacturing are 2 entry modes that have more risks, but more controls than exporting and licensing entry methods. By adopting this entry model, 2 or more companies form joint venture in which each company provides complementary competitive advantages (Doole and Lowe, 2001). Practically, the operational process of joint venture may vary slightly from one to another. Given the obvious reasons, most joint ventures adopt the format by setting the new joint company up in the host country where they manufacture products (manufacturing company) or provide services to local customers (service company). Finally, foreign manufacturing by direct investment is the highest risk mode in which a firm manufactures their products in overseas and sells them to the local markets. Pros and cons of each entry mode group have been synthesised in table 2.4.

Table 2.4 Pros and cons of main entry modes

Entry methods	Advantages	Disadvantages
Indirect exporting	• Lease expensive • Low risk	• Low control • No market knowledge gained
Direct exporting	• Partial or full control over the foreign markets • More and quicker information feedback • Better protection of trademarks	• Higher startup costs • Greater information requirements • Higher risks than indirect exporting
Licensing	• Control operation in some way • Risks are limited	• Profits must be shared • Lack of contact with customers
Joint ventures	• Reduces political risks • Shared knowledge costs and benefits	• Conflicts in interests • May become locked into long-term investment
Sole manufacturing Venture	• Retain central control • Sensitivity to local conditions	• Labour relation problem • Conflicts between HQ and local management

Source: Adapted from: Bennett (1998), Wild and Han (1999),

Stonehouse et al (2000) and Bradley (2002)

Classifications of entry modes listed above are largely based on considerations of costs, control, benefits, and risks. Although there are a range of options of entry modes, companies still attempt to seek new pathways to expand their business across borders differently and innovatively. Of note, internet entry mode has been recognised as an alternative path for firms entering foreign markets in recent years. Cateora, Graham and Ghauri (2000) emphasise that although in its infancy, the internet must not be ignored as a foreign market entry method. They point out that internet marketing, at the very beginning, focused on domestic sales. However, a surprisingly large number of firms, including both MNEs and SMEs (to be discussed in the next section), start receiving orders from foreign customers. However, Cateora, Graham and Ghauri (2000) do not clarify the 'physical distance' regarding internet foreign entry method. It is questioned whether the internet entry method is appropriate and realistic for firms expanding their businesses from Asian continent to European continent.

In summary, due to both disadvantages and advantages of each entry method, it is apparent that no one mode is ideal for all businesses. To select the most appropriate model, firms make entry decisions based on many factors (Stonehouse *et al*, 2000; Bradley, 2002). These determining factors vary between MNEs and SMEs due to their different characteristics, such as size, marketing experiences, and different management styles. Consequently, this leads to distinguishable foreign market entry method choices between SMEs and MNEs.

2.4.2 Entry Modes Choices by SMEs

Different entry modes represent varying levels of control of risks (Gemes-Casseres, 1990; Hennart and Park, 1993; Lampel and Jaffe, 1996). Each entry mode involves certain resource commitments (Tse and Pan, 1997). MNEs have great managerial and financial resources that commit them to high risk taking and control (Nakos and Brouthers, 2002). Therefore, they normally have more options of entry mode choices in comparison with SMEs (Papadopoulos, 1988) and prefer high-control modes such as sole manufacturing venture and joint venture (Agarwal and Ramaswami; 1992). Other international scholars (e.g. Chung and Enderwick, 2001; O'Gorman and McTiernan, 2000) argue that SMEs have limited options in their choices of foreign entry mode because of some constraints. Theories of MNEs entry mode choices should not be directly applied to SMEs.

As discussed in section 2.2.3, comparing with their large competitors, SMEs generally lack the financial and managerial resources (Nakos and Brothers, 2002). Such ownership disadvantages normally prevent SMEs from adopting high-control entry modes (O'Gorman and McTiernan, 2000). Several studies have confirmed that SMEs prefer low investment and non-equity entry modes such as licensing and exporting (Agarwal and Ramaswami, 1992; Erramilli and D'sSouza, 1993; Zacharakis, 1997).

Given the considerable differences between SMEs and MNEs, a number of studies have identified that exporting is the most used entry mode adopted by SMEs (Cavusgil and Nevin, 1981; Burton and Schelegelmilch, 1987). Agreeing with Papadopoulos (1988), Doole and Lowe (2001) suggest that SMEs are limited to exporting to their international operations because this model is with relatively little commitment and limited associated risk comparing with other high-risk modes. This view is supported by Carstairs and Welch's (1982) research in which they found that exporting entry mode was highly adopted by Australian SMEs.

As mentioned in section 2.4.1, attracting foreign customers by internet has an increasingly important role in firms' internationalisation, in particular the SMEs (Quelch and Klein; 1996; Hamill, 1997; Dool and Lowe, 2001). By using a mail survey, Fraser and Stonehouse (2000) invested SMEs in The North of Englandin a wide range of industries. Their findings show that certain numbers of SMEs used internet to sell their products. This result is consistent with Quelch and Klein (1996) who argue that the internet leads to more rapid internationalisation of SMEs as it makes SMEs reach a global audience cheaply and more easily.

37

However, other studies (Shan, 1990; Horn, 1990; Acs and Audretsch, 1990; Choo and Mazzarol, 2001) have found that a wide variety of entry modes are actually adopted by SMEs beyond exporting and internet modes, such as joint venture and wholly-owned subsidiary. Interestingly, the Australian Department of Foreign Affairs (DFAT, 1995) investigated 650 SMEs from different countries in Australia. The results indicate that various entry modes have been employed by SMEs such as sole manufacturing venture, agents, distributor networks, strategic alliances, licensing, and joint ventures. DFAT's survey shows that, amongst these modes, sole manufacturing venture and independent agents are 2 of the most popular foreign entry modes among these investigated SMEs from different countries. Moreover, Yap and Sounder (1994) suggest that SMEs may use high control entry modes serving niche markets in the host country by providing innovative products and unique services. Their argument is extended by Nakos and Brouthers (2002) who note that SMEs may service niche markets more effectively than MNEs.

In summary, studies into SMEs' internationalisation indicate that SMEs do not limit their options to low control and low risk entry modes in internationalising their activities, but use various resources to employ a wide range of market entry modes in both equity and non-equity formats. However, it is of note that conclusions of the above SME research primarily drew upon questionnaire surveys that hardly explain in-depth why SMEs select a particular mode of entry. Undoubtedly, further investigations of SME entry mode choices, especially from a qualitative perspective, are needed.

2.4.3 Internationalisation Process and SMEs' Entry Modes

The conventional international theory suggests that firms start international activities when they have developed domestic competitive advantages (Buckley and Casson, 1976). Once these firms operate in the overseas markets, its internationalisation is to be a gradual, sequential process through different stages (Johanson and Wiedersheim-Paul; 1975; Johanson and Vahlne, 1977; Luostarinen, 1979; Cavusgil and Nevin, 1981). This is well known as international stage theory, which is also called the incremental model.

Incremental stage theory was first proposed by Johanson and Wiedersheim-Paul (1975). By investigating 4 Swedish SMEs, Johanson and Wiedersheim-Paul (1975) explore that a series of stages of internationalisation occur incrementally for a firm's foreign expanding. A firm begins to internationalise its operation by pursuing the following stages gradually: 1) importing and/or exporting (direct/indirect) 2) build up own sales subsidiary in host country 3) foreign investment (JVs or overseas production). The basic assumption of the incremental model advotes a firm's internationalisation is the consequence of a series of incremental decisions. As many SMEs normally lack the management knowledge and resources, these obstacles prevent them from selecting high control and high risk entry modes that require large resource commitment. Instead, SMEs initially expand their foreign business by choosing low risk entry modes such as exporting and selling abroad via independent representatives. Johanson and Wiedersheim-Paul (1975) emphasise in their stage module that through learning from foreign markets in host countries, firms gain more knowledge that stimulates their international business by involving further controls.

In addition to Johanson and Wiedersheim-Paul's incremental model, Johanson and Vahlne (1977) studied firms' internationalisation activities by examining how managerial learning drives internationalisation. Their research suggests that a firm's initial foreign expansion starts with low risk by targeting physically close markets and then expand to more physically distant markets with increased experience over time. Meanwhile, several empirical studies support the incremental model (Boter and Holmquist, 1994; Cavusgil, 1984; Coviello and Munro, 1997; O'Gorman and McTiernan, 2000).

However, the incremental approach to internationalisation has come under criticism. Cannon (1993:43) critically identifies that "stage theory cannot be rigidly applied". He argues that the case of a small firm with high technology innovative products does not follow the incremental internationalisation patterns when it expands its business internationally. Moreover, other studies (Millington and Bayliss, 1990; Hedlund and Kverneland, 1984; Whitelock and Munday, 1993) found that some firms do not internationalise in a step-by-step process but leapfrog into internationalisation. A British study of 43 foreign direct investment cases found that 36% of United Kingdom companies established manufacturing subsidiaries when first entering the US markets (Newbould et al, 1978). Further to these criticism, Lindqvist (1988) and Bell (1995) argue that the pace and pattern of SME international growth and choices of entry mode are largely influenced by inter-firm relationships such as variety of network relationships (Benito and Welch, 1994) rather than depending on only the knowledge.

SME market entry decisions are more dynamic and complex than MNEs. It is difficult to explain in a simple way (Kumar and Subramaniam, 1997). For example, Katsikeas (1996) and Dool and Lowe (2001) argue that the vast majority of research of internationalisation is based on firms in the US and other Western developed countries. Given the considerable differences between Western and Eastern countries in many aspects, simple generalisations can be misleading. Therefore, to provide more precise insights for SME managers, more empirical research in line with the choice of market entry modes has been conducted by taking country differences into account.

2.4.4 Different Entry Mode Choices from Country Levels

National culture differences lead to different business cultures that further affect firms' strategic decisions (Hofstede, 1998) such as entry mode choices (Kogut and Singh, 1988). Tse and Pan (1997) argue that firms from same country may follow certain patterns when expanding their business internationally. On the contrary, firms from different countries may adopt different entry modes. For example, although research indicates that USA firms' entry modes are more flexible comparing with firms from other countries, patterns are still identified contextually. In one of their studies, Dunning and Pearce (1985) found that USA firms tend to venture alone when they enter Western foreign markets. Interestingly, in a recent study of USA firm market entry choices, Tse and Pan (1997) confirmed that joint venture and exports are USA firms' preferred choices in entering Chinese markets due to lacking of knowledge of local markets, political risks, and uncertainties. Not the same as USA firms, relying on their high quality and famous brand, Western European firms' entry mode choices are consistent to Johanson and Wiedersheim-Paul (1975) and Vahlne's (1977) incremental stage model. These Western European firms tend to start their internationalisation activities by adopting the low risk entry mode such as exporting. With increased knowledge and experiences in foreign markets in time, they consider expanding their business through joint ventures. Finally, these companies would utilise the wholly-owned subsidiary entry mode (Tse and Pan, 1997). The findings of Tse and Pan (1997) also reveal that Japanese firms prefer to high control modes from long term orientation. For example, Hood, Young and Lalls (1994) and Williams (1999) indicate that Greenfield entry mode is favoured by Japanese companies rather than merger and acquisition when entering the UK markets.

Of note, findings above are mainly based on Western and Japanese MNEs. In the context of SMEs'

internationalisation, a few studies indicate that SMEs from different country intend to use different

entry modes as well. Nakos, Brouthers and Moussetis (2002) found that Dutch SMEs are more

preferred non-equity entry modes comparing with Greek SMEs when entering Central East European

countries. Nakos, Brouthers and Moussetis (2002) themselves suggest that further studies should

focus upon SME entry mode choices at country levels so that international researchers can improve

their understanding of SMEs' internationalisation on country basis.

Choo and Mazzarol (2001) examined the choices of market entry modes of SMEs between Australia

and Singapore. Their findings show that Australian SMEs are limited to exporting or agent entry

modes. With more options, Singaporean SMEs were more likely to consider licensing, joint venture,

and manufacturing entry modes particularly when entering Southeast Asian countries. Evidently,

different economic positions and business cultural varieties distinguish firms' foreign entry mode

choices from country to country. Drawing upon above research findings, it is proposed that CSME

managers may have different entry mode choices comparing with SMEs from Western developed

countries. In the next section, factors that influence firms' foreign entry mode choices will be

discussed in detail.

2.5 Different Theoretical Frameworks and Entry Mode Choices

Examining international entry mode choices of SMEs is important as it is significantly related to

SMEs' performance (Lu and Beamish, 2001, Nakos, Brouthers and Moussetis, 2000). However, how

to choose the mode of entry is a very difficult question to answer in general terms. The market entry

decision is a function of the interaction of various factors. There are many factors that, controllable and uncontrollable, affect managers' decision making of the entry mode choices (Root, 1994). To find out the variety of factors that influence a firm's choice of entry mode, many international researchers have developed a range of theoretical frameworks from different perspectives across several disciplines, such as economy, marketing, strategic management, and organisational behaviour (Hymer, 1976; Vernon, 1966, 1979; Buckley and Casson, 1976; Dunning, 1980, 1985, 1988; Anderson and Gatignon, 1986, 1988; Hill et al., 1990; Erramilli and Rao, 1990, Root, 1994).

Being a crucial issue in international strategic decisions, factors influencing the choice of entry mode have been critically discussed by economists and marketing experts. Many prominent modes and theories have been developed in past decades, such as the stage model (Johanson and Wiedersheim-Paul, 1975; Johanson and Vahlne, 1977), network theory (Johanson and Mattsson, 1988), transaction cost analysis model (Anderson and Gatignon, 1986), and resource-based theory (Capron and Hulland, 1999; Conner, 1991; Hunt, 2002; Ekeledo and Sivakumar, 2003). With different theories applied, each theoretical framework provides different academic insights to help international researchers understand why a certain entry mode offers lower cost than others and why certain factors have to be considered in a manager's entry decision-making over others. In the following discussions different models and frameworks are to be reviewed and criticised.

2.5.1 Stage Model

The stage model (Johanson and Wiedersheim-Paul, 1975, Johanson and Vahlne, 1977) is also known as the incremental model which has already been discussed in the section 2.4.3 with the focus of the entry mode process, factors influencing the mode change patterns have not been explicitly discussed. In this pattern-oriented approach, experiential knowledge of the foreign markets is the key factor influencing firm's entry mode choices in different stages. Logically, Johanson and Wiedersheim-Paul (1975) indicate that each stage, from low risk to high control model, involves increased commitment. This commitment increases when firms learn more from the foreign markets (Bilkey and Tesar, 1977; Cavusgil, 1984; Kedia and Chokar, 1986). In particular, firms become less uncertain about the foreign markets when they move from one stage to another. It is because they gain more experiential knowledge in a particular foreign market (Calof and Beamish, 1995). However, stage theory suffers from some key problems. It can not explain why some firms established their first manufacturing branches before setting their sales subsidiaries (see detailed examples in section 2.4.3). Moreover, moving to a new stage is determined by not only experiential knowledge but other factors, such as stimuli and other mediating factors associated with the internal and external environment (Calof and Beamish, 1995).

2.5.2 Transaction Cost Analysis Model

The Transaction Cost Analysis (TCA) model was initially developed by Anderson and Gatingnon (1986) on the basis of MNEs. TCA model suggests the entry mode choice can be exclusively determined on a least-cost basis. The underlying rationale for the entry mode choice in transaction cost analysis is efficiency. According to Anderson and Gatingnon (1986), the choice of entry mode is based on the most efficient organisation structure for coordinating its international productive activities (Cannon, 1993). Many factors giving rise to transaction costs have been identified, such as transaction cost relating to vertical integration and marketing productivity problems (Anderson and Weitz, 1986), environment and strategic factors (Hill, *et al*, 1990), information impacts, uncertainty and complexity (Jones and Hill, 1988). This TCA model is extended into the service industry by Erramilli and Rao (1993). Most interestingly, Nakos *et al* (2002) investigated Dutch and Greek SMEs and concluded that TCA mode is applicable in the context of SME international market entry mode choices. Their findings suggest that SMEs prefer equity modes when making asset specific investment, but tend to adopt non-equity modes of entry while making less asset specific investment.

Although TCA model has been widely examined and applied in the research of foreign market entry mode choices by many researchers (e.g. Erramilli, 1990; Nakos and Brouthers, 2002; Palenzuela and Bobillo, 1999; Taylor and Zhou, 1998), it was criticized that TCA model is ambiguous and difficult to measure (Decker and Zhao, 2004). This model excludes non-transaction benefits. Meanwhile, it largely neglects government-imposed factors which normally impact a firm's entry modes choices (Anderson and Gatignon, 1986; Tse, Pan and Au, 1997). Moreover, the TCA model fails to take strategic and competitive context into account in relation to firm's entry mode choice (Madhok, 1998).

2.5.3 Resource-Based Theory

Another theory relating to firms' choices of entry mode is resource-based theory. Underlying the resource-based theory, a firm's entry mode choice is based on considerations of firm-specific resources that afford the firm's competitive advantages. There is a fit between the firm's resources and external opportunities (Capron and Hulland, 1999; Conner, 1991; Hunt, 2002). Nakos and Brouthers (2002) argue that two major transaction costs are important in deciding SME entry mode choices: market transaction cost and control cost. They claim that market transaction cost is related to the asset specificity of the investment required when making a new foreign entry. Asset specificity could be the physical or human resources that are unique for company to complete a specific task (Williamson, 1985; Williamson and Ouchi, 1981; Wernerfelt, 1984). Moreover, Malhotra et al (2003)

45

address that firms' other resources such as financial information and relation could also influence a firm's entry mode choices. The specific mode of foreign entry depends on the type of resource advantage. Nakos *et al* (2002) found that SMEs tend to adopt non-equity modes of entry when asset specificity is low but prefer equity modes of entry when asset specificity is high.

2.5.4 Emergence of Network Theory

According to Emerson (1981), a network can be described as a set of two of more connected business relationships. This relationship could be built from competitors, suppliers, customers, distributors and government (Axelsson and Johanson, 1992; Sharma and Johanson, 1987; Johanson and Mattsson, 1988). More generally, this relationship is either interorganisational or interpersonal (Coviello and McAuley, 1999). Network theory suggests that network relationships influence initial market entry mode choices (Malhotra *et al,* 2003; Coviello and McAuley, 1999; Morsink, 1998).

It is recognised that there is a growing body of literature highlighting the potential influence of network relationships on the firm's internationalisation (Johanson and Vahlne 1992; Ghauri and Henriksen, 1994; Bell, 1995; Coviello and Martin, 1999). Going further to motivations of internationalisation, international researchers suggest that a firm's decision regarding entry is relevant to its business networks. This network relationship facilitates a firm's outward expansion and influences its initial market entry decisions (Axelsson and Johanson, 1992; Mayer and Skak, 2002).

The assumption in the network theory is that relationships built through business activities can help firms to gain access to resources and markets (Malhotra *et al,* 2003; Johanson and Mattsson, 1988). Lacking of resources has been identified as a natural constraint in SMEs business activities, particularly its internationalisation. Established foreign networks can help SMEs expand their international businesses efficiently (Carter and Jones-Evans, 2006). Research examining network issues in the context of SMEs is increasing. Many studies led by international researchers (Coviello and Munro, 1997; Coviello and Martin, 1999; Chetty and Holm, 2000; Johanson and Mattsson, 1988; Mayer and Skak, 2002) have shifted their attention to using network theory to explain SMEs' internationalisation activities. In their survey of New Zealand-based software small firms, Coviello and Munro (1997) indicate that international market growth patterns and entry mode choices of small firms are influenced by close relationships with its inter-firms, such as clients, suppliers and customers. Before good relationships are built firms tend to prefer low cost entry mode when entering the foreign counties. In contrast, the high cost investment entry mode may be adopted when firms' network relationships are well developed. This view is supported by Bell (1995) and Lindqvist (1988), as well as Johanson and Mattsson (1988).

Closely examining the current network research in relation to SMEs internationalisation, it is recognised that most authors successfully explained the Western SMEs' internationalisation process and entry mode choice, but failed to reveal SMEs approach in the context of Asian countries in this issue. With the changing roles of Asian firms in the global markets, the analysis of Asian firms' foreign market entry strategy based on the network approach has been increased. In the context of Asian MNEs, Sim and Pandian (2003) studied Taiwanese and Singaporean textile and technology companies and their findings highlight that networks and alliances play an important role in Asian MNEs entry strategy choices, particularly the ethnic networks in the Asian region. In such networks, firms' cooperative activities are based on ethically linked personal connections ('Guanxi') that provide firms the country-specific knowledge of local markets and distribution system because these connections enable them to share similar cultural heritage and management attitudes. Being different from the international literature on Western SMEs, networks of Asian firms are largely based on ethnic and cultural foundations rather than networks developed through business clients and partners. This view is supported by Hamilton (1996). Through above discussions, it is apparent that the ethic and social embedded networks and relationships ('Guanxi') are key features of Asian firms. Unfortunately, this specific relationship has not been well studied underlying the context of Asian enterprises (Sim and Pandian, 2003), especially Asian SMEs.

It is noted that all the theories having been discussed above examine firms' market entry mode choices from single factor aspect. However, one thing is asserted that "no single theory can be expected to satisfactorily encompass all kinds of foreign-owned value-added activity simply (Dunning, 2001: 176)". One could hardly recommend a specific strategy for all situations as each theoretical framework contains its own pros and cons. Each single mode is imperfect due to the neglect of other relevant important factors (Decker and Zhao, 2004). Therefore, a framework integrating multiple theoretical perspectives is more appropriate in explaining the complex entry mode selection decision. Accordingly, Dunning (1980, 1988) integrates different factors synthetically and developed the eclectic mode, which is one of the most well-know and widely adopted theoretical frameworks in relation to entry mode choices. Comprehensive understanding of Dunning's (1980, 1988) framework can help international researchers to understand entry mode choices systematically.

2.5.5 Dunning's Eclectic Theory

To modify transaction cost theory by adding non-transaction cost benefits, Dunning (1980, 1988) developed an eclectic model that has been widely used in exploring firms' entry mode choices by international researchers. Dunning suggests that 3 sets of factors will affect a firm's entry mode choices: Ownership advantages (O), Location advantages (L), Internationalisation advantages (I). O-advantages cover a broad range of potential sources which could be tangible (natural resources, capital manpower etc.) or intangible (brands, knowledge, organisation skills, etc.). L-advantages consider the local market size, physical and political infrastructure, income capital, etc. I-advantages refer to the ability of a firm to leverage its domestic competitive advantages abroad by internalising markets (Dunning, 1993). The eclectic framework has improved TCA mode by integrating firms' assets power (O-advantages), market attractiveness (L-advantages) and cost of integration (I-advantages) together. Dunning's (1980, 1988, 1993) eclectic mode suggests that the more OLI advantages the firm obtains, the more likely the firm prefers more integrated modes of entry, such as wholly owned subsidiary entry modes.

More than just adding values to TCA model, many scholars admite that Dunning's (1980, 1988) eclectic framework is superior to many other single theories as it synthesises many important factors by integrating them into the entry mode choices. OLI model has been widely examined and extended by many researchers (Kogut and Singh, 1998; Vernon, 1983; Hill, Kwang and Kim, 1990; Erammilli and Rao, 1993; Pan and Tes, 2000; Nakos and Brouthers, 2002; Brouthers, Brouthers and Werner, 1999) and supported by many empirical studies (Brouthers and Werner, 1999; Nokas and Brouthers, 2002).

In one of their SME international studies, Nakos and Brouthers (2002) sampled 133 Greek SMEs, investigating their foreign investments in the Central and Eastern European (CEE) markets. Their findings indicate that SMEs' entry mode choices highly depend on their ownership advantages. Their

49

empirical study suggests that Dunning's eclectic framework is applicable in predicting SMEs' entry mode selection in CEE markets. Moreover, to explore the usefulness of Dunning's eclectic theory, O'Gorman and McTiernan (2000) conducted a study of small and medium-sized Irish hotel groups entering international markets. The findings conclude that SMEs must develop both ownership advantages and organisational capacity to transfer them into certain international markets.

Unarguably, OLI framework has done an excellent job in explaining a firm's foreign market entry mode choices. However, the practical values of Dunning's framework have been questioned by a few scholars. Decker and Zhao (2004) argued that OLI framework intends to explore all important factors influencing entry mode choices but it is impossible to do so practically. Dunning himself (1980) points out that OLI is too much 'paradigm' and too little of a 'model' for researchers and practitioners. Moreover, Buckley and Casson (1998: 540) point out that 'its (OLI) complexity appears to have created a degree of confusion amongst scholars, which only a formal modeling exercise can dispel'. Generally, Decker and Zhao (2004) argue that many existing theoretical frameworks focus upon only one or two factors (size, culture etc.) and neglect other relevant important elements such as strategic goals.

In summary, the preceding theories in the context of firms' entry mode choices have been discussed. Stage theory emphasises firms' experiential knowledge and its impact on a firm's incremental entry mode choices. Transactional cost analysis is based on the conception of economic efficiency. Moreover, resource-based theory is more focused on the fit between organisational resources and international opportunities. By transposing the social exchange perspective of social networks into business networks, network theory indicates that the actors in the business network, such as suppliers and customers and distributors play important roles in SMEs international business activities. Nevertheless, as discussed earlier, each single theory has its drawbacks. To overcome the criticism, eclectic framework can be used to explain firms' international entry mode choices in a comprehensive way.

Overall, the foreign market entry mode choice is a very complicated process. Reviewing the past research, a large number of influencing factors in light of firm's entry mode choices from different theoretical perspective have been created. However, only a few of them provide insights to international decision makers from practical perspective. Some of them are complex and ambiguous and make decision makers confused. For example, Nakos and Brouthers (2002) investigated 133 Greek SMEs in entering the CEE markets. Their findings indicate that international experience did not appear as an influencing factor that affected Greek SMEs' entry mode choices. However, same authors in the same year, by sampling Greek SMEs again, Nakos, Brouthers and Moussetis (2002) in their other article '*Greek and Dutch SMEs Entry Mode Choice and Performance: A transaction Cost Perspective*' state that international experience played a significant role in these SMEs entry mode choices. By reviewing these two studies carefully, the author found that both data were collected by sending 450 questionnaires to Greek SMEs. Presumably, the same collected data was used for these two studies, but the results were contrastive. Consequently, research in exploring the influencing factors and firms' entry mode choices has to be carefully designed and conducted. In order to produce more precise research outcomes, main influencing factors from both theoretical frameworks and empirical studies in light of firms' entry mode choices are to be systematically synthesised in the next section

2.6 Synprojectof Main Influencing Factors

Due to the importance of entry mode choices, international researchers have given influencing factors
and the choice of entry mode special care and attentions (e.g. Dunning, 1980, 1989; Buckley, 1998;
Erramilli, Agarwal and Dev, 2002; Doherty, 2000). Based on different theories discussed above, a
large number of studies try to either test or extend these theories by identifying certain single or
multiple factors. However, some of the results contain many seemingly unrelated considerations and
give little consideration of research method systematically (Anderson and Gatignon, 1986; Cannon,
1993). From a practitioner's perspective, no decision makers will decide their market entry mode by
considering a solo determinant factor. To provide managers with guidance of choosing optimal entry
modes, the comprehensive review of influencing factors and entry mode choices is much needed. The
following summary of key factors tries to provide a systematic basis for the choice of the entry mode
with focuses of a set of factors: firm-specific factors, product-specific factors, strategic factors,
culture factor, and decision maker's characteristics.

2.6.1 Firm's Ownership Advantages

To test the validity of the existing theories of foreign market entry mode choices, various empirical
studies have been conducted in this field regarding firms' ownership advantages (e.g. Anderson, 1997;
Anderson and Svensson, 1994; Brown, Dev and Zhou, 2003; Whitelock, 1995, 2002; Woodcock,
Beamish, and Makino 1994). The findings of these studies indicate that firm size, international
experience, and knowledge know-how are 3 key influencing factors. Research in relation to these
factors has mainly sampled international MNEs from developed countries, but some SME studies are
increasing currently.

Based upon surveys of MNEs, the findings of early literature surrounding **firm size** show 2 interesting results. Some researchers assert that the bigger the firm is, the more likely it is to adopt high control entry mode (e.g. Ali and Camp, 1993; Erramilli and Rao, 1993; Kogut and Singh, 1988; Caves and Mehra, 1986). Others conclude that the size of a firm is not an important predictor in firms' entry mode choices (e.g. Evans, 2002; Reuber and Fischer, 1997). Moreover, by sampling SMEs in the given situation, Nakos and Brouther (2002) found that there is no significant difference in Greek SMEs' entry mode choices considering the firm size. However, in one of their studies, Shi, Ho and Siu (2001) conducted a survey by sampling Hong Kong SMEs entering Mainland China. The findings indicate that firm size is likely to affect the selection of entry mode. Relative larger Hong Kong SMEs prefer to wholly owned subsidiaries in mainland China as they have financial capacity to handle international expansion.

International experience has been recognised as another important factor which affects a firm's entry mode choices in the past research (Kim and Kogut, 1996; Mudambi, 1998). However conflicts appear among the research. Studies by Eramilli (1991) and Anderson and Gatignon (1986) indicate that a firm's international experience has positive correlation to high-level control model. The more international experience a firm possesses, the more likely the firm adopts an entry mode with higher level of control. This finding is supported by many researchers (e.g. Evans, 2002; Herrman and Datta, 2002; King and Tucci, 2002; Anderson and Gatignon, 1986; Reuber and Fischer, 1997). However, other studies report contradictory evidences to suggest that a firm's international experience is not instrumental in its entry mode decisions (Kogut and Singh, 1988). Sometimes it has a negative relation to firms' entry mode choices (Chung and Enderwick, 2001).

Of note, above empirical studies are mainly focused on MNEs entry mode choices. Having discussed earlier, underlying the context of Greek and Dutch SMEs entering CEE markets, two studies by Nakos and Brouthers (2002) and Kakos; Brouthers and Moussetis (2002) represented contradictory results. The former showed that firm international experience was not a significant predictor in SME entry mode choices. However, the latter indicated that Greek SMEs with great international experience prefer equity modes of entry with higher control. Shi, Ho and Siu's (2001) research based on Hong Kong SMEs entering the mainland China supports Nakos and Brouthers (2002) and shows that international experience does not seem to affect the selection of entry mode.

Deriving from the resource-based theory (Capron and Hulland, 1999; Conner, 1991; Hunt, 2002; Denekamp, 1995), existing research indicates that **know-how knowledge** has a certain impact on a firm's entry mode choices. Dunning (1988) argues that a firm's specific knowledge of know-how is an important ownership advantage. It is normally difficult to be transferred and articulated (Hill *et al,* 1990; Kim and Hwang, 1992). Therefore, a company with know-how knowledge is more likely to use high control mode of wholly-owned subsidiary since the knowledge know-how as a tacit component can not be easy transferred and maintained. Moreover, the know-how knowledge as an intangible resource is normally highly protected by firms to sustain their competitive advantages. Purposely, firms with special knowledge know-how prefer a wholly-owned subsidiary mode when entering international markets (Dunning, 1988; Kogut and Zander, 1993).

Considering conflicting results discussed above, it is necessary to conduct more contextual empirical studies regarding firm size and international experience factors and get in-depth understanding of ownership advantages and their impacts on firms' strategic market entry choices more precisely and systematically.

2.6.2 Strategic Factors

Companies cannot make their business decisions solely based on economic factors, but usually have to pay extensive attention to non economic conditions (Anderson and Gatignon, 1986). Given the consideration of strategic importance, a number of international researchers claimed that managers' strategic views and firms' strategic goals actually affect a firm's entry decisions (e.g.Almor, 2001; Isobe, Makino and Montgomery, 2000; Shi, Ho and Siu, 2001; Hill, Huang and Kim, 1990). In other words, firms may be driven by strategic objectives rather than selecting the most efficient method of foreign market entry (Cannon, 1993).

Reviewing the prior empirical studies, strategic factors examined in light of firms' entry mode choices include long-term or short-term internationalisation strategy (Ghemawat, 1991), timing of entry strategy (Delios and Makino, 2003; Silvakumar, 2002; Isobe, Makino and Montgomery, 2000), objectives of market entry (Bradely, 2000, Shi, Ho and Siu, 2001), global or multi-domestic strategy (Anderson and Gatignon, 1986; Hwang, 1988; Hill, Hwang and Kim, 1990). Ghemawat (1991) claims that firms aiming for long-term international expanding prefer entry mode with high level of control. In contrast, the short-term expansion strategy leads to low cost mode choices.

In their eclectic model, Hill, Hwang and Kim (1990) integrate strategic factors into the entry mode choices and found that firms pursuing a multi-domestic strategy will favor low-control entry modes because multi-domestic strategy requires each subsidiary in the foreign country to have its own market functions. The products may vary between nations according to the preferences of different customers. In contrast, firms pursuing a global strategy prefer high-control entry modes. This is because, Hill, Hwang and Kim (1990) further explained, achieving a high level of coordination requires a high degree of control over the operations of different national affiliates. By considering marketing strategic factors, Cannon (1993) proposes that firms adopting market diversification strategy prefer low control entry mode as objective of diversification strategy is to achieve a high level of return from low level of resource allocations. If firms employ market concentration strategy, they intend to choose high control entry mode because these modes allow firms to control foreign markets. It is noted that both strategic factors proposed by Hill, Hwang and Kim (1990) and Cannon (1993) are again based on MNEs from theoretical perspective. No further empirical research has been carried out to test their hypotheses.

Extending the idea of strategic influencing factors into SMEs international context, Shi, Ho and Siu (2001) sampled 123 Hong Kong SMEs and investigated their market entry mode choices in their entries of mainland China. The findings of the research show that 2 strategic factors have significant influences on Hong Kong SME entry mode choices. They are export-oriented strategy and market-seeking strategy. Shi, Ho and Siu's (2001) statistical results indicate that Kong SMEs following an export-oriented strategy prefer setting wholly owned subsidiary with highest control to pursue profits and growth by manufacturing low cost products in mainland China and exporting them to other countries. Differently, small Hong Kong firms following a market-seeking strategy prefer joint venture entry mode to expand their market shares in mainland China. To the author's best knowledge, none of other empirical studies have been conducted by considering firms' strategic factors underlying Asian SMEs market entry mode choices. This research is to fill the gap by investigating CSME managers' entry mode choices when entering The North of England markets.

2.6.3 Product-Specific Factors

Product as a core component of business obviously should be taken into great consideration when strategic decisions are made (Root, 1998). Product factors in the target markets play a large role in a firm's decisions of market entry mode choices. However, this category covers different analyses as it involves wide elements of products. For example, to discover influences of product factors on firms' entry mode choices, some empirical studies investigate product images and reputations (Lee, 1986; Anderson and Gatignon, 1986), others focus on products in relation to customer services and life cycle state of the product in the target markets (Lee, 1986; Harrigan, 1983; Davidson, 1982).

Regarding entry mode choices, in his well-known book *Entry Strategy for International Markets*, Root (1998) divides products into 4 different types: differentiated products, standard products, service-intensive products, and technology-intensive products. Due to the unique features of these different products, Root (1998) further claims that if a firm's products are highly differentiated, the company will prefer the exporting entry mode since "such products can absorb high unit transportation cost and high import duties and still remain competitive in a foreign target country (p.13)". Standard products favor local production through contract manufactures or equity investments to keep its low cost advantages. However, this finding is mainly derived from US companies' international business activities. It is assumed that this conclusion will not be applicable into Asian firms' internationalisation due to contrasting conditions of labour and materials cost between Western and Eastern countries. Root (1998) argues that firms with service-intensive products must find a way to perform their services in the foreign markets as they cannot export. These types of companies can locate their services by setting up local branches and subsidiaries. Moreover, technological intensive products push a company toward either licensing entry modes or equity investments to protect their know-how knowledge (Dunning, 1988; Kogut and Zander, 1993).

2.6.4 National Culture Influences

Another most commonly investigated factor in light of firms' internationalisation in the prior studies is national culture. Root (1998:237) asserts that "cultural differences can affect any and all entry strategy decisions: the choice of entry mode, the control of entry operations". Many other international researchers also claim that cultural factors are key elements to be considered by managers in their foreign market entry mode choices (e.g. Dunning and Bansal, 1997; Nordstrom and Vahlne, 1992; Kogut and Singh, 1988; Brouthers and Brouthers, 2001). Socio-cultural factors influence a company's choice of entry mode because differences of the cultural values, language, social structure, and ways of business management on the foreign country differ strikingly from the home country (Dunning and Bansal, 1997; Johanson and Valhne, 1975; Kogut and Singh, 1988, 1999; Hill et al, 1990; Root, 1998).

In the broad sense, Hofstede (1980) defines culture as a collective programming of the mind which distinguishes the members of one human group from another. This generic term is made up of a host of interrelated elements, such as family, language, and communication, government and policy etc., (Baligh, 1994; Dunning and Bansal, 1997; Makino and Kent, 2000; Mitra and Golder, 2002). In Hofstede's (1994) culture research 5 dimensions were identified: power distance, individualism versus collectivism, masculinity versus femininity, uncertainty avoidance, and long-term versus short-term. Cultural similarities and differences from national level have close relevance to a firm's internationalisation (O'Grady and Lane, 1996; Dunning, 1997; Nakos and Brouthers, 2002) as Hofstede (1994:1) states that "the business of international business is culture".

Reviewing previous studies, the cultural distance has been frequently claimed to influence the selection of entry mode (Kogut and Singh, 1998; Nakos and Brouthers, 2002; Dunning and Bansal, 1997; Kim and Hwang, 1992). With provided large-sample statistical evidences, Kogut and Singh's (1988) study based on the data of 228 entries into the United State markets shows that the social culture factor has a negative relationship with control modes. Their findings indicate that the greater the cultural distance between the home and host countries, the more likely a firm would prefer a joint venture entry mode to reduce the risk of uncertainty in those markets. This statement is supported by a number of international researchers (e.g. Catignon and Anderson, 1998; Agarwal, 1994; Erramilli and Rao, 1993). However, other empirical studies provide evidences showing that the distance of national culture presents a positive relationship with the high level of control entry mode, such as wholly owned manufacturing subsidiary (Padmanabhan and Cho, 1996; Delios and Ensign, 2000). These researchers claim that the greater the cultural distance between the home and host countries, the more likely a firm prefers to establish their own sole ventures to avoid multi-culture management issues when entering foreign countries. In contrast, Root (1998) claims that great cultural distance leads to non-equity entry modes (e.g. exporting) that limit a firm's commitment in the foreign country. Conflictions discussed above require more empirical data to make concrete theoretical statements in the context of organisational and managerial preferences by firms from different nations.

Beyond the general characteristics of national culture differences, some empirical studies investigated a few cultural components and their influences on a firm's entry mode choices. Fisher and Ransinghe (2000:353) argue that "companies may be influenced more by certain cultural characteristics than by general perceptions of cultural difference". Previous studies show that the most influential cultural component in relation to firm's entry mode choice is the level of uncertainty avoidance (Edwards and Buckley, 1998; Fisher and Ransinghe, 2000). For instance, a company's confidence in its ability to manage business difficulties in foreign markets tends to influence its choice of level of control (Andeson and Gatignon, 1986; Caves and Mehra, 1986; Kogut and Singh, 1988).

By investigating Singapore building and construction industry companies, Fisher and Ransinghe (2000) explored that uncertainty avoidance is listed as a dominant trait in a situation involving foreign investment. Their findings show that firms whose native country's culture is defined by a higher level of uncertainty avoidance have a strong preference to choose joint venture entry mode. Moreover, from a cultural perspective, Dunning and Pearce's (1985) research reveals that if possible, American firms tend to venture alone when they enter foreign markets because of American higher individual and lower uncertainty avoidance cultural features. Tse and Pan (1997) found that Japanese firms prefer a high control mode by pursuing long-term orientation (dominant Japanese culture). For example, Greenfield entry mode is favoured by Japanese firms rather than merger and acquisition modes particularly in entering the UK markets (Williams, 1999).

Studies discussed above based on Western MNEs show that national culture has a significant influence on a firm's foreign market entry mode choices. Building upon these findings, the consideration of the Asian culture impact on Asian SMEs internationalisation has to be paid. Intensive studies have identified that Asian cultures distinguish from Western cultures in many different ways (Hofstede, 1980, 1986; Redding, 1990; Trompenaars, 1993; Hodgetts and Luthans, 1997). For example, rooted in Jewish, Christian, Greek, and Roman background, Western thinking is analytical while Eastern thinking is synthetic as it is rooted in Confucianism, Buddhism, and

Hinduism. The basic differences between Eastern thinking and Western thinking inevitably lead to different management assumptions (Hofstede, 1994). Consequently, the strategic decision making of Asian SMEs market entry mode choices needs to be seen particularly in its cultural embeddings.

2.6.5 Decision Maker's Characteristics

Drawing upon the strategic management and entrepreneurship literature, a number of researchers have attempted to identify decision makers' characteristics and its influences on firms' international business activities (e.g. Calof and Beamish, 1995; Chetty and Campbell-Hunt, 2003; Reid, 1981; Chetty, 1999; Suarez-Ortega and Alamo-Vera, 2005). According to Thomas *et al* (1991), the background of CEOs in large organisations is strongly associated with firms' strategic choices. Extending this idea into the international business context, the choice of entry mode may be affected by decision makers' personal characteristics.

There is a growing support that decision makers' characteristics have certain influences on their international strategic decision making. However, the research has predominantly focused on the relationship between the international experience of top managers and the degree of firms' internationalisation based on large organisations (Athannassiou and Night, 2000; Carpenter and Fredrickson, 2001; Reuber and Fischer, 1997). Very limited research has been conducted to explore the decision maker's characteristics and its influences on firms' choices of foreign market entry mode. Reviewing the existing studies, there are only 2 empirical studies have been carried out by Herrman and Datta (2002, 2006) that directly investigated CEO's characteristics and its effects on the choice of entry mode. In their first study, Herrman and Datta (2002) investigated 126 CEOs successions based on large organisations (sales over $250 millions) and examined the relationship between successor

CEO characteristics and their choices of entry mode throughout 271 foreign market entry events. The results indicate that with increasing position tenure, CEOs favored full-control entry model as greater legitimacy in their position goes along with higher levels of confidence and experience. Moreover, CEO's personal international experience also pushes them towards to a full-control mode since greater international experience provides CEOs with knowledge and confidence in the target foreign markets. In their very latest research, Herrmann and Datta (2006) surveyed 78 US large companies based on their 380 foreign market entries. The findings show that the old CEOs, compared with younger CEOs, are more likely to choose joint venture as their entry mode choice as they have greater experience in working with partners.

In SME sector, researchers also attempt to investigate what role decision makers' characteristics play in their internationalisation decision making (e.g. Reid, 1981; Cavusgil, 1984; Chetty and Campbell-Hunt, 2003). From different perspectives, a number of empirical studies explore SME owner managers' characteristics and their international business activities. Calof and Beamish (1995) found that decision makers' attitudes (e.g. risk taking) propel a firm's internationalisation. By examining the exporting development process, Suarez-Ortega and Alamo-Vera (2005) investigated 286 Spanish wine-growing SMEs. Their findings indicate that managers' educational level, experiences abroad and their foreign language proficiency are positively associated with the level of exporting development and affect the degree of exporting process, export intention, export propensity, and export intensity. However, Suarez-Ortega and Alamo-Vera (2005) did not further investigate how these factors actually affected Spanish SMEs' other entry mode choices such as joint venture.

Additionally, a few studies have claimed that decision makers' past experience (Calof and Beamish,

1995) and level of education (Simpson and Kujawa, 1974) have certain influences on SMEs' international business performance. However, these studies from SME sector predominantly focused on the pace of SMEs' internationalisation rather than their entry mode choices. Calof and Beamish (1995) claim that decision makers' characteristics determine how they perceive the benefits, costs and risks of internationalisation. To submit to Calof and Beamish (1995), decision makers' characteristics discussed above will affect SMEs' initial entry mode choices. Theoretically, Kumar and Subramaniam (1997) propose that decision makers' personalities such as knowledge, abilities and motivations affect the final choice of a particular entry mode. However, there are no empirical studies that have explored this issue directly in SME sector.

2.7 Entry Mode Decision Making Process

From a practical perspective, the decision making process of entry mode choices has caused a number of researchers' attentions (e.g. Root, 1994; Kumar and Subramaniam, 1997; Pan and Tes, 2000; Young *et al* 1989; Reid, 1981). These leading scholars argue that a firm's entry mode choices should be regarded as a multistage decision making process instead of focusing on influencing factors only. Drawing upon this assumption, this section is to discuss the key features of entry decision making process approaches focusing on Root's (1994) comparing all entry modes approach and the hierarchical mode by Kumar and Subramaniam (1997) and Pan and Tes (2000) beginning with a review of two strategic approaches adopted in firms' entry decision making: rational and cybernetic strategy.

2.7.1 Rational Strategy versus Cybernetic Strategy

Making decisions is without doubt one of the most important functions of management. The outcome of decisions may determine a business survival (Lu, 1996). Managers' managerial behaviour can be understood through the study of decision processes and decision contexts (Pettigrew, 1988, 1989). Managers use different strategies and approaches to make their management decisions. Drawing upon different strategy schools, rational decision-making strategy (Mintzberg, Ahlstrand and Lampel, 1998) and cybernetic decision-making strategy (Lindzey and Aronson, 1985; Kumar and Subramaniam, 1997) are reviewed in this study.

Rational decision-making is a deliberate process of conscious thought. Managers adopting this approach make their decision-making as deliberate as possible (Mintzberg, Ahlstrand and Lampel, 1998). A rational decision-making process requires massive resources commitment such as collecting and analysing data, holding planning meetings etc. (Johnson and Whittington, 2006; Porter, 1996). In contrast, the cybernetic decision-making strategy draws on Simon's (1955) assumption that human brain can not obtain a rational solution to problem by considering all elements as it has a limited analytic capability. Extending Simon's (1955) idea into managers' strategic decision-making, Steinbruner (1974) propounds a cybernetic model of decision-making. Steinbruner (1974) states that only limited relevant factors can be taken into account by decision makers in making their strategic decisions. Moreover, rational strategy requires typically large amount of time and money. For cybernetic strategy, in contrast, lesser resources are spent on information collection (Kumar and Subramaniam, 1997). Since the rational decision-making mode requires massive resources commitment, it is best suitable for MNEs rather than SMEs that are more likely to use cybernetic decision strategy because most SMEs lack of resources to gather comprehensive information (Steinbruner, 1974; Kumar and Subramaniam, 1997).

Applying the cybernetic strategy into managers' international decision-making, Kumar and Subramaniam (1997) argue that one of the important steps in a firm's entry mode choices is to decide the decision strategy which decision makers adopt. Taken for granted, international strategic decisions are more complex compared with domestic businesses in a number of ways. Externally, international business often involves foreign currencies, different political and legal systems, and various cultures cross national boundaries. Internally, international organisations face greater challenges to configure and develop their available resources effectively to meet companies' international expansion (Johnson, Scholes and Whittington, 2006). All these factors make international strategic decision-making a very unstable and dynamic process due to a lot of uncertainties and unpredictability (Aharoni, 1966; Ghauri and Holstius, 1996; Griffin and Pustay, 2005; Johnson, Scholes and Whittington, 2006).

In one of his studies, Buckley (1998) indicates that the role of uncertainties of internationalisation looms large in SMEs' decision-making. Plus due to bias of information acquisition and time constraints, SME managers normally take short cuts and inadequate evaluations in their international decision making. Further to Buckley's (1998) suggestions, Kumar and Subramaniam (1997) assumed that strategic entry decision-making for SME managers is unfamiliar and uncertain. The decision context for SME managers is complex and dynamic. The decision-making environment is less-accountable. Consequently, SME decision makers tend to use less formal and less elaborate strategy in their entry decision-making. As Kumar and Subramaniam (1997) assert that a cybernetic decision-making model is more suitable for SME managers in deciding their strategic entry modes. However, Kumar and Subramaniam's (1997) theoretical hypoprojecthas not been further tested by empirical research.

2.7.2 Entry Decision Process by Comparing All Entry Modes

Successful internationalisation requires good strategic decision-making of entry mode choices. The decision process in foreign market entry mode choices is a critical and an important strategic procedure (Kumar and Subramaniam, 1997; Nakos and Brouthers, 2002). A process-orientated mode provides decision rules for decision makers who can apply these rules to their entry mode choices. However, little work has been done at identifying the decision making process in light of firms' strategic entry mode choices (Decker' and Zhao, 2004).

Root (1998) develops a decision-making approach by comparing all entry modes at the same levels (see figure 2.2). This decision model integrates 3 aspects over the entry mode decision planning and process: the availability of company resources, risk and nonprofit objectives. Figure 2.2 shows that decision makers start by reviewing all entry modes. With both advantages and disadvantages in mind, external and internal influencing factors are analysed on the basis of reliable information. Drawing upon the outcome of analysis, feasibility of entry modes can be decided. The feasible entry modes include, as Root (1998) claims, all possible entry modes to penetrate the target county within the company's resource and commitment capabilities. After feasible entry modes are screened, comparative analyses of profit contribution, risk and nonprofit objectives need to be conducted among these feasible entry modes. Finally, decision makers bring the analytical results together for an overall comparative assessment and rank the feasible entry modes to decide the most appropriate entry mode.

Figure 2.2 Foreign market entry decision process

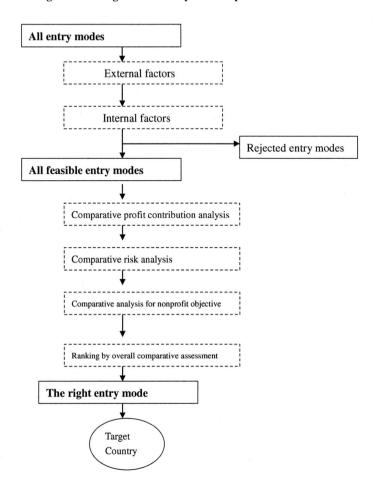

External factors

Internal factors

Rejected entry modes

All entry modes

All feasible entry modes

Comparative profit contribution analysis

Comparative risk analysis

Comparative analysis for nonprofit objective

Ranking by overall comparative assessment

The right entry mode

Target Country

Source: Root (1994) *Entry Strategies for International Markets.*
San Francisco: Jossey-Bass Publishers.

Root's (1994) entry mode decision process shown in figure 2.2 is based on the assumption of rational decision-making strategy. Decision makers make their entry mode choices in a deliberate way by screening massive information and spending large amounts of money. Root (1998) proposes that managers should consider all the modes of entry together at the same level when they make entry mode decisions. Moreover, he asserts that all the factors have the same level of relevance for all entry modes of entry. Root's (1998) comparing all entry modes approach seems more suitable for large companies, but SME managers less favour it. Alternatively, a hierarchical decision making mode is introduced by other international researchers.

2.7.3 The Hierarchical Process of Entry Mode

Having discussed above, decision makers adopting rational decision-making strategy in their entry mode choices normally consider all of the entry modes into account at the same point of time instead of just examining some entry modes and critical factors (Pan and Tse, 2000; Kumar and Subramaniam, 1997). However, as discussed earlier, it is assumed that decision makers have a limited analytical capacity (Simon, 1955). They sometimes adopt a set of critical factors to simplify a complex decision into a hierarchical process, especially for SME managers as they normally do not have enough time and resources to evaluate all alternatives at the same time (Kumar and Subramaniam, 1997).

Based on a sample of over 10,000 foreign entry activities into China, Pan and Tes (2000) empirically developed a process-orientated hierarchical mode in light of firms' market entry mode choices (see figure 2.3).

Figure 2.3 A hierarchical entry decision-making model

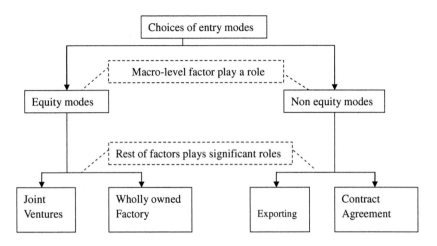

Sources: Adapted from Pan and Tse (2000) 'The Hierarchical Model of Market Entry Modes'.
Journal of International Business Studies, 31(4), pp535-554.

The hierarchical model shown in above proposes that entry modes can be reviewed as equity and non-equity entry modes at first instance. At this level, macro-level influencing factors often play a role. After equity or non equity entry modes are decided, decision makers should move down to next lower level and decide which specific mode within equity or non-equity is to be further considered. A set of micro-level factors are further invested to determine the choice of wholly owned operations or joint ventures in equity–based modes, and contractual agreements or export in non-equity based modes. However, in their empirical study, Pan and Tse (2000) did not clarify the size of these sampled companies (MNEs or SMEs). Moreover, this model does not indicate what kind of decision rules a decision maker might apply to make their choices (Decker' and Zhao, 2004), more 'process-oriented studies that investigate how managers make entry mode decision are needed' (Pan and Tes, 2000: 545).

2.7.4 A Contingency Framework for the Mode of Entry Decision

Drawing on the contingency theory, Beach and Mitchell (1998) developed a contingency mode of entry decision that is supported by Kumar and Subramaniam (1997) theoretically (see figure 2.4).

Figure 2.4 A contingency model of entry decision

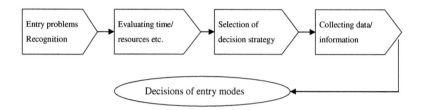

Source: Adapted from Kumar and Subramaniam (1997) 'A contingency framework for the mode of entry decision'. Journal of World Business, 32(1), pp53-72.

As shown in figure 2.4, this contingency entry decision-making process consists of 5 stages. The first stage involves entry problem recognitions (the entry decision-making context). Once the problems have been identified, decision makers move to the next stage evaluating the entry tasks. At this stage, Kumar and Subramaniam (1997) suggest that 3 questions should be asked: what factors that affect the modes have to be considered, where information on these factors can be collected from, and how much is going to cost to get this information. As a third stage, a decision strategy to solve the entry problem has to be selected. Both rational decision-making strategy and cybernetic decision-making strategy can be adopted at this stage. In the fourth step, information consistent with selected strategy should be collected. Finally, considering all the outcomes of previous 4 stages, the actual choices of foreign market entry modes will be decided when entering the foreign markets.

Critically, the contingency framework of entry mode decision is too 'general' to provide greater implications for the managers in practice. As the authors themselves suggest "how managers actually make the mode of entry decision should be further investigated (Kumar and Subramaniam, 1997:69)". Another issue is that this contingency framework that is theoretically proposed has not been empirically studied. In spite of its flaw, Kumar and Subramaniam's (1997) framework still provides greater insights to help decision makers in their foreign entry mode choices.

To sum up, a market entry mode choice is one of the most important issues and critical strategic decision as it has strong impact on a firm's future decisions and operations in the international markets (Root, 1994; Decker and Zhao, 2004). Previous research in this area largely focuses on the relationship between factor and entry mode and little attention has been put on the entry mode decision-making process. Indeed, the latter is essential for manager or a team of managers from practice perspective. Most importantly, more empirical studies building upon exiting entry decision-making process model should be carried out, especially from a practical perspective.

2.8 Chapter Summary

This chapter has reviewed why MNEs and SMEs are seeking internationalisation and how they choose their strategic market entry modes. Existing literature suggests that a foreign investment decision is a very complicated social process. It involves a variety of individual and organisational behaviours and is influenced by different elements at different stages. Intensive studies have been carried out on a Western MNEs basis. However, the FDI theory in relation to SME entry mode choices has not been comprehensively developed, especially those Asian SMEs from developing countries entering Western developed countries. It is recognised that explanations of 'why some modes of entry offer lower costs than others and why certain circumstances seem to favor certain entry modes over others' have not been fully explored regarding SME entry mode choices.

Moreover, the present literature generated from empirical studies has not given greater attention to research 'problem-setting (context)' and research 'methods design'. Consequently, conflictive results appear. To avoid these problems, it is important to design research methods with special care and attention by considering the research context where empirical research results are built. This research, as mentioned in Chapter One, will pay particular attention to foreign market entry mode choices with specific focus upon 'How do CSME Managers Make their Strategic Entry Mode Choice when Entering the UK'. It is hoped that more contextual research outcomes will be achieved. In fulfilling this purpose, the next chapter provides a discussion of the research approach used to achieve the research objectives set out for this study.

CHAPTER THREE

RESEARCH METHODOLOGY AND METHODS

3.1 Introduction

In the last chapter existing literature on choices of entry mode has been reviewed. Building upon the research gaps identified, research questions for this study emerged. To find the most suitable way to conduct empirical research, this chapter moves the discussion to methodology and methods adopted for this research. Drawing upon Crotty's (1998) epistemological paradigm, the philosophical debates and the positioning underpinning this study are discussed at the beginning of this chapter. With a claim of social constructionism and interpretivism as epistemological and philosophical stances, the details of the author's justification of why a qualitative methodology and semi-structured interview research method are selected for this study will be discussed. This is followed by the ethical considerations and the limitations of the research. Much of this chapter is concerned with the way in which the author collects appropriate data to explore the research questions.

3.2 Understanding Research Philosophies

Any research philosophy the researcher adopts contains important assumptions about the way in which he or she reviews the world (Saunders, Lewis and Thornhill, 2006; Luckman, 1967). The knowledge and how it is developed is an important issue in social research. The relationship between philosophy and social science has a long history. In contrast to natural science social science focuses on the intellectual life of human beings. Research in this area is based on assumptions about how the world is perceived and how people can best understand it (Bryman, 2001; 2004). These assumptions are important to help researchers in developing their research strategy and underpin research methods (Saunders, Lewis and Thornhill, 2006; Eastery-Smith *et al.,* 2002; Kumar, 1999; Crotty, 1998).

3.2.1 Ontology and Epistemology

Social ontology is concerned with 'what is' within 'the nature of existence' (Crotty, 1998: 10). In the philosophical tradition, ontology refers to the subject of existence (Hughes and Sharrock, 1997). It has been termed by philosophers as social scientists' assumptions about reality (Durant, 1953; Saunders, Lewis and Thornhill, 2006). Sitting alongside ontology, epistemological assumptions concern how a researcher begins to understand the world and communicate this as knowledge (Denzin and Lincoln, 2003; Burrell and Morgan, 1979). It is influenced by assumptions of ontology about the way the world operates (Saunders, Lewis and Thornhill, 2006; Morgan and Smircich, 1980). Epistemology deals with the nature of knowledge and is concerned with providing a philosophical grounding for researchers to decide how they can ensure that knowledge is adequate and legitimate (Maynard, 1994). It directs researchers to justify research methodology underpinning the research inquiry and clarify the research design. According to Crotty (1998), there are 3 main epistemologies: objectivist, constructionism and subjectivism. Social constructionism is the epistemology the author holds for this research.

3.2.2 Social Constructionism

Objectivism assures that "social phenomena and their meanings are independent of social actors (Bryman, 2004:16)". In this position, meaning exists "apart from the operation of any consciousness (Crotty, 1998: 8)". Ontologically, objectivism advocates that the meaning of social actions is independent. Researchers, taking this philosophical position, view the world as existing naturally

74

there (Burrell and Morgan, 1979; Crotty, 1998; Robson, 2002). In contrast, subjectivism assumes that meaning is imposed on the object by the subject (Bryman, 2004; Burrell and Morgan, 1979; Crotty, 1998; Denzin and Lincoln, 2003). Subjectivists hold the view that an object is meaningless in itself in the generation of meaning. The meaning emerges from an individual's mind that emphasises the importance of the subjective experience in the creation of the social world (Morgan and Smircich, 1980). This objectivist-subjectivist debate leads to the third epistemological approach: constructionism which brings objectivity and subjectivity together (Crotty, 1998).

According to Crotty (1998), a constructionism view is that meaning cannot simply be described either objectively or subjectively. On the one hand, this philosophical approach claims that the world is meaningless in itself and there is no objective truth, "truth (or meaning) comes into existence in and out of engagement with the realities in our world....meaning is not discovered, but constructed (Crotty, 1998:8-9)". Without a mind, meaning (or truth) does not exist. On the other hand, constructionists believe that creativity of meaning is not reliable if social researchers only judge the 'truth' according to personal feelings or intuitions rather than according to objective reasoning and judgment, this consciousness leads to a subjectivism epistemology. Constructionists hold the strong belief that meaning is associated with objects but it is constructed out of something.

To extend this, constructionism consideration raises the question of 'how meanings are constructed and whose meanings count'. Anderson (1998) and Crotty (1998) claim that beliefs and meaningful reality are socially constructed. As shared meaning, social reality is co-constructed, modified and reproduced through social life. Creation of knowledge does not take place in isolation. What we take to be knowledge of the world is a production of historically situated interchanges among people

(Greenwood, 1994; Gergen, 2003). This is the key concept of a social constructionism stance originally developed by Berger and Luckmann (1967) in their book *The Social Construction of Reality*.

As suggested by Crotty (1998) and Marshall (1994), social constructionists insist that society is produced by human beings. The social world is an interpretive net woven by individual and groups. From their viewpoint, the social phenomena exist not just 'out there' but in the minds of people who construct meanings and knowledge through an on-going dynamic social process between individuals (Gergen, 1985). Moreover, Crotty (1998) emphasises that a social constructionism shapes the way in which people look at the world holding their culture on them. As noted by Crotty (1998: 54), "we are inevitably viewing it through lenses bestowed upon us by our culture. Our culture brings things into view for us and endows them with meaning". People, either individual or groups, depend on culture to direct their behaviours and organise their experiences. Social reality is a function of shared meaning (Marshall, 1994). However, function does not exist without culture. It can be seen that humans do not create the natural world but make sense of 'the world' through their culture that is already embedded. These socially constructed meanings can be explored in different ways.

An interpretivist approach looks for "culturally derived and historically situated interpretations of the social life-world (Crotty, 1998: 67)". From an interpretivist point of view, to understand a particular social action, meaning in an action must be found and interpreted, and constructed afterwards (Denzin and Lincoln, 2003; Crotty, 1998; Saunders, Lewis and Thornhill, 2003). Social researchers adopting an interpretative stance face "a double interpretation: the researcher is providing an interpretation of others' interpretations" (Bryman, 2004:15).

In summary, the aim of social research is to produce insights (Ghauri and Gronhaug, 2005; Chalmers, 1999; Marshall and Rossman, 1995; Hollis, 1994; Silverman, 1993). These insights, to be accounted as knowledge, must be justified as a 'true' belief. In the act of justifying, all research is based on researchers' own assumptions about how the world is perceived and how people can best understand it (Burrell and Morgan, 1989; Crotty, 1998; Strauss and Corbin, 1998).

3.2.3 Philosophical Paradigm of This Research

Different ways of viewing the world shape different ways of researching the world (Crotty, 1998). Based on the belief that reality is socially constructed by individuals and determined by the way in which researchers interpret and understand it, the author claims that this research takes the social constructionist position to guide the author's research design and methodology throughout this study. As suggested by Crotty (1998), individuals construct meanings in different ways, even in relation to the same phenomenon. Reviewing the existing internationalisation theories and concepts, they are mainly created on the basis of Westerners' experience and understanding. It is questioned whether the knowledge socially constructed through Westerners' cultural lens would be applied in practice by Easterners.

Cohering with the social constructionist viewpoint, the interpretivist paradigm is adopted for this research to study CSME managers' individual experience of their entry mode choices. For SMEs, the foreign market entry decision, in some sense, is the manager's individual determination. Given the subjectivity, CSME managers' individual experience and understanding of the international phenomenon have to be interpreted. Underlying a social constructionism paradigm, it is important to

77

explore how CSME managers construct their knowledge of the entry mode choices and how each individual manager interprets and gives meanings of this phenomenon. In other words, the CSME manager's subjective experience of the fact (the matter of entry mode choice) from his or her individual point of view enables the researcher to make more sense of their meanings and help the author to understand their world in relation to the phenomenon this research investigated.

3.3 Research Methodology and Methods

Building upon the researcher's epistemological and philosophical paradigms, the rationale of research methodology employed for this study will be discussed in this section. In addition, the methodology and methods adopted in the previous studies are also reviewed critically.

3.3.1 Qualitative Research Methodology

Research methodology is a strategy or plan of action that shapes the choices of particular research methods. It must enable researchers to achieve the desired outcomes (Ghauri and Gronhaug, 2005; Mason, 2002; Crotty, 1998). The term of 'qualitative research' means any type of research in which findings are not arrived at by statistical procedure or other means of quantification. Qualitative researchers are interested in social interactions and the meanings of these interactions (Dey, 1993; Wolcott, 2001; Holliday, 2002; Flick, 2002; Marris, 2000). In other words, a qualitative research is pragmatic, interpretive, and grounded in the lived experience of people (Marshall and Rossman, 1999; Gill and Johnson, 1997; Oakeshott, 1998). Qualitative researchers attempt to capture meanings in its natural data setting (Bryman, 2001; Robson and Foster, 1989; Black and Champion, 1976). This research adopts social constructionism with the purpose of exploring CSME managers' individual decision-making experience in relation to their entry mode choices. The researcher is interested in these CSME managers' "lived experiences, behaviours, emotions and feelings (Strauss and Corbin, 1998:11)". It is designed as an explorative study with a focus of CSME managers' personal experiences. This consequently leads to the choice of qualitative methodology which enables the author to probe the unique and typical meanings of CSME managers' international experiences and interpret their social world in greater detail.

3.3.2 Research Methods

Reviewing the prior empirical research in relation to the entry mode choice, a number of methodological critiques are issued by international business researchers (e.g. Moffat and Wood, 1995; Nakos, Brouther and Moussetis, 2002; Siu and Kirby, 1999; and Shi, Ho and Sui, 2001). Almost without exception, previous empirical studies in this area were based on a sample survey (Dunning, 1988; Anderson and Gatignon, 1986; Erramilli and Rao, 1990 etc.). By adopting a survey research method, researchers are often limited by influencing factors which were pre-hypothesized from a positivism perspective. However, restricting to selected factors may easily lead to wrong or inconsistent conclusions. It is difficult to get deeper insights in entry mode decision making (Zhao and Decker, 2004). Also, the sample quality for the survey is difficult to control (Zhao and Decker, 2004). Most empirical research in prior studies sets out to test the relationship between influencing factors and entry modes (cause and effect) by using quantitative hypotheses. However the questionnaire survey method adopted in the past studies cannot provide a richness and depth of understanding to the international entry mode choices by exploring the decision makers' experiences. This is why a different philosophical approach and methodology are employed for this study.

Taking the above criticisms into account, a quantitative survey based upon positivist approach is not suitable for this research since CSME managers' international experience is not easy to be understood by survey data. CSME managers' entry mode decision involves many social factors. Such a complicated issue needs further in-depth exploration (Nokos and Brouther, 2002). To reveal and understand CSMEs managers' subjective managerial experiences, in-depth and rich data are necessary and essential. Considering this research is exploratory in nature, being consistent with social constructionism and interpretivism, a qualitative research method is appropriate to answer the research questions of this study.

There are numerous qualitative research methods. To ensure the chosen research method is adequate and consistent with the philosophical stance outlined earlier in this chapter, the semi-structured interview is employed as the data collection technique in this research. Interview is a relatively informal style that involves at least 2 or more people with a conversation or discussion (Kahn and Cannell, 1957). Rather than a 'question-answer' format, qualitative interview is more active and interactive between researchers and informants and thus makes it highly attractive for the collection of qualitative data (Bryman, 2001; Ghauri and Gronhaug, 2005; Manson, 2002; Saunders *et al*, 2000). There are different types of interview in qualitative research. The most recognised categories of interview are structured interviews, semi-structured interviews, and unstructured interviews (Bryman, 2001; Ghauri and Gronhaug, 2005; Saunders et al, 2002; Wengraf, 2001) Different purposes of research questions lead to different types of interviews.

This research adopted semi-structured interviews instead of structured interview and unstructured interviews. The structured interview technique is not suitable for this study because it does not give the researcher opportunities to probe deeply in discovering new clues (Easterby-Smith *et al.*, 2002).

In contrast, an unstructured interview gives interviewees the opportunity to talk freely about the events. However, many social researchers (e.g. Bryman, 2001; Ghauri and Gronhaug, 2005; Johnson, 2001; Strauss and Corbin, 1998; King, 2004) claim that an unstructured interview is very complex and hard to control. As a new qualitative researcher, it is risky to adopt this technique and control the interview effectively. In fact, Mason (2002:62) argues that the term 'unstructured' interviewing is a 'misnomer' because "no research can be completely lacking in some form of structure". In this sense, the unstructured interview is not appreciated either for this research. Consequently, the semi-structured interview is the most suitable research method to gain insights of CSME managers' decision making experience for this study. King's (2004) template analysis method is then used as a data analysis method for this research. The details will be discussed in section 3.6.2.3.

3.4 Research Design

Research design is clearly guided by the research strategy. A research strategy should be consistent with the purpose of the research. It involves decisions of how data is to be collected and analysed in relation to the research questions. Cohering with the epistemology and philosophical approaches the author claimed earlier for this study, the research design is outlined to offer the guidance for the author to conduct this research consistently during the whole research process (See figure 3.1).

By taking a social constructionist paradigm this study aims to interpret CSME managers' individual international business and management experience from a qualitative perspective. By adopting the qualitative methodology semi-structured personal interviews are designed to collect rich data that enables the researcher to probe in-depth understanding of CSME managers' entry mode choices. Considering the nature of the qualitative interview data, qualitative data analytical techniques are chosen for this research, such as the narrative and template analysis.

Figure 3.1 Research Design

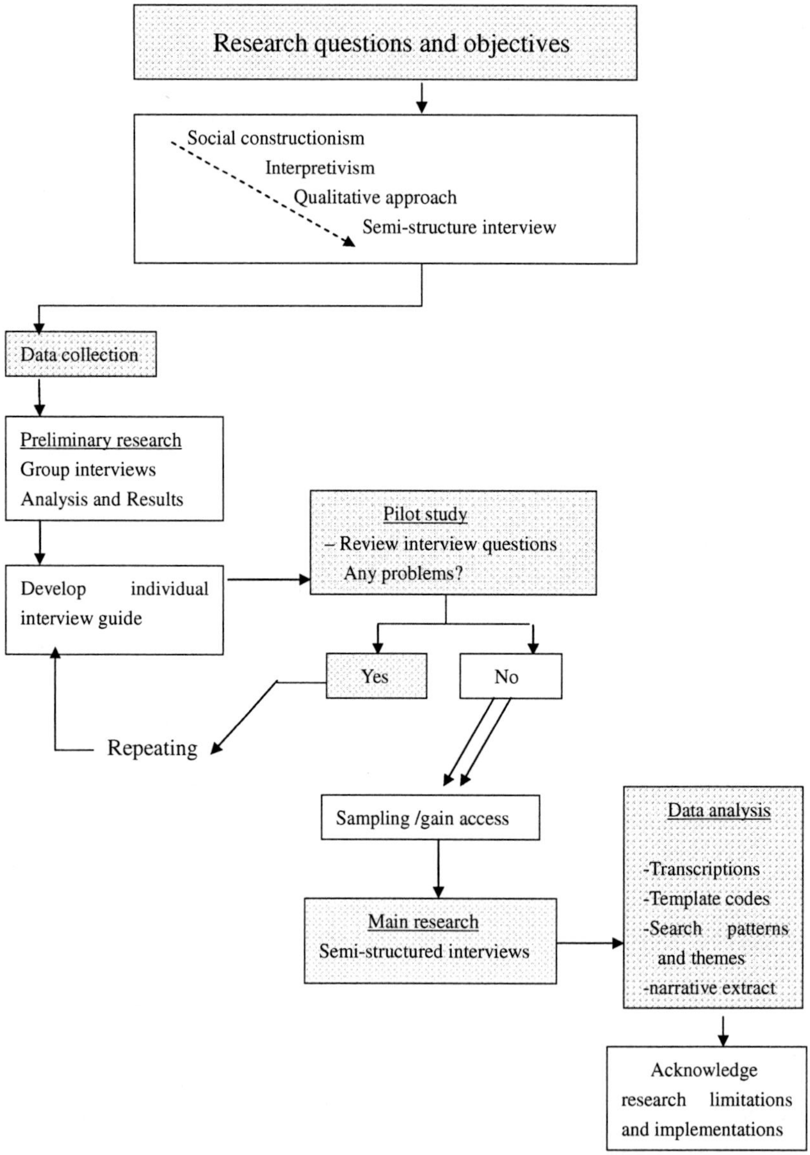

As noted, qualitative research is complex, dynamic and endlessly creative and interpretive (Denzin and Lincoln, 2003). No matter how the research has been deliberately designed, some practical issues always rise during the research process. In order to conduct the research efficiently, research action plans have to be piloted before the main study is conducted (Ghauri and Gronhaug, 2005; Mason, 2002; Saunders, Lewis and Thornhill, 2004).

3.5 Pilot Studies

Traditionally, pilot study is the most commonly used technique to test the validity of the questionnaire in quantitative research. Like Bell (1999) and Saunders, Lewis and Thornhill (2004) advised, it is essential to give the project a trial run. Otherwise, there is no way to ensure that the research is running successfully. In qualitative research, a pilot study also plays an important role in the research process. Designed for different purposes, one pre-research focus group interview and 3 individual interviews were conducted. The purposes and the details of conducting group interviews and individual interviews are explored next.

3.5.1 Focus Group Interviews and Preliminary Research

The focus group is a special type of group interacting with each other to gather information for the special purpose (Bryman and Bell, 2004; Ghauri and Gronhaung, 2005; Krueger and Casey, 2000). Focus group interviews can be designed to justify the methodological techniques for the main study; to try out a definition of a research problem, or to identify key informants (Fontana and Frey, 2003).

As 'pre-research' (different from pilot study), the focus group interview in this study was employed for two purposes. First, the focus group interview was designed to explore interviewees' understanding of theoretical concepts and some specific terminologies related to foreign market entry

mode choices. Warren (2001) argues that most of the qualitative interview is to derive interpretations

from interviewees' talks. Interview participants are to be viewed as meaning makers (Holstein and

Gubrium, 1995). Their understandings of the research questions directly influence the interaction of

'asking questions and getting answers'. Outcomes of this focus group were used to develop the first

draft of the interview guide for the main research. A good qualitative research design is to "blend of

intellectual and practical concerns (Mason, 2002:44)." As the foreign market entry mode choice is

very dynamic and complex, both intellectual and practical issues have to be taken into account.

Before the focus group interview was conducted, invitation letters were sent to seven selected CSME

managers by e-mail. Four of them (one from service sector and 3 from manufacturers) confirmed that

they could make it. Finally, 4 participants attended the focus group interview. To encourage all

participants to talk freely, the interview was carried out at a comfortable place to enable participants

feel relaxed. An unstructured in-depth questioning technique was employed for this group interview.

It lasted 2 and half hours and conversations were recorded. Before the conversations of the focus

group ended participants were asked to clarify whether they were familiar with some terminologies

and relevant knowledge involved in the research area (see appendix I).

After the group interview, the recorded conversations were transcribed in Chinese and then important

narratives from interviewed managers were translated into English. In addition, an interview

summary report was written, which included the interviewee's unusual reactions (for example, are

they excited? confident? doubtful? etc.). Interestingly, the results of this focus group interview show

that one manager had never heard of turnkey contract entry mode, another manager was confused about merger and acquisition. The findings indicate that CSME managers' intellectual knowledge regarding foreign market entry mode choices had to be taken into account when designing the research questions for individual interviews. Based on the outcomes of the focus group interview, the first draft of semi-structured interview questions was ready for pilot study.

3.5.2 Pilot Individual Interview

Asking questions and getting answers is a much harder task than it may seem at first. No matter how carefully the interviewer words the questions, the written word always has a residue of ambiguity (Fontana and Frey, 2003). Enabling the data to be collected and analysed properly, it is essential to ensure the interviewees have no problems with understanding and answering the questions. A pilot study helps researchers to achieve these goals.

For the pilot study, 3 individual face-to-face interviews were undertaken amongst 3 CSME managers who are from different industry. Only one interview was tape-recorded. The other 2 participants were not so comfortable with their conversations being taped, but file notes were produced. On average, each interview took one hour. At the end of the interviews, the participants were asked to give comments and suggestions they would like to add to the interview questions. Data collected from the recorded pilot interview were analysed by adopting Miles and Huberman's (1994) framework through 3 stages: data reduction, data display, and finally drawing and verifying relationships and key themes, as well as patterns. Moreover, King's (2004) template data analysis was also trialed in this pilot study. The results and feedback from the piloted interviews helped the author in checking out whether the designed interview questions were suitable or reliable to gain valuble data for this research. Accordingly, the justification of the original designed questions was conducted.

3.5.3 Justification of Research Design

As many social researchers have suggested (e.g. Denzin and Lincoln, 2003; Mason, 2002), qualitative research is a creative and dynamic reflexive process, but initial decisions of the research strategy may need to be changed during the research process. To ensure that the data are generated and analysed effectively, the research design was justified from 3 aspects based on the results of the piloted individual interviews.

First of all, semi-structured interview questions were modified. Initially, 3 resources were used to create the interview guides: literature, the author's own international experience and results of focus group interviews. The first draft interview guide included 25 questions in total. According to several managers' suggestions, some questions were taken out, and one question was added. The final draft of the semi-structured interview guide comprised 20 questions (See Appendix II). Moreover, the interviewed managers advised that the interview time should be strictly controlled to one and a half hours. After a trial, King's (2004) template data analysis was chosen as the data analysis technique for the main study.

3.6 Main Research

As discussed above, a small-scale pilot research was conducted to refine the interview questions by checking out the problems associated with answering the questions, as well as the time of completing each interview. This pilot study enabled the researcher to assess the reliability of the designed questions and ensured the appropriateness of the data analysis technique for this research. After these preparations, the researcher commenced the main research with clear directions. This section will discuss the main research conducted for this study and explain how the data collection and data analysis activities were properly organised in helping the researcher to achieve the research aims and objectives.

3.6.1 Data Collection

Bryman and Bell (2003) claim that the interview has become a most important method widely employed in qualitative research. The use of interview can help researchers to collect reliable data that are relevant to the research questions and objectives (Saunders, Lewis and Thornhill, 2006). Being consistent with the social constructionism and interpretivism philosophical approaches, a qualitative semi-structured interview was adopted for the main research in this study. A good quality of interview requires a great deal of detailed and rigorous planning. Details of who was interviewed, how interviewees and organisation were approached, and how the actual interviews were conducted will be discussed in this section.

3.6.1.1 Sampling

Primarily, sampling is mainly associated with quantitative research to test hypotheses and very little has been explored in the context of qualitative research. However qualitative research does demand strategic considerations in sample selections. Representative sampling is the most commonly used technique in quantitative research, but the least commonly used in qualitative research because 'the key issue for qualitative sampling is how to focus, strategically and meaningfully, rather than how to represent' (Mason, 2004: 136). In this research, the focus is on individual CSME managers' experiences of foreign market entry decision making, particularly their entry mode choices. To gain an in-depth understanding of this issue, it is apparent that the representativeness and the size of the sample are less important in this circumstance (Wolcott, 2001; Bryman and Bell, 2003; Saunders,

Lewis and Thornhill, 2006). For the purpose of this research, in deciding the sample types and size, the researcher adopted both purposive sampling and sequential sampling.

In order to ensure the selected samples could provide a rich detail and fit the purpose of this research, extra attention was given to this issue before the final sampling decision was made. The data profile of this study includes CSMEs that set up their businesses through the connection of local government, as well as those set the businesses individually. To answer the research questions and meet the research objectives, the author selected the samples purposively for this study based on her subjective judgments. The decision of the nominated interviewee list was judged with considerations of both interviewees' characteristics (the author used to work for one CSME in Gateshead and knew some CSME managers through meetings and Chinese social events) and the opinions of the manager from One North East Regional Developed Agency who is in charge of the Asian foreign companies' investments in the North East of England. In order to choose the best interviewee, interview informants' individual intelligence, knowledge, time, and ability to reflect their experience were also taken into account for this research.

In deciding the sampling size of this research, the key idea of theoretical sampling was applied. Accordingly, theoretical sampling is "an ongoing process rather than a distinct and single stage (Bryman, 2004: 305)". It is to carry on sampling theoretically until a category has been saturated with data. This technique is termed sequential sampling by Ghauri and Gronhaug (2005). They suggest that the aim of using a sequential sampling is to add new samples continually until final conclusions are arrived at. In this research, both purpose sampling and sequential sampling were mainly adopted. The final sample size was adjusted by the researcher as an on-going process. Although qualitative research is particularly good at "constituting arguments about how things work in particular contexts, rather than representing the full range of experience (Mason, 2004: 136)", but still a certain number of samples is needed to make meaningful sense in relation to the research. Initially, 10 interviews were planned to be carried out as a minimum. Instead of fixing the sample size completely, the author determined if new insights still continued appearing after the 10 interviews, undoubtedly, more interviews would be conducted. As a matter of fact, in total 10 interviews were conducted in the main research finally.

3.6.1.2 Approaching the Participants

As most of the targeted potential interviewees are the owners of CSMEs, it did not bring the author much trouble to get the organisational authority for this research. Only one interviewee required the researcher to contact their parent company in China first. As suggested by Johnson (2000), access to targeted organisations and interview informants is extremely difficult since not all targeted interviewees have sufficient motives or interests to be interviewed (Johnson, 2000). In this research, the author made good use of her personal contacts she established before approaching the potential participants. Due to the personal Guanxi relationships, the targeted participants made very positive responses when they were approached by the telephone conversations. In gaining access to interview participants, strong personal links and the Chinese culture of 'Guanxi' played important roles in this case. With permission, 10 formal interview were conducted after informed consent was signed by all interview informants (see details in 3.8, the ethical issues section)

3.6.1.3 Semi-Structure Interview

As confirmed earlier, the semi-structured interview designed for this research provided an opportunity for the researcher and interviewees to interact each other. This built upon Ghauri and

Gronhaug's (2005) and Bryman's (2004) interview frameworks. The interview process of this

research involved 4 main steps: 1) preparing interview, 2) pre-interview, 3) main interview and, 4)

post interview. The process of the conducted interview in this research is demonstrated in the

following figure (see figure 3.2).

Figure 3.2 The process of interviews

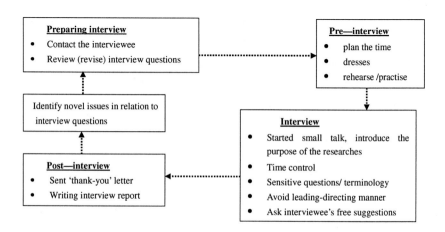

Source: Adapted from Ghauri and Gronhaug (2005) and Bryman (2004)

To avoid misunderstandings caused by language obstacles, all interviews were conducted in Chinese.

Following the above process, each interview began slowly with a small talk. Some simple questions

were asked as an 'icebreaker' at the beginning. To get the ball rolling efficiently, extra attention was

paid to not moving the conversation too quickly. At the end of each interview, the researcher asked the

interviewee's permission to have a follow-up conversation if there were any problems in relation to

the interview. Moreover, the researcher also invited the informant to make contact with the researcher

by either telephone or e-mail if there were any points they would like to add after the interview. The following table contains the information of all the interviews conducted in this study.

Table 3.1 Summary of conducted interviews

Org.	Pre-interview	Interview	Post-interview
A	• contacted by e-mail and phone • Informed consent signed • interview questions were sent to interviewee one day early by e-mail	• 1.5 hrs lasted • (tape recorded + notes) • Interviewee read the interview questions before the interview	• sent thanks-letter • filed the tape and the interview notes • made memo
B	Same as above	• 1.5 hrs • Half recorded + notes • Interviewee read the interview questions	• Sent thanks-letter • Made phone call, confirmed some answers (notes part)
C	Same as above A reminder phone contact	• 1.5 hrs • Only notes/ as interviewee wasn't comfortable with tape-recording • Interviewee got the interview questions in advance, but had no time to prepare it	• Sent thanks-letter • Filed the tape and interview notes • Made phone call, confirmed some answers
D	Same as above Verified the equipment was working properly—batteries Spare batteries	• 2 hrs • MP3 recorded + notes • Interviewee got the questions and prepared it	• Sent thanks-letter • Filed the tape and the interview notes • Made memo
E	Same as above Made sure to have enough of all items needed—pens, pencils and papers	• 1.5 hrs (MP3 recorded +notes) • Interviewee didn't check e-mail—didn't knew details of the interview questions before the interview	Same as above
F	Same as above	• 1 hour (Recorded) • Interviewee was briefly informed with the major interview questions by telephone 24 hrs in advance before the actual interview conducted	Same as above
G	Same as above	• 1 hour (Recorded) • Interviewee was briefly informed with the major interview questions by telephone 24 hrs in advance before the actual interview conducted	Same as above
H	Same as above	• 1 hour and 15 minutes (Recorded) • Checked if interviewee got the interview guide one day before the interview	Same as above
I	Same as above	• 1 hour (Recorded) • Interviewee didn't feel well due to illness	Same as above
J	Same as above	• 1 hour and 20 minutes (Recorded) • Interviewee well prepared the interview questions in advance	Same as above

Among these 10 interviewed CSME managers, seven are male and 3 are female. Nine interviews were tape-recorded and one was not (the reason was discussed in research reflexivity in Chapter Six).

As the above table indicates, the researcher prepared all interviews elaborately in advance. In particular, the post-interview process enabled the researcher to reflect the prior interview in a critical manner. This ensured that the quality of collected data would help the author to understand and gain insights of the phenomena this research investigated. However, data without interpretations and analysis are less meaningful. To capture the richness and fullness of the meanings, the collected data were creatively and strategically analysed in next stage.

3.6.1.4 Data Transcription

After each interview, while the memory was still fresh, the author listened to the recorded tape immediately. By doing this, the main purpose was to check whether the interview data was properly recorded. If not, the author would contact the interviewee to make another appointment as early as possible. After the data was confirmed, the recording was transcribed as soon as possible in Chinese at first. Transcribing of interview is not just a simple technical task of writing down the words onto a piece of paper; it is creative activity. Wengraf (2001:209) argues that while the researcher is transcribing the taped interview, "a flood of memories and thoughts will be provoked; these memories and thoughts are available only once". Accordingly, memo notes were made when ideas were stimulated by re-hearing of the recorded data for each interview. To manage the transcripts in an effective way, each transcript of the interviews was arranged into the designed table (see table 3.2) to enable the interview data to be retrieved with ease.

Table 3.2 Format of the transcription of the interview

Box No.	Notes	Transcript	Special notes
001		Interviewer:	
002	New categories	Informant:	Paused for 3 seconds
003	......	......	......
004	......	.....	

As table 3.2 shows, in the 'special notes' column, tone of voice, pause and disturbances were all noted for each transcript. After the transcript was done, the author went back to listen to the recording again to double check whether the conversation was accurately transcribed. If there were no issues, the summary report of the interview was produced for each interview. This summary report includes the general interview information and reflexivity of the interview from both interviewer and interviewee's perspectives. Finally, all the relevant documents for each interview, including transcripts, informed consent, field notes, research summary reports, were labeled and filed.

3.6.2 Analysing Data

Given its nature of uniquely rich data feature, how to analyse qualitative interview data has remained at the heart debate of the social qualitative research. Although numerous volumes have been published on the techniques of qualitative interview data analysis (Bryman, 2004; Denzin, 1989; Daniels and Cannice, 2004; Krueger and Casey, 2000; Ghauri and Gronhaug, 2005; Miles and Huberman, 1994; Strauss and Corbin, 1998), qualitative researchers still have been known to be overwhelmed with the vast accumulation of data and struggled with finding analytical approaches for the massive data. Clearly, there is not a single standard approach to qualitative data analysis. No matter what approaches researchers wish to use, they must understand that qualitative data analysis should be creative, strategically and internally consistent. Following up this key principle, the data analysis approach adopted in this study was mainly based on Miles and Huberman's (1994) approach and King's (2004) template analysis.

3.6.2.1 Data Analysis Strategy

To ensure that data analyses are "systematic, sequential, verifiable, and continuous (Krueger and Casey, 2000: 128)" a data analysis strategy was deliberately designed for this study (figure 3.3).

Figure 3.3   General strategy of data analysis

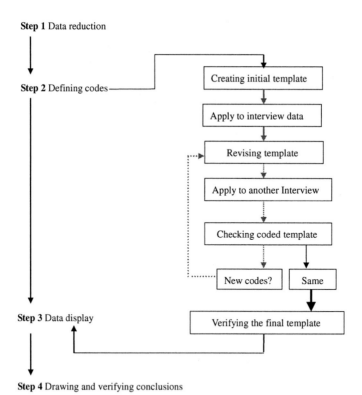

As indicated in figure 3.3 the general strategy of data analysis presented above includes 4 main steps: data reduction, developing coded template, data display, and finally drawing conclusions. This strategy has been employed to guide the data analysis throughout this study. As a sequential, evolving, and on-going process, the details of each step is discussed next.

3.6.2.2 Data Reduction Process

Facing the mass of collected interview data, the key question is about what can be done with the 'products'. There are potentially a wide range of activities that can be used to 'do something with the products'. A data reduction is normally first carried out for interview data. It refers to "the process of selecting, focusing, simplifying, abstracting and transforming the data that appear in written-up field notes or transcriptions (Miles and Huberman, 1994: 29)". The process of the data reduction this research followed is illustrated in figure 3.4.

By adopting the data reduction process presented in figure 3.4, the researcher produced a large number of written notes, memos, narrative extracts, as well as some English translations of key sentences and important quotations. During the data reduction process, extra attention was paid to what CSME managers said and why their words are important. Through this process, it was realised that data reduction occurred continuously throughout the whole research process. From the beginning the researcher was conscious about the issue of data collection until final conclusions were drawn and verified.

Figure 3.4 Data reduction process

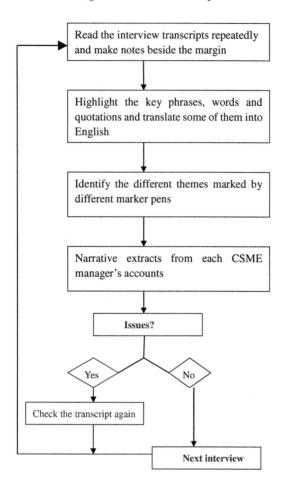

3.6.2.3 Narrative Extract

According to narrative theory, people create themselves through narratives (Carr, 1986). In research it

is common for participants to frame accounts into stories about themselves. Generally, stories about

people take two forms: life stories and people's narratives of particular experiences (Riesman, 2004).

Narratives are dictated by the social and cultural context in which the narrators live. By conducting a narrative analysis, researchers can understand the social world and the narrators' parts in it. This assumption is consistent with the social constructionists' viewpoint as narratives are social constructions that are developed in everyday social interactions. They are shared means of making sense of the world (Murray, 2003).

One important aim of this research was to gather rich qualitative data by exploring CSME managers' personal decision-making experience. It focuses upon how these CSME managers made their entry mode choices. The researcher is interested in meaning-making of the individual CSME manager in co-constructing their international decision making experience. Narrative is particularly valuable for individual sense-making in this case. On the first reading of the transcript of each semi-structured interview data, CSME managers' personal narratives were interpreted. Narrative extracts from 10 individual CSME managers were produced to illuminate their international decision making experiences with particular focus upon their entry mode choices. Interpreting CSME managers' narratives helped the researcher to develop coding schemes. Many different approaches to coding can be used. This research employed King's (2004) thematic template analysis method as main data analysis technique.

3.6.2.4 Coding and Thematic Template Analysis

A code is a label attached to a section of a text. It indexes a theme or issues in the data which has been identified by researchers as important to their interpretations. Coding also reduces the text so that text can be displayed in an explicit form for researchers' interpretations (Crabtree and Miller, 1999). Coding is a dynamic and fluid process (Strauss and Corbin, 1998). There is no one correct or ideal way for data coding (Bryman, 2004; Miles and Huberman, 1994).

Template analysis recommended by King (2004) was selected as the most suitable code technique for this research due to 2 reasons.

First, template analysis focuses on themes identification by interpreting collected textual data. As a flexible approach, template analysis can be tailored to the requirements of the researcher. It also works well for this research which seeks to explore perspectives of CSME managers' different experiences within a contextual constructionist position. Moreover, template analysis is relatively less time-consuming. It can handle a larger data set. Most importantly, template analysis is a somewhat structured approach to handling data rather than complete loose form (King, 2004; Nadin and Cassell, 2004).

Taking the factors discussed above into account, as a new qualitative researcher, template analysis makes the author feel more comfortable to handle the mass of the collected qualitative data of interviews and answer the research questions properly. The key feature of template analysis is that the template is revised continually as an ongoing process (King, 2004). Basically, researchers adopting a template analysis need to produce a list of codes identified from the textual data. Hierarchically, these codes ('template') are organised into different higher-levels (broad higher codes) and low levels (detailed lower-order codes). Building upon King's (2004) template analysis, the process of how to develop the template was presented below (see figure 3.5).

Figure 3.5 The process of template development

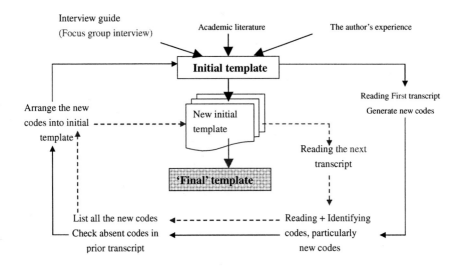

The template analysis uses of a priori codes. These pre-defined codes constitute the initial template to present the themes and patterns. Template analysis normally starts with at least a few pre-defined codes which help guide analysis (King, 2004). First, defining codes of the interview text started with a preset of initial codes. The pre-defined codes of this research were derived from 3 sources: interview guide derived from outcomes of the focus group interviews, academic literature, and the researcher's own international practical experience. As mentioned in section 3.5.1, this research conducted a focus group interviews as a preliminary research. The main purposes of this focus group interviews included: obtaining general background information about this research topic from CSME managers' perspective, learning how these respondents talk about their understanding of the phenomenon such as attitudes, perceptions and opinions. The outcomes of the focus group interviews were used to develop the semi-structured interview questions. It provides insights into categories of investigated research problems and facilitated the development of the initial template.

In this research, the pre-defined codes guided the researcher to carry out the template analysis at the first stage and helped the researcher to focus on areas of greatest relevance to her research questions. These pre-defined codes were created as prior themes that were treated as higher-order codes. By reading and re-reading the interview text, the provisional template of codes was developed by adding new themes whenever and wherever new themes emerged. During the process, if the interesting text did not fit the exiting codes, the new theme was created by labeling it at the side of the transcript of interview. Simultaneously, the quotations wherever the new codes were identified were always marked by different colors.

After the first round of reading and coding was completed, re-reading the transcripts and checking the codes, especially new codes, was conducted with extra care. Once 2 rounds of reading and coding finished, all developed codes identified from the first interview transcript were listed and these new codes were arranged into the initial template. The revised template with new developed codes was used as the new preliminary template to analyse all interview transcripts one by one. From the initial to final template, each individual interview transcript was reviewed very carefully by adding new codes and dropping redundant codes throughout. This process continued until no new codes emerged from the interview text. Then the final template resulted with the saturation of this process for this study.

The following example can be used to graphically illustrate this analytical process (see table 3.4). The provisional template presented in table 3.4, as discussed earlier, was derived from current literature, the researcher's personal international business experiences, and the interview guide plus some indications developed from the focus group interviews. By doing this, the topic guide is fairly structured, with the interviewer defining in advance most of the research areas the researcher investigated are covered. In this research, the researcher constructed the provisional template very carefully to serve it as an initial guide applying it into the interview data.

Table 3.3   Provisional Template

---

1. Motivations **(Higher order)**
   - Push factors **(Lower order)**
   - Pull factors
   - Entrepreneurial factors
   - Strategic factors
2. Entry mode choices **(Higher order)**
   - Exporting **(Lower order)**
   - Joint venture
   - Wholly-owned subsidiary
3. Influencing factors **(Higher order)**
   - Internal factors   **(Lower order)**
     - Firm-specific factors **(next level order)**
     - Product-specific factors
     - Strategy-specific factors
   - External factors **(Lower order)**
     - Culture factors
     - Networks
4. Decision making process **(Higher order)**
   - Decision making strategy **(Lower order)**
   - Taking all entry modes at same level
   - Considering entry mode hierarchically

Based upon the above constructed initial template, the researcher systematically reviewed the full set of interview transcripts to identify the interview text that were relevant to the research aims. If the text was identified as an issue in the relevance to the research question, but it was not covered by the existing code, it was added as a new code. For example, after re-reading an interview text, a new code emerged in the 'entry mode choice' theme. The following is one of the interview quotes:

To be honest, we did not intent to expand our business to other EU countries in the first year at all. All we wanted to do was to fully concentrate on the UK markets. However, it was unexpected we got 3 e-mails from other EU countries in the first 6 months. All of them found us by visiting our bilingual-home page. Now we have stable orders from the Italian customer every year.

〔**Manager Q**〕

From this interviewed CSME manager's narrative, internet entry mode emerged as a new code underlying the higher order code of 'entry mode choices'. It was inserted into the provisional template (see figure 3.5).

Figure 3.6 An example of developing the template

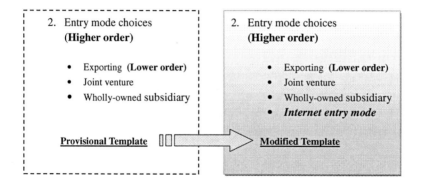

As an on-going process, all interview data were reviewed and the preliminary template was revised by inserting new codes or replacing some of the existing codes until the final template was resulted.

3.6.2.5 Data Display and Relationship between Themes

According to King (2004), the hierarchy template may not reflect relationships between the themes. Complementally, maps, matrices and other diagrams can be used to explore and display template analysis findings (Crabtree and Miller, 1999; King, 2004). The purpose of data display is to help researchers define relationships between themes and draw appropriate conclusions. There are a few methods that can be employed to display qualitative data. When a full linear template is produced, a matrices data display approach can be used to identify relationships between themes (Miles and Huberman, 1994; Nadin and Cassell, 2004). Taking the form of a table, a matrix normally is employed to summarise qualitative data along multiple dimensions (Miles and Huberman, 1994; Ryan and Bernard, 2003).

Nadin and Cassell (2004) compared matrix analysis and template analysis and clarify that it is impossible to construct a matrix for every category in the final template. However, some matrices can be constructed with certain categories in different levels. Borrowing this idea from Nadin and Cassell (2004), a matrix for some created codes in the template was produced and included information about what new codes were added, what codes are deleted or justified comparing the previous initial template, why all these happened, and what quotations from the interview text could be used to support the insertion of new codes or deletion of initially defined codes. Except created matrices, the author also used other diagrams and charts to organise the data diagrammatically, for example, categorising quotations by looking for underlying 'commonalities and differences' of the same themes or patterns throughout the interview data.

During constructions of matrices, one key principle was followed in this research: reduce complex information into selective and simplified forms to easily understand configurations (Miles and Huberman, 1994). These matrices indicated what was happening to the interview text and directed the researcher to move on the next step of analysis, drawing and justifying conclusions in an efficient way.

3.6.2.6 Drawing Conclusions

Drawing conclusions is a main stream of data analysis activities. As the editor of International Business Review, Ghauri (2004:120) indicates that many qualitative researchers "have considerable difficulties in drawing conclusions". To get the analysis done efficiently, a mixture of analysis techniques should be used strategically, such as comparisons based on pattern seeking, clustering (Ghauri, 2004; Miles and Huberman, 1994). The researcher adopted different approaches to interpret the data at this stage.

Before any formal conclusions were drawn (a small number of informal conclusions may be there when the author developed template codes or data display), the author looked through all forms of documents which were already conducted during the research such as the template, the research summary reports, field notes, etc.. This was followed by revisiting the research aims and objectives. By doing this, the researcher tried to build up a full picture and attempted to draw conclusions systematically and sequentially. Afterward, the author looked deeply at 'commonalities and differences' among different interview text and then compared them with the preliminary modes or factors developed from prior empirical studies in relation to entry mode choices through existing literature. In particular, if differences were identified, the places where these new insights emerged in the original transcript were traced and re-looked. Then all the relevant quotations were printed and cut and presented on the ground (similar like Krueger and Casey's LONG-TABLE APPROACH, 2000). The general process at this stage was reading the transcripts, thinking about them, studying them, comparing them, and finally concluding them. Logically, the author generated ideas and propositions through the interactive process by moving backwards and forwards amongst the research questions, existing literature, collected and analysed data.

3.7 Final Research Stage

As mentioned in Chapter One of the introduction to the thesis, the most important purpose of this research to make an original contribution to practice rather than only focus on theoretical contributions. To enhance the practical contribution, a further research for this study was conducted. Four CSME managers and one senior governor from the CSME sector were interviewed after the data analysis was completed. Two interviews were conducted in England. The interviewed managers were the participants in the first round of the interview at the data collection stage. The other 2 CSME managers, who are considering expanding their business in the UK, were interviewed in China during the summer of 2006. Both of them were not involved in the first round interviews. The interviewed governor in China is a president of CSME Bureau at Provincial level and he plays an important role in CSMEs' policy making.

Due to time limitations, each interview lasted about only 20 minutes in average. Three interviews were tape recorded. With a deep understanding of the particularly hierarchical power of Chinese culture, the author made great efforts to get permission from the senior governor to record his interview. Differing from the first round interviews, the author briefly presented the findings and results of this research first, and then asked the interviewees to make comments. Two interview transcripts were conducted. Field notes were made for another 3 interviews. Afterwards, data was analysed by looking at those participants' narrative extracts to make senses of each individual's comments and feelings. Their opinions towards the outcomes of this research brought great insights to this study from a practice perspective. Moreover, their positive feedback enhanced the trustworthiness of this research.

3.8 Ethical Concerns

A code of ethics provides ethical principles for social research (Bryman, 2004, Robson, 2002). There are a range of useful codes of ethics established by professional committees. In this research, the author followed a code of ethics by the University Ethics Committee at Northumbria University at Newcastle. Ethics arise at a variety of stages throughout the duration of a research project in social research and involve issues such as privacy of participants, informed consent, deception etc. (Bryman, 2004; Saunders, Lewis and Thornhill, 2000; Zikmund, 2000). In this research, the ethical concerns mainly focused on the researcher and research participant roles and relationships in the nature of the selected research method of face-to-face qualitative interview. With particular considerations of the 'power relationships' and 'privacy issues', ethical issues for this study were spread into 3 stages: gain access, data collection, and data report.

As mentioned earlier, some of the samples were targeted through the researcher's own personal relationships with CSME managers. Considering the feature of strong Chinese 'power distance' culture (Hofstede, 1984, 1994), although the researcher used 'guanxi' to get access to the organizations, the author did not attempt to put any pressures on intended participants (Robson, 2002; Saunders, Lewis and Thornhill, 2000; Sekaran, 2000). To reduce hierarchical influences to a minimum, the researcher repeatedly stated to the participants that they are completely free in deciding whether to be interviewed at the first contact. They were told that they had absolute rights to refuse to take part interviews at anytime during the research process. The author believes this did not transgress any ethical issues and did not impact the quality of the collected data.

In gaining access, there was another issue which arose in relation to the 'power relationships' ethical considerations. One potential participant agreed to accept interview individually in the UK but insisted that permission must be authorised from the headquarters in China. Bearing this case in mind, the author kept thinking 'whether there is harm to any participants' during the research process.

Privacy is another major ethical issue in social research (Bryman, 2004; Robson, 2002; Saunders, 2003; Sekaran, 2000). The most commonly used approach regarding privacy issues is to send informed consent to participants. The details of informed consent vary dependent upon the nature of the research (Saunders, 2003). In this research, all participants were provided with a well prepared informed consent letter. This letter includes full information about participation rights and use of the data, such as purpose of the research and participants' privacy protection. All details can be found in Appendix I. Practically, great care was given in maintaining each participant's right to anonymity in particular (Easterby-Smith *et al*, 2000; Saunders, Lewis and Thornhill, 2003).

During the data collection stage, the author also reminded herself that privacy has to be maintained even though the participant has already agreed to take part in the research. Before the interview started, it was clearly communicated that the participant had the right to withdraw from the interview whenever they want. They could also decline to respond to the question if they though that it went beyond the scope of the access agreed during the research process (Cooper and Schindler, 2001). In the duration of the face-to-face interviews, the researcher strictly followed the ethical concern which indicated by Saunders, Lewis and Thornhill (2003) and Sekaran (2000): avoid pressing the participant for a response.

Ethical considerations were also maintained during the data reporting stages. As a special ethical group within a small social committee in the North of England, many CSME managers who were interviewed know each other. To maintain the anonymity, extra attention was paid in reporting this research to prevent any participants and organisations to be identified by 'piecing together' the characteristics that were revealed in this study (Sunders, Lewis and Thornhill, 2006).

3.9 Limitations of the Primary Research

Without doubt, qualitative interview has its own advantages and disadvantages due to the nature and characteristics of this research method itself. Reviewing this study, limitations of this research were realised. Reflecting upon the research process, some of the practical issues made certain limitations during the qualitative interviews. For example, the author realised that some of her personal interview skills, such as how to probe questions to get rich and deeper meanings, how to control the conversations of the interview etc., were underdeveloped initially. These might be the bias that slightly caused limitations at the very beginning of data collections stage. However, during the research process, the author has incrementally built up her qualitative research ability and her confidence also has boosted at the later stage of this research.

3.10 Chapter Summary

Overall, this chapter has explained why social constructionism has been chosen as the epistemological position that led to the author's choices of interpretivist paradigm and qualitative approach for this research. Building upon the qualitative methodology assumption, it was described how qualitative interview method fits the research question of this study and how it helped the researcher to achieve research objectives. Furthermore, details of data collection and data analysis are presented transparently in order to provide readers with a clear picture of how this research was actually carried out. Moreover, throughout the discussions, ethical concerns with specific focus of Chinese 'power distance' culture were addressed. It implies that 'cultural awareness' might be a big issue for international researchers in the context of Chinese business management research. To end this chapter, the author identified her initial practical weaknesses of conducting qualitative research as a consideration of the limitations for this study.

CHAPTER FOUR

FINDINGS AND DISCUSSIONS

4.1 Introduction

As argued in Chapter Two, little has been done to investigate the choice of entry mode of SMEs from developing countries entering developed countries, either conceptually or empirically, particularly from a qualitative perspective. Drawing upon the data collected, this chapter sets out to present and analyse the findings of this study. It begins with a brief historical review of Eastern Asian foreign investments in the North of Englanddrawn from secondary sources, followed by profiles of researched CSMEs in this study. The rest of the chapter provides the findings that emerged from the data and reveals CSME managers' individual experiences in relation to their entry mode choices when entering the North of England markets. By providing direct evidence from the data, the key findings and discussions of this research are presented by exploring 1) the motives of CSME managers' outward investments in the North East of England, 2) influencing factors and its impact on CSME managers' entry mode choices, 3) entry decision strategy and processes adopted by CSME managers. Throughout the chapter, the findings are synthesised in light of the current theory base.

In presenting the interview data, participants' narratives were selected to illustrate the themes and points that have emerged over the course of template analysis. CSME managers' narratives presented in this chapter are the marked interview text that evidentially illustrated where each coded theme was derived from during the data analysis.

4.2 A Historical Overview of East Asian Investment in the UK

From the mid 1980s, the world economic structure has been revised. There are strong indications that the twenty-first century will be characterized as an Asian era of regional trading blocks (Dunning, 1998; Ohmae, 1985, Mohotra, Ulgado and Agarwal, 2003). The rapid rise of the developing Asian countries has broken down America's domination in business. The leading international business scholar Dunning (2002), in his autobiographical article states that he spent as much time in Asia and the Pacific, notably Korea, Hong Kong, Taiwan, and The Peoples Republic of China, as he spent in the Western countries. Of note, international business research has made dramatic progress in the last few decades. The pattern of foreign investment by Western-based firms in developed countries has been well documented (Nakos, Brouther and Moussetis, 2001). However, less attention has been paid to the phenomenon of Asian firms from developing countries entering Western developed countries.

Foreign investment in the UK has grown considerably in recent years. According to Child, Faulkner and Pitkethly (2000:142) "the UK has been the most popular destination in Europe for oversea investors throughout the twentieth century". The scale of inward FDI in the UK has been large and growing continuously in the twenty-first century. Not only FDI from developed countries but the UK also has a long history in attracting East Asian investment and it "acted opportunistically by promoting its more peripheral regions in securing East Asian investment (Garrahan and Ritchie, 1999: 2)". Although all EU members made great efforts to try sharing Asia's dynamism, the UK still remains in its position as the favorite destination for foreign investors compared to other EU members, particularly in the North of England (Garrahan and Ritchie, 1999).

Historically, the economy of the North of England (as a state-managed region) heavily relied on coal, steel and shipbuilding manufacturing industries (Robinson, 1990). With the decline of these traditional industries in 1970s, this region has been suffering from the highest unemployment, the lowest average weekly earnings, and the lowest economic activities rate. The proportion of the region's businesses surviving longer than 3 years is the lowest in the UK (The North East Chamber of Commerce, 2002). The long-term economic decline in the North has led to a regional policy of attempting to attract increasing foreign inward investment. In the last decade, this region has claimed more foreign investments from East Asian than any other regions in this country (Garrahan and Ritchie, 1999).

East Asian economic miracle has led to its outward investments not only in developing countries but developed countries (Sideri, 1995; Conte-Helm, 1999; Burdis and Peck, 1999; Stone, 1999). Due to the growth of the emerging economies of East Asia, since 1980s, East Asian investment in the North of Englandhas expanded rapidly (Cone-Helm, 1999; Stone, 1999). Taking Japan as an example, before 1986 there were only 7 Japanese firms in this region but this number had increased to 29 by 1995 (see figure 4.1 below).

Figure 4.1 FDI in the North of Englandby East Asian firms

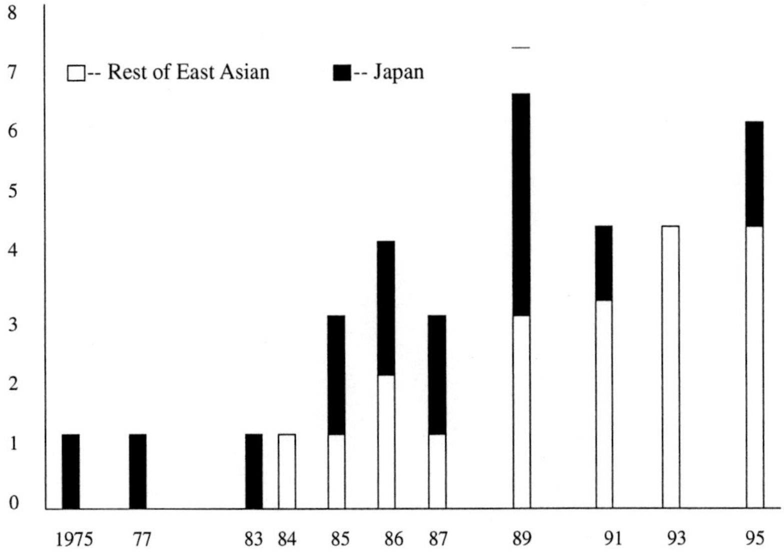

Taken from: National Economic Research Unit, FDI North Database (1999)

As figure 4.1 shows, before 1990, East Asian investment in the North of Englandwas dominated by Japanese companies. From 1991 inward investment of other East Asian countries in this region has grown, such as Corporation, the computer company from Taiwan, Onwa TVs from Hong Kong, and Samsung Electronics from South Korea etc. (NERU, 1999). Most recently, CSMEs from mainland China have become new foreign investors in The North of England.

4.3 Chinese Firms' Outward Investment

It has been noted that outward foreign investment from developing countries is growing at a fast rate. According to UNCTAD (2004), over past 15 years, annual foreign investment outflows from developing countries have grown faster than those from developed countries. In 2003, outward FDI

113

from developing countries accounted for over one-tenth of the world's total stock and 6% of the world total outward flows (see figure 4.2).

Figure 4.2 FDI outflows from developing countries (Billions of dollars)

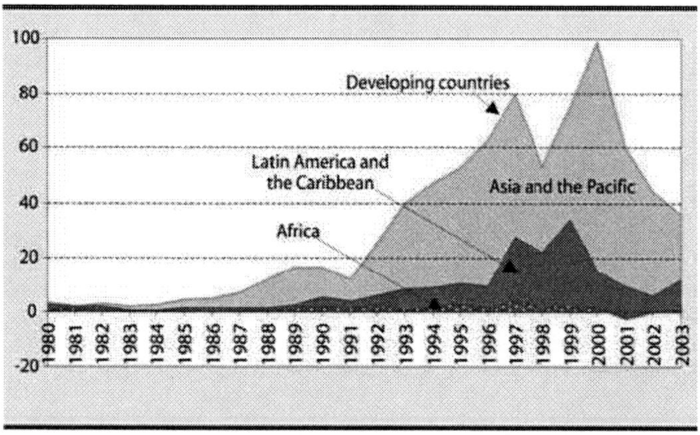

Taken from: United Nations Conference on Trade and Development
FDI Database (2004)

Figure 4.2 shows that Asian foreign investment increased dramatically between 1980s and 1990s. Asia has become the largest and fastest growing outward investor in the developing world comparing with Latin America and the Caribbean and Africa. Among these Asian outward investors, China FDI outflows grow rapidly (Child and Yu, 1996; Xiang, 2001; Xiao, 2000; Liu, Buck and Shu, 2005). To apprehend the significance of Chinese firms' international activities in the North East of England, it is necessary to review China's foreign outward investment development.

From the 1980s to the 1990s, China's average annual FDI outflows rose from $450 million to $2.3 billion. Its outward FDI stock had reached $37 billion by the end of 2003 (see figure 4.3). According to UNCTAD (2004), China ranked number 58 in the Outward FDI Performance Index between year

2001 and year 2003 among total 128 countries.

Figure 4.3 China outward FDI stock (Billions of dollars)

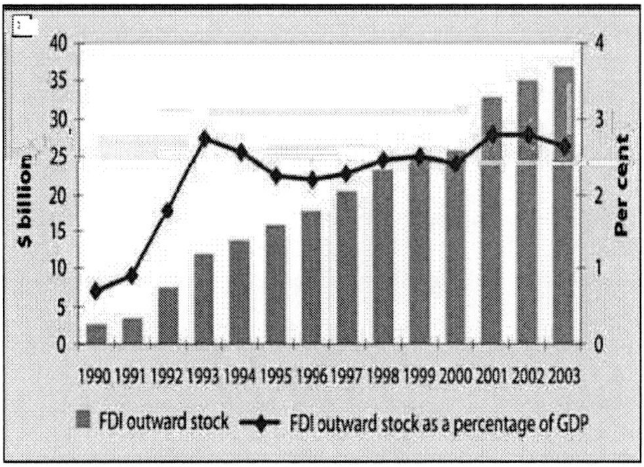

Taken from: United Nations Conference on Trade and Development
World Investment Report (2004)

With the increase of the foreign investment, Chinese firms' formal amount of money invested in

oversea markets raise every year. Comparing with $6.33 billion foreign investment in 1999, at the end

of 2000, this figure exceeds $7.6 billion (Annual Report of China Foreign Trade Committee, 2000).

In year 2002, Chinese firms involved 350 non-financial and 75 product processes and trade foreign

investment projects. The invested money arrived $9.83 billion (National Bureau of Statistic 2002,

China Statistic Yearbook, 2002). According to the China foreign economic trade white book (2002),

there are 5,976 Chinese firms have invested oversea markets till the end of 1999. The figure of

Chinese firms' outward investments by the end of year 2002, which was the first year when China

joined WTO, rose to 6960, an increase of 15% over its position two years ago. Traditionally,

distribution of Chinese foreign investment flows towards other Asian developing countries rather than developed countries. However, it now spreads over different areas in the world. It is evident recently that Chinese foreign investment outflows are not only located in neighbouring countries, but also in Africa, Latin America, North America and Europe such as the UK.

According to the One North East database (2004), there were only 20 operating Chinese firms at the North of Englandin year 2002. This figure had increased to 48 by the end of year 2004. All these Chinese companies come from mainland China, and most of them are SMEs. These CSMEs involved a wide range of industrial sectors: computer component and software, textile and garment, agriculture, construction material, fashion jewellery, soft drink etc. Although these CSMEs' foreign investments in the North of Englandare still in the very young stage, it has drawn attentions of Government development agency in England and local governments. For example, One North East, Gateshead and Newcastle city councils have launched a number of support projects to encourage Chinese companies' investments in the local area. It is believed that empirical investigations of these CSMEs' foreign investments in the North of Englandwill offer great insights to facilitate their performances of internationalisation.

4.4 Research-Based CSMEs' Profile

As discussed in Chapter Three, a semi-structured interview was adopted as the data collection method for this study. In identifying research samples, 10 CSME managers were selected purposively for the main study among the CSMEs operating in the North of England. Data from 10 interviewed CSME managers formed the primary data to fulfil the purposes of this project (see table 4.1).

Table 4.1 Brief of investigated CSMEs

Business sector	Company/ Products	Entry mode choices
Fashion industry	Jewellery Company	Overseas sales office
Garment industry	Ties Company	Overseas sales office
Textile industry	House Soft Decoration— *Cushions, table clothes etc.*	Joint Venture
Beverage industry	Chinese Beverage (soft drink)	Overseas sales office
Food industry	Chinese Food Company	Wholly-owned subsidiary
Plastic industry	Packing Supply Company *Plastic packing products*	Overseas sales office
Computer industry	Computer accessories Company	Overseas sales office
Service industry	Chinese Herb Company Web Design Company Chinese Consultant Company	Wholly-owned subsidiary Wholly-owned subsidiary Wholly-owned subsidiary

As table 4.1 indicates, the 10 selected CSMEs in the North of England include both manufacturing firms and service companies. Among these samples, there was a wide range of industries involved such as the jewellery industry, textile industry including garment and house soft decoration, the food industry including soft drink and Chinese food, the computer industry including accessories and software design, Chinese medicine and consultant services. In terms of the firm size, most of the parent companies from manufacturing sector employ more than 300 people. Parent companies from service sector employ fewer than 20 people in mainland China. The period of foreign investments of each CSME in the North of England varies from two to eight years.

The interviews were conducted over a period of 13 months. Each interview lasted 1 hour and twenty minutes in average. 9 of them were tape recorded. Transcripts have yielded more than 60,000 words (in Chinese characters). As the general purpose of this research is to explore CSME managers' foreign entry mode choices on basis of these managers' individual historic experiences, each interviewee was asked to reflect their motives and feelings during their entry mode choices. Meanwhile, brief information of both the parent company and its foreign investments overseas were provided by these participants at the beginning of each interview.

When conducting this research, extra care regarding the ethical issues has been paid by considering the Chinese culture characteristics. For example, some interviewees criticised Chinese Government SMEs policies, the anonymity of names of individual and institutions became a sensitive issue due to Chinese hierarchy and power distance cultural characteristics in this sense (Hofstede, 1980, 1998). Taking some ethical issues into account, when presenting the findings, the author has used fictional names of both individual and companies to avoid the participants and companies being recognised. In table 4.1, the author highlighted only the products and services of the interviewed companies instead of giving their real names. Moreover, considering the small size of the Chinese ethic group in the North of England, the individual identity is worried if the participant's personal profile is revealed coupled with the company profile. It is therefore only the company profile is provided for each case in this study.

Presenting the brief of the research profile above provides relevant information in helping the researcher to understand the setting of the scene and the research context underlying this study. Following this, findings and analysis of this study are explored and discussed.

4.5 Motives of CSME Managers Entering the North of England

In fulfilling the research aims of this project, one objective is to explore what factors actually drove

CSME managers deciding to entry the North of England markets. Through the ongoing process of

selecting, simplifying and abstracting the collected interview data, 4 sets of factors emerged. They are

1) push factors, 2) pull factors, 3) managers' entrepreneurial characteristic factors, and 4) strategic

factors. Each of them will be discussed in this section.

4.5.1 Push Factors

According to the listed themes developed in the template, 3 kinds of push factors, as higher-order

codes, emerged from CSME managers' narratives: 1) release of Government control, 2) Chinese

Government supports and incentives of going abroad, 3) avoiding pressures of competitions from

both Chinese and foreign companies in China. The following are the detailed findings of these push

factors based upon CSME managers' responses during the interviews.

4.5.1.1 Release of Government Control

Every interviewed manager emphasised that CSMEs' internationalisation was partially a result of a

release of Government control. In their interviews, participants highlighted how important and

powerful role the Chinese Government plays in CSMEs' international business activities. In order to

control and govern CSMEs' international activities, relevant regulations and policies are rigorously

regulated by the Chinese Government. Compared with SMEs from Western developed countries,

CSME managers all expressed that CSMEs' internationalisation was restricted heavily by the

Chinese Government, particularly a decade ago. Owner manager P from the Packing Supply

Company illuminated his feeling of difficulty in pursuing their international business many years ago.

> *Before, as an SME owner manager, I felt that there are a lot of constrains ....In the mid of 1980s, one of my overseas friend (Chinese) introduced the first foreign customer to me. At beginning, we only did exporting to this customer. As business relationship between us went very well, this foreign customer later proposed to form a joint venture. At that time, although there were a few Chinese companies, mainly large firms, involving overseas investment, my instinct told me that this was a great opportunity for my business. After further investigation, we submitted our application.... it just like a stone dropped into the sea .....*

Manager P's narratives reflected other managers' experience. **Managing Director F** from the fashion company continued expressing this feeling from general respect.

> *A decade ago, it was so difficult for CSMEs to do business abroad. From central Government to local institutions, perhaps dozens of application forms and documents have to be filled before you were permitted to invest business in foreign countries.*

Both participants recalled their experiences from the negative side to contrast the better situation recently regarding the Chinese Government control. They further confirmed that from a central controlled plan system to the free-market system since 1979, the Chinese Government gradually realised the importance of shifting from 'over intervention' to 'liberalisation'. As a result, the Chinese Government relatively (not completely) released some controls in relation to CSME managers' business activities. These managers admitted this change has inspired their initial motives of 'going abroad'.

4.5.1.2 The Chinese Government Supports and Incentives

From his reflections, owner **Manager T** indicated that Chinese Government support was a key factor that drove him seeking business opportunities overseas. He commented that the Chinese Government launched a number of favourable foreign investment regulatory policies not only for inward FDI but also outward investments. Manager T recalled, in 1999, the Chinese Government carried out the 'going global' strategy to encourage both large Chinese firms and CSMEs to integrate their business into international markets. By doing this, the Chinese Government released a policy of reducing the control power of foreign currency exchange restriction. *"This is a big news for CSMEs, like us"*, Manager T continued, *"Chances of investing overseas is there for us, but we had no channel to convert US dollars. Doing international business without $ is like a skilled house wife could not make meal without rice (old Chinese saying)"*. Agreeing with Manager T, 3 other managers all asserted that the tightly foreign currency control by the Chinese Government used to be a big constraint factor for CSME managers to involve international business in the past. Manager H further elaborated:

> *The restriction of purchasing foreign currency made our [international] business such difficult before... but now situation is different. Government's policy of foreign exchange has been changed, it gives us [SMEs] more opportunities to think about and invest oversea markets.*

Elsewhere, **Manager M** mentioned that the new exporting policy launched especially for CSMEs in 2004 drove them expanding their international business positively. The Chinese Government announced that CSMEs that possess RMB 500,000 can export products directly to their overseas clients instead of through large trading companies. *"Before the new policy was launched, our international business largely relied on trade agents. Those agents make money on the commissions, thereafter not much money left for us."* This used to be a common issue that prevented some CSMEs from expanding business internationally. Manager G confirmed this point: *"because of the low margins (SMEs relying on trading company for exporting), I know a few CSME managers quit their exporting....but some of them already started again now"*.

Moreover, participants illuminated that the Chinese Government supports pushed them going international as well. For example, **Manager T and M** confirmed that many Chinese provincial SME Bureau assigned special persons who look after CSMEs foreign investment. Some of them play fairly positive role in helping CSME managers seeking international overseas opportunities and supporting them expanding internationally. Overall, the favourable outward investment polices and Government support revealed in this research have changed these CSME managers' business conceptions and made them realising that 'going international' is an effective strategy to survive when facing fierce competitions in domestic markets.

4.5.1.3 Fierce Competition in Domestic Markets

Evidently, the domestic market competition in China is an important factor that pushes CSME managers seeking overseas business opportunities. Every interviewee strongly addressed that fierce competitions from both foreign and domestic companies brought them increasing competitive pressures intensively. Manager B from the beverage company described this situation as "a nightmare". He reinforced that for CSMEs, intense competitions from foreign companies in China are tremendous. They are not just competing with foreign MNEs but also overseas SMEs. He gave an example to emphasise his comments:

> *There is a Canada beverage manufacturer that entered China in 1983, they initially targeted higher-level income Chinese customers, and earned great profits in the past. However, a few years ago, this Canada company started to launch low cost beverage (5 RMB/ per bottle, equals 33 pence /per bottle) fighting to survive in Chinese market. That was a big threat for many CSMEs in this sector.*

Manager C and E confirmed Manager T's comments. From their accounts, Chinese customers are more inclined to buy foreign products particularly from Western developed countries for certain historical and cultural reasons. They pointed out that:

> *Comparing with local Chinese firms, most foreign companies are competitive due to their high quality products. However, prices of their products are normally higher than Chinese products. Shifting their strategy from differentiation and quality to low-cost (by foreign) SMEs put many CSMEs into extremely difficult positions.*

To reinforce his point, **Manager B** from the beverage company went on to continue his comment:

> *3 years ago, this Canada company launched 3 RMB /per bottle (20 pence/per bottle) low-cost fruit juice....low-cost is not unique advantage for Chinese companies any more. It's time for CSMEs to think about how to specialize their core business....'going out' is a positive way to help CSMEs leverage their market capabilities.*

Manager Q claimed that the vicious competition from local Chinese companies is another factor pushing CSME managers to consider going international. He further explained that after more than 20 years political and economical reforms, China is changing rapidly. Nevertheless, as most developing countries, the Chinese market still retains many problems and issues. Unsophisticated markets and unsound economic regulations provide soil for growth of vicious competition. *"Some Chinese business men want to play the game, but don't follow the game rules"*, Manager Q indicated, *'Price-war in China makes many CSMEs surviving hardly in Chinese markets"*.

Additionally, manager W believed that the competition is not only a factor pushing CSMEs internationalisation in manufacturing industries but service sector. He confirmed that:

Service sector has been liberalized for foreign direct investments relatively in China in the past ten years such as insurance, business consultant companies. Especially, after China jointed WTO, this market is more open. For example, the financial service, like bank industry, is going to be deeply involved by foreign companies, such as RMB services.

Manager W affirmed "*We know the competition is going to be worse in service sector....fighting up against foreign MNEs competitors in China? It's difficult. To survive, we must seek alternative way in such a competitive market*". Overall, from CSME managers' narratives, it is acknowledged that push factors on home country basis, such as the Chinese Government incentives and support, and intensive competitions and pressures from both domestic and foreign companies in China, pushed CSME managers thinking and seeking international business opportunities actively.

4.5.2 Pull Factors

In the cases of investigated CSMEs, 2 pull factors emerged from participants narratives which facilitated CSME managers' business investments in the North of England, these pull factors includes 1) British Government support, especially from One North East, the regional development agency, 2) network encouragement from host countries.

4.5.2.1 Govenment Support from the Host Country

Among the 10 interviewees, 6 participants admitted that One North East, the Dvelopment Agnency of the England, played a very positive role in their determinations of entering the North of England markets. As **Manager P** confirmed, to attract more Chinese companies investing in the North East of UK, One North East has established their offices in Beijing and Shanghai in China. In the last few years, One North East has organised many workshops in China to introduce business environment and favourable FDI policies in the North of Englandfor potential Chinese investors. Most importantly, One North East emphasised that as a regional development agency, they would provide comprehensive supports to Chinese investors. These events triggered and encouraged many CSME managers' intentions of investing in the North of England. In early of this interview, manager P explained:

> *Before attending Mr. X's presentation (from One North East) , we really hesitated over the choices between going abroad or still stay in China....we made out decision as we know that we can have comprehensive supports from One North East, they have office in China, we can communicate each other, this is crucial for us.*

Three other owner managers from the manufacturing sector expressed their comments from same point of view.

> *For me, 'One –stop shopping' supports from One North East was true encouragement....for many CSME managers, language and cultural barriers are obvious, these barriers affect many aspects doing business overseas. Being aware of this, One North East assigned a alliance manager, who speaks both mandarin Chinese and English. From initial marketing investigation to business proposal, from accommodation to office rental, this manager gave us great supports.*

> *(Owner Manager T)*

> *Moreover, One North East works jointly with International Departments of local city councils to provide CSME managers free basic legal and consultant services. In early market investigating stage, the alliance manager gave us many supports and valuable advices. These 'superb services' from One North East really built up our confidence to our further investments in this region.*

> *(Owner Manager Q)*

Before (I) came to England, two of my friends who had businesses in France invited me to go to France, but to be honest, I didn't feel comfortable, it's not because I don't trust my friends, just because Oh....One North East's supports made me feel more confidence. Dealing with Government agents (One North East) means 'less risk' and 'safer' to me.

Owner Manager M)

From what Manager P, T, Q and M explained, it is revealed that Government supports from the host country had a considerable effect on CSME managers' decisions of investing in the North of England. Being consistent with Chinese low-risk taking business culture, managers in the case of this study expressed their willingness of dealing with Government to make them 'feel' safer.

4.5.2.2 Network Supports

When reflecting what other factors encouraged these CSME managers investing in the North of England, 4 interviewed managers disclosed that their investments were driven by their networks in the UK. These connections are either their personal contacts or potential customers. One owner Manager F from a Chinese textile company explained that:

In 1973, through a friend in Hong Kong, I came to know a British business man who was a managing director in a British textile company in the North of England. He appreciated the low cost of our products. I was really impressed by the design and quality of their products. I believed that corporation between us would bring great profits for our company. However, it was impossible to do so at that time due to various reasons.

Manager F explained that by then China was not open to the Western world yet. Political and economic controls in China in 1970s made this alliance just a dream. "*Luckily we have been keeping the relationship between us*", Manager F continued that "*after the Chinese Government launched*

126

open door policy in 1978, very soon, this friendship turned into business partnership". From initial exporting products to this British textile company till forming the joint venture partnership, *"I believe"*, manager F affirmed that *"the contact with this British business company was one of the important factors that encouraged us to invest business in this region (the North East of England)"*.

Three other managers also noted that contacts and business networks in the foreign countries had certain impact on CSME managers' business determinations overseas. It was asserted that China open door policy provides many opportunities for not only large Chinese companies but SMEs to build business networks with foreign companies abroad. **Manager M and G** indicated that to seek more business opportunities abroad, except attending some international trade fairs in China, they also attend to 2 big trade fairs abroad. One is Frankfurt trade fair in Germany, another one is Birmingham trade fair in April every year in the UK. Via these trade fairs, these managers built up their business contacts and further developed these contacts into business partners. **Manager G** narrated:

> *From stand decoration to products selections, plus other expenditures, attending abroad trade fairs cost us a lot of money, but it was worth it. Luckily, through these international trade fairs, we have built many business contacts and built our business networks in the foreign countries, some of them already turned to our foreign business partners.*

Manger M from the jewellery company illustrated how his international business activities triggered by their business networks in the UK as well. He explained that:

> *We went to Birmingham trade fair in 2002, next to our booth was a British lady who has been doing jewelry business for more than 20 years in the UK. This lady is very interested in our rings and necklaces and impressed by their low prices. She suggested - if we can change our design more Western style, there would be a great potential markets for our products in the UK....this business relationship has been kept after the fair. She gave us a lot of help for our businesses in the UK.*

From these participants' perspective, CSME managers' foreign investments in The North of Englandwere somehow shaped by their business networks in the UK formally (Government) or informally (networks). Business networks in the host country encouraged these CSME managers expanding their international businesses positively.

So far, external motives of CSME managers' investments in the North of England(emerged from the interview data) have been explicitly brought into the discussions. Additionally, CSME managers also highlighted some internal factors which had relative impact on their decisions of foreign investments in this region.

4.5.3. Managers' Entrepreneurial Factors

Additional to the external motives, some participants recognised that CSME managers' strong personal preference of internationalisation was a key factor to enter the North of England markets. Manager M emphasised that external motives may lead an organisation to consider the possibility of launching business abroad, but they are not sufficient condition for the foreign investment decision. This is evident in manager M's comments where he indicated that the company may lose markets in home country but still decide not going abroad. To confirm this point, a number of interviewees claimed that they were initiators of their foreign investment projects in the North of England. They believed that for most of CSMEs, especially for small companies, the managing director's (most of them are owners as well) 'personal thoughts' hold the power over a firm's internationalisation decision. Adding to this point, manager T commented that some CSME managers may not think risking their business abroad even a foreign opportunity appears if they have no intention of going abroad at all. Manager P further gave an example to reinforce manager T's comments:

A few years ago when we had no foreign customers, as a marketing manager, I met Mr. Z who was a marketing manager from another CSME. His factory by then already had some well established foreign business partners in United States, the UK and France. Via his networks, Mr. Z knows a French customer who was seeking business partnership with Chinese firms and asked me if we were interested in this business (Mr. Z's factory did not manufacture that product at the moment). My instinct told me it was a good opportunity. Therefore I spent quite lot time to discuss this with Mr. Z. However.....my boss completely denied my proposal, and insisted that foreign market is too risky.

From **Manager P's** continued narratives, it is noted that his company started doing international business in the foreign markets only after the ex-general manager retired. *"Our new general manager is a kind person who is optimism, openness and willing to take risks"*, Manager P commented, *"He is very interested in overseas markets, especially the foreign markets in the Western countries because he believes that doing business in the Western developed countries is more interesting and could enable us to learn more than doing business in the neighboring countries"*. This exemplified that CSME managers' personal preferences of 'going abroad' turned into an important factor that determines CSME managers' foreign investment decisions. Two other interviewees, **Manager M and Manager B** expressed the same comment. For them, doing business in England was somehow their personal intents and preference. **Manager M** explained that

I started my own business when I was 15 year old. In the last 25 years, honestly, I made good money on my business and built sufficient business experience in China. However I had never been doing business in the foreign countries before I came to England. Everybody says that doing business abroad is difficult than doing business in China, I am a kind person who enjoys challenge, that's why I am here....I know that each CSME manager has his/her own reason to come England, for me, it's simply- I just want to see the world outside China and experience different things.

To reinforce manager M's point, manager B affirmed that *"I did not deny that some external forces do drive CSME managers thinking and doing business internationally. However, you can take the horse to the water, but you cannot make it drink"*. It is apparent that above discussions explored how CSME managers' strong individual preferences affected their determinations of investing in the North of England markets.

Another emerged theme in this research is that managers' intention of gaining entrepreneurial freedom. Among these interviewed CSME managers, more than half of them used to either work or study in Western developed countries, such as the UK and Switzerland. Three managers obtained their business management degrees from foreign universities. **Manager P** who used to study in the UK commented that *"Knowing more Western business management styles makes me feel that it is difficult to become a real entrepreneur in China because there are still some Government and institutional restrictions that constrain Chinese entrepreneurs"*. Another **Manager W** with same opinion continued that *"One of the important reasons why I determined to come here (the North East of England) was because I do not want others to take control of my business activities"*. He believed that doing business overseas gives him more opportunities to gain entrepreneurial freedom than in China. These managers' narratives demonstrated that these interviewed CSME managers have desires for business autonomy. They recognised that doing business in England enables them having opportunities for this desire.

4.5.4 Strategic Factors

During the data analysis, another emerged theme that shaped CSME managers' investment in The North of Englandwas the strategy factor. In answering the question '*Why did you decide to invest your business in this region',* some participants put more weight on firms' strategic objectives internally rather than concerns of external factors. Entering the North East of England, for some CSME managers, was to 1) gathering direct information, 2) expectations of growth in local market, 3) and developing their own international managerial expertise.

Manager Z explored that he initially wanted to gather first hand market information by investing in England. He explained that *"Gaining efficient market knowledge of England can help us to understand the Western business better and enhance our international business performance in other Western developed European countries".* Additionally, **Manager T** pointed out that one of the important motives for him was to seek niche market growth in the North of England markets. More specifically, Manager T asserted that their company targeted overseas Chinese in the UK as their customers in the North of England markets. During the last few years, they have built a market niche by selling traditional Chinese food successfully.

For other CSME managers, they claimed that their initial intentions of entering the North of England markets were to build up their own international expertise teams for further international expansion from long-term views. In his reflection, **Manager M** noted that *"Setting business venture in England could improve and enhance our staff's international knowledge and practical experience that reinforces our foreign customer services for now and future".* Manager M indicated that currently they have more than 400 employees in China, last year they recruited two foreign jewellery designers, one is from Italy and another is from South Korea. Their products, as manager M stated, have a great potential selling well in the European markets. *"We just moved a small step in our international business expanding at the moment. Invading the Western markets is one important goal for us. We* *want to prepare our own international expertise in a long-term commitment by investing in the North of England markets*", Manager M emphasised.

4.5.5 Discussion

Summarising the findings of the motives of CSME managers' foreign investments in the North of England markets, 4 groups of factors are regarded as important motivations by CSME managers. They are push factors, pull factors, entrepreneurial factors and strategic factors. The first 2 groups are mainly connected with external factors in line with Government policies and supports, plus the competition conditions in the home markets and networks in the host country. The last 2 groups of factors concern the entrepreneurial and strategic aspects from firm's level. Throughout CSME managers' reflections of their investments in the North of England, it is evident that each CSME manager had different experiences in deciding whether or not to enter foreign markets. In some cases, owner managers regarded external factors as more important than internal factors. For other cases, entrepreneurial and strategic factors are primarily important in shaping their foreign investments. Going beyond the surface level of the findings, the synprojectand further discussion on CSME managers' initiatives of entering the North of Englandwith consideration of theories discussed in Chapter Two are provided next.

From CSME managers' clarification, external factors that shaped their foreign investments in the North of England markets can be discussed in several aspects.

- In terms of the CSME managers' motives of entering the North of England markets, the findings revealed that the *Chinese Government liberation to FDI and supports are of primary importance in encouraging CSME managers going abroad*. This finding corroborates Griffin and Pustay

(2005) and Rugman's (2006) statements that economic changes, government power and market liberation play important roles in motivating both SMEs and MNEs' foreign investments (as mentioned in section 2.3). Clearly, comparing with Western SMEs, international business activities of CSMEs are more intervened by the Chinese Government due to the characteristics of Communist political and central planned economic systems in China. As discussed in section 2.3.2., although one of the important Chinese economic reforms is to increase Chinese enterprises autonomy (Nolan, 2002), inheritance from the planned economy makes CSME managers hard to act entrepreneurially (Child and Tse, 2001). Uncertainty reforms in China, in particular policy issues, still remain a deep problem in line with CSME managers' determinations of going abroad. However, although some Chinese Government interventions are still there, many hurdles of foreign investments have been eliminated. Regulatory FDI policies provide a favourable condition and create more opportunities for CSME managers operating across national boundaries.

- Furthermore, it was evidenced that *heavy competition in China has become another considerable factor driving CSME managers to look for opportunities in the North of England markets.* This finding is consistent with Buckley (1998) who indicates that as push factor, competition from foreign international companies in home markets exceptionally push SMEs seeking new markets. The competition from both foreign and domestic companies in China makes CSME managers feel difficult to survive. The declining home market pushes CSME managers to seek opportunities in international markets (Donckels and Aerts, 1998; Erdener and Shapiro, 2005; Lall, 1983; Griffin and Pustay, 2005; Rugman and Collinson, 2006). This can be explained by the fact that with large numbers of foreign companies suddenly flow into Chinese markets, many

133

Chinese companies, both MNEs and SMEs, feel unable to compete with many foreign companies. As this research exemplified, price-war and intensive competition in China push CSME managers looking for foreign investment opportunities in different regions in the world, such as the North of England. This conclusion supports Child and Rodrigues (2005) who state that domestic competitions in China drive both Chinese MNEs and CSMEs seeking business opportunities overseas.

- This study also implied that *Government supports in the host country played an important role in attracting CSME managers' decisions of investing in the North of England markets*. As discussed earlier, 'superb services' offered by the One North East, the Government regional development agency in England, were highlighted by CSME managers in their reflections of initiatives of entering this region. These CSME managers confirmed that it was relatively easier to set up businesses in the foreign country with Government helps. This finding makes connections with Chinese business culture. Influenced by Chinese hierarchy and power distance culture (Hofstede, 1980; 1998), most interviewed Chinese managers asserted that strong Government support from host country made them feel relatively protective. This finding confirmed Buckley (1998) and Fujita's (1998) comments that host Government incentives drive SMEs internationalisation.

- The last external factor is *the business networks in the host country*. Several international researchers (e.g. Rugman and Collinson, 2006; Erdener and Shapiro, 2005) suggest that the determinants of FDI for MNEs are normally in relation to the market size, physical infrastructure, political environments, and effective governance at the political and economic levels (see section 2.3). This research, however, does not completely support what the previous studies discovered based on MNEs' internationalisations. According to this study, no indications have been given to confirm that market size of host country was apparently a pulling factor to attract CSME managers entering the North of England markets. Instead, this research identifies that networks in the host country indeed encouraged CSME mangers entering this region. Comparing with Fujtia's (1998) claim that SMEs may be pulled into foreign markets by their business partners who are large firms, this research extended Fujtia's (1998) findings by discovering the network that encouraged SMEs' foreign investment could be managers' personal contacts, social networks and even potential customers rather than just large firms. In this case, links can be made between networks and the Chinese Guanxi culture that discussed in Chapter Two (see section 2.3.1). It has been evident that having faith in 'Guanxi' networks in host country, CSME managers believed that doing business with someone they know in the foreign countries could help them to reduce uncertainties and risks in some ways. Generally, they believe that Guanxi business philosophy could work outside China as well.

Turning from external factors to internal elements, a number of new findings have been discovered during the data analysis in this study. Considering the entrepreneurial issue, 2 factors were identified in relation to CSME managers' decisions of entering the North of England. One of them has not been discovered in previous empirical studies.

- This study explored that CSME managers' *personal interest of internationalisation appeared as one important incentive factor.* According to some CSME managers' narratives, evidences in this research suggest that external drivers were not sufficient condition for them determining foreign investment. Some companies may lose markets in China, but they might still decide not going abroad. In this case, the decision makers' personal preference seems crucial important in driving their overseas investments. The existing literature (as discussed in section 2.3.1) claims that entrepreneur's attitudes determine their business behaviours (Cater and Jones-Evans, 2006). CSME managers' personal preferences of entering the North of England markets reflect their risk-taking entrepreneurial attitudes (Brochhaus, 1980; Buchanan and Di Pierro, 1980). Moreover, this finding also supports Buckley (1998) and Fujita (1998) who argue that investing in the foreign country is a result of entrepreneur foresight for SMEs. Evidently, Gerhard's (2000) findings, which indicated that Austrian SME managers' personal preference of internationalisation motivated them entering the US markets, is applicable in the context of CSME managers entering The North of England markets.

- Another finding of this research reveals that *seeking strategic freedom to act entrepreneurially* was considered of importance for CSME managers. This finding has not been discovered in past surveys among Western SMEs. From mainstream theories (Pleitner, Brunner and Habersaat 1998; Karmel and Bryman, 2002), SMEs have the advantages of flexible management styles comparing with MNEs (as mentioned in section 2.2.2). However, there are many external constraints that make CSME managers unable to enjoy strategic freedoms. This can be linked back to the discussion of Chinese political and economic system in Chapter Two (see section 2.3.1). Due to the Chinese political system of Communist Party and central controlled economic system, varieties of policies and regulations by Chinese Government largely constrain CSME managers' strategic freedoms (Child and Tse, 2001; Nolan, 2001). Although the Chinese Government is trying hard to increate Chinese enterprise autonomy, it still needs time for CSME managers to enjoy the strategic freedom as much as the Western SME managers do.

Internationally, 2 strategic factors were also discovered in motivating CSME managers entering The North of England markets.

- Deriving from their narratives, it is evident that some CSME managers intended strategically to *seek niche markets* in the North of England. Being similar with international motives of British SMEs (Naude, 1998) and Austrian SMEs (Gerhard, 2000), CSME managers also intended to seek market growth in the host country. However, the difference is that large market size is an attractive factor for SMEs from Western developed countries, particularly when they entering the emerging markets. CSMEs in The North of Englandwere interested in particular niche markets.

- Moreover, this research disclosed that some CSME managers intended to *build international and management expertise from long-term orientation.* Gerhad (2000) identified that one of the main motives of internationalisation by Austrian SMEs is to develop and acquire direct market knowledge in the foreign countries. It is evident that CSME managers in this study have the same orientation with Austrian SME managers. More than that, some CSME managers also have strategic intentions to develop their own staff's international knowledge from long-term thinking. According to existing literature, many SMEs are lack of strategic planning due to limited managerial resources (see section 2.2.2). However, this research shows that some CSME managers who are well educated in specialist in business management have clear long-term views. They realised that, with massive FDI inflows in China, cost-leadership strategy does not work profitably for CSMEs in long-term view. To survive, they must prepare themselves to improve their competitive advantages by integrating into international markets.

In summary, based on above discussions, some different motivations in relation to CSME managers' determinants of entering the North of Englandhave been highlighted in this research. It seems that these investigated CSME managers paint a more complex picture. The findings of this research imply that existing theories and explanations in terms of motives of firms' internationalisation must be modified before fully applying into CSME cases. With mixed results, different motives of internationalisation lead to varieties of market entry mode choices.

4.6 Entry Modes Adopted by CSME Managers

Drawing upon the narratives of CSME managers in exploring what entry modes they adopted when entering the North of England markets, 3 types of entry modes emerged. They were 1) Low-control mode: direct exporting through overseas sales subsidiary, 2) Medium-control mode: Joint venture, 3) High-control mode: wholly-owned manufacturing subsidiary. Interestingly, amongst these entry modes, the format of joint venture adopted by one CSME was operationally different from normal joint venture (see section 2.4.1). Moreover, internet emerged as an entry mode, triggered by some CSME international activities unintentionally in other European countries such as Denmark, Italy etc... In this section, the findings of entry modes adopted by CSME managers in The North of Englandwere reported followed by discussions of the findings.

4.6.1 Direct Exporting: Setting Overseas Sales Subsidiary

After analysing data, the findings showed that among of the CSME managers, 5 of them chose direct exporting (setting overseas sales subsidiary) as the initial choice of entry mode when first entering the North of England markets. Drawing upon the data, these 5 companies are all from manufacturing sector. 5 interviewed CSME managers explored that direct exporting enables them to maintain their low cost of products and flexible services. Moreover, these CSME managers asserted that direct exporting seemed a trend currently for Chinese manufacturing companies. From these managers' point of views, indirect exporting entry mode should be abandoned if possible. Setting up company's own overseas sales subsidiary is a better choice comparing with using third party such as sales agents and distributors. Manager P from the packing company illuminated the advantages and necessary of setting overseas sales offices by saying that:

> *Comparing with 20 years ago, setting our own sales office in the UK could be just a dream for us, things are changed now. With the advanced technology and convenient transportation, it is a realistic option for CSMEs now. There are many benefits in doing so. One is for sure clearly, if you want to make more profits, you must get rid of the third sales parties. Using whatever trading companies in home country or local sales agents or distributors in the host country, it is obvious that you have to pay commissions to them. In doing this, it is difficult to find your own foreign customers. Setting overseas sales office enable us contact to foreign customers directly which helps us to develop foreign markets.*

More than just cutting off commissions, **Manager B** from the soft drink company added that:

> *Using indirect exporting prevents us from gaining local marketing knowledge. Comparing with Western SMEs, CSMEs far more lack of international experience. To keep using third sales parties is making this even worse. Personally, I think setting overseas sales offices enable CSMEs to have better links with foreign customers in the host country. In the long-term view, this will provides more opportunities for us to develop more business networks internationally.*

From these CSME managers' standpoints, taking over indirect exporting entry method by setting overseas sale branch can avoid commission payments to third parties. Furthermore, this also enables them to take a chance learning from international markets directly and building close relationship with their foreign customers.

4.6.2 Joint Venture

Interestingly, in this study, only one investigated CSME manager adopted joint venture entry mode

when he initially entered the North of England markets. This Chinese-British joint venture was

formed in 1990s. The initial idea of forming this joint venture was to exploit each company's

complementary competitive advantages. In this case, the Chinese company wanted to exploit their

British partner's marketing knowledge by combining their own low cost product advantage. To

reinforce this point, **Manager F** excitedly stated that

> *This* (joint venture mode) *is a very effective model. We have been
> running it successfully for years. Using this entry method enables us to
> make fully use of both our competitive advantages. Our products sell
> well in the EU markets simply because these products not only featured
> with Western designs but are in relative low prices comparing other
> similar products manufactured by Western companies.*

From Manager F's comments, given the obvious labour and material reasons, cost of manufacturing

products in the UK is absolutely higher than in China. How did they possibly keep control of the low

cost? Figure 4.5 below presents the manufagturing process of sofa cusion in the joint ventures. As

figure 4.5 indicates, as the first step, the British partner plays an important role in product designs as

they have great experiences of the Western markets. Once the final product design is confirmed by

both partners, the Chinese partner manufactures the product parts that require low cost materials and

intensive labours in China and shape these parts to England. At the next step, the British partner

completes the final products in their premise in England. Finally, the completed products are sold by

entering the British partner's sales networks in the UK and other EU countries. Of note, in this joint

venture format, cushion cases that required intensive labours (cutting and sewing) and easy to ship

were manufactured in China. The fillings and assembling that require relative less labours were

produced by the British partner in England. By doing this, the finally completed products are still competitive in the Western markets by remaining its low cost advantage but with Western style

designs.

Figure 4.4 The operation process of the Chinese-British joint venture

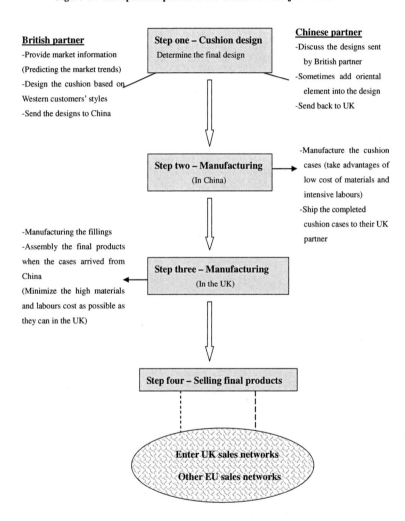

During the data analysis, the researcher further probed this phenomenon in discovering why only one

CSME used this joint venture mode. It was evident that because many business activities in this entry mode operate separately in two countries, both partners have to highly corporate effectively and

efficiently. Without well established relationship, it is very risky by using this entry mode. Further to

this point, **Manager F** commented that:

> *I believe that one vital factor for adopting this entry mode is to develop a good relationship with your overseas partners. From my personal experience, many corporations between two partners have to be mutually adjusted as we are not physically located in one country and working face-to-face everyday. Therefore, good relationship, again, and trust are extremely important.*

The interviewed manager revealed that his British partner, the managing director, came to China and

made some connections with Chinese people in early 1973. He is very familiar with Chinese culture

and its management system. Additionally, this British founder has a very good personal relationship

with the Chinese founder. Given the special relationship between these two founders and the typical

product, it might be argued that this is a very unordinary case and the experience explored in this

specific situation is very contextual. However, giving the pictures of different contexts is one of the

important research purposes and reasons why qualitative research has been chosen for this study.

4.6.3 Wholly-Owned Manufacturing Subsidiary

The findings of this research also indicate that building up wholly-owned manufacturing subsidiary

turned out as an interesting method for CSME managers. According to the data, 4 of them used this

high control and high risk mode as their choices when first entering the North of England markets.

Details of these 4 wholly-owned subsidiaries are illustrated in table 4.2 below.

Table 4.2 Chinese wholly-owned subsidiaries in the UK

Company	Products	Market context	C. advantages
Company **A**	Computer web-design	SMEs in the UK	Low cost/flexible service multi-language service
Company **B**	Financial and consultant services	business involves both China & UK	Multi-culture knowledge and low cost
Company **C**	Manufacturing Chinese food	Chinese overseas customers	Unique products (Niche market)
Company **D**	Chinese Herb M. & treatment	Both Western & Eastern customers	Unique knowledge (Differentiation)

As shown in table 4.2, among of these 4 wholly-owned subsidiaries, 3 of them are service firms and one belongs to manufacturing sector. **Company C** is a small Chinese company that manufactures traditional Chinese food. The manager from this company explored that *"Our main customers are overseas Chinese nationalities. We make good profits as nobody competes with us"*.

The other 3 service companies all tended to use their special know-how knowledge to expand their businesses in the North of England markets. **Company A,** the small computer software firm, labeled themselves as a niche marketer. As numbers of British and Chinese companies involving the international business activities between China and the UK is rapidly increasing, there is a large demanding of bilingual-language web design (Chinese-English) business. Similarly, **Company D** uses their special Chinese herbs and traditional treatments to expand their business. Both companies offer distinctive (highly differentiated) products and services to their customers. To protect their knowledge know-how, wholly-owned subsidiary, from these CSME managers' accounts, is the most suitable entry mode.

Company B is another service company that adopted wholly-owned subsidiary entry method when initially entering the North of England markets. **Manager W** from company B explained that

> *Our customers include two groups. One is the British SMEs that want to involve business in China but cannot afford expensive consultant fees to seek large consultant companies. For them, we are the right one because we can provide them valuable services with low charge. Reversely, we also provide consultant services for the CSMEs entering the UK markets. We help them solve visa issues, aid them developed their business plans etc. again, prices we charge are lower than British consultant companies. We can survive, simply, because we have these special advantages.*

In summary, the 4 interviewed CSME managers above explored that they had similar purposes to choose wholly-owned subsidiary entry mode when they initially entered the North of England markets. Clearly, they had similar market objectives: focusing on niche markets and being eager to exploit their specialized know-how knowledge than explore local resources. In other words, the strong forces (unique knowledge in one or two segments) in their specialized markets made these CSME managers concentrated on profits rather than market share when they decided to employ wholly-owned subsidiary entry mode.

4.6.4 Internet Entry Mode

According to the data collection and analysis, interestingly, the findings of this research revealed that internet as an entry mode has become another option for some CSME managers to expand their business into other EU countries. However, it was not initially planned and expected. Both **Manager Q** and **Manager M** explored that:

> *To be honest, we did not plan to expand our business to other EU countries in the first year at all. All we wanted to do was to fully concentrate on the UK markets. However, it was unexpected that we got 3e-mails from other EU countries in the first 6 months. They found us by visiting our bilingual website.*
>
> 〔**Manager Q**〕

> *We asked an IT expert in China designed beautiful home page for our UK branch. The pictures of our jewellery look amazing on the internet. During the first 3months, we had been working extremely hard to develop our sales networks in England and tried on Scotland as well. The interesting thing was that we got our first customer from Denmark via internet. It was absolutely unexpected.*
>
> 〔**Manager M**〕

Among the interviewed CSME managers, many of them had spent reasonable money on designing their web sites. Via internet, some Chinese manufacturers got their orders from foreign customers unintentionally. However, no service CSME was approached by foreign customers from outside the UK. In other words, internet entry mode was only active for manufacturers but not service providers in cases of CSMEs. Overall, as an interesting finding, it shows that the internet provides CSMEs with a shop window to foreign customers from other EU countries, such as Italy, France, and Denmark.

4.6.5 Discussion

This study has discovered 4 different entry modes that are adopted by CSME managers when entering the North of England markets: setting overseas sales branch, joint venture and wholly-owned manufacturing subsidiary. Additionally, internet as an unexpected entry mode aided some manufacturing CSME managers successfully attracted their foreign customers from other European

countries. To find out how these findings extended the understanding of SMEs market entry mode

choices, further discussion is to be provided by linking to the theories discussed in the literature

review.

According to existing literature, many international researchers (e.g. Nakos and Brouthers, 2002,

Papadopoulos, 1987) admit that SMEs have limited entry options comparing the MNEs because of

their financial and managerial constraints. Consequently, these SMEs prefer to choose low cost and

low risk entry modes such as exporting and licensing (Agarwal and Ramaswami; 1992; Chung and

Enderwick, 2001; O'Gorman and McTiernan, 2000; Agarwal and Ramaswami, 1992; Erramilli and

D'sSouza, 1993; Zacharakis, 1997). However, linking to the significance of CSMEs context,

arguments above are not fully supported by this study. It is clearly evident that these investigated

CSME managers employed a wide range of low-risk, middle-risk and high-risk entry modes. It

implies that a wide array of options can be selected by SME managers according to the given situation.

This outcome reinforced the survey results of the Department of Foreign Affairs of Australia (1995)

that explored SMEs from different countries employed various entry modes when entering Australia.

Moreover, the 4 wholly-owned subsidiary cases in this study strongly supported Yap and Sounder

(1994) who argued that high risk and control modes are likely to be adopted by SMEs, especially if

they serve the niche markets in the host country by providing innovative products and unique services

(see section 2.4.2).

In addition, the illustrations presented in this study do not capture the stage process theory which

emphasises that a firm's internationalisation is to be a incremental process from low to high risk mode at different stage (Johanson and Wiedersheim-Paul; 1975; Johanson and Vahlne, 1977; Luostarinen, 1979; Cavusgil and Nevin, 1981). This study has revealed that some CSME managers did not internationalise in the manner suggested by stage model. By no prior presence in the UK, 3 Chinese service companies and 2 manufacturing companies in this research moved either through joint venture or directly investment to the North of England markets. These findings corroborated some international researchers' criticisms of stages theory (e.g. Millington and Bayliss, 1990; Hedlund and Kverneland, 1985; Whitelock and Munday, 1993).

Moreover, through semi-structured interviews, this research provided an opportunity to probe how the Chinese-British joint venture actually operated in their manufacturing process. This is an emerging new finding in that the joint venture employed by the CSME manager operationally differed from the common format of joint venture. As discussed in section 2.4.1, following the assumption and key principle of joint venture concept, once 2 foreign companies decide to form a new joint venture, they often build up manufacturing plant in the host country to manufacturing products or provide services to their customers (Dool and Lowe, 2001). However, the findings of this study have shown that this CSME manager created a unique operational model by combining Chinese products' low cost advantage and British partner's marketing knowledge. This Chinese company avoided the high material and high labour costs in the UK. This is the most concerning issue for many Chinese companies that intend to adopt either joint venture or wholly-owned manufacturing subsidiaries. Therefore, this Chinese-British joint venture model could give other CSME managers some valuable insights and great aspirations.

Another interesting finding of this study was the internet entry mode. As discussed in section 2.4.2, although selling products via internet has been recognised as an effective path for firms entering the foreign markets. However, internet in the context of foreign market entry mode choices has not been well studied (Quelch and Klein; 1996; Hamill, 1997; Dool and Lowe, 2001; Fraser and Stonehouse, 2000). Derived from CSME managers' narratives, it was discovered that internet selling became an entry method triggering some CSMEs' internationalisations outside of the UK markets without expectations. This implied that once company entered the market, there are probably more demands than the firm first thought. Consequently, this finding suggests that CSME managers may strategically think of the EU as a whole single market rather than only prepare for the UK markets when they initially consider their entry strategic choices.

In summary, research data in this study turned out that the CSME managers entering the North of England initially employed 4 different market entry methods. Direct exporting, especially setting up overseas sales branch, intends to take over indirect exporting entry mode in the case of CSMEs. Moreover, this research implies that firms including SMEs could employ more than one entry mode simultaneously. Also, internet as an entry mode should be further investigated particularly in SMEs' international expansions as suggested by Fraser and Stonehouse (2000). Joint venture entry mode adopted by the CSME in this study implies that there is no ideal and standard market entry strategy for different firms entering even the same markets. Each firm can select the most appropriate entry method according to the given situation they face. Most importantly, SMEs should use their unique resources and capabilities (such as the specific good relationship in the case of the Chinese-British join venture in this study) to best transfer them into foreign markets without eroding their values. It is difficult, but SMEs can use their advantages of flat structure and flexible decision making process that enable them act more creatively and innovatively in their entry mode choices.

4.7 Key Factors Influencing CSME Managers' Entry Mode Choices

With the recognition of 4 different entry modes employed by CSME managers, this section turns to what and how certain factors influenced their market entry mode choices. After initial entry modes were discovered, participants were further asked to explore why they chose the particular entry mode when they first entered the North of England markets. Driving from the data analysis, the findings revealed that 5 sets of factors, including 1) firm-specific factors, 2) strategy-specific factors, 3) product-specific factors, 4) decision makers' personal characteristics, 5) as well as networks and culture factors, played important roles in CSME managers' entry mode choices when entering the North of England. Details of these specific factors related to the identified entry modes are presented and discussed below.

4.7.1. Firm-Specific Factors

By asking the participants to decide what factors led to their different selections of entry modes, a number of themes emerged based on firm-specific factors. According to the themes and codes developed in the template, it was discovered that 3 firm-specific factors, including low-cost advantage, flexibility and special knowledge know-how affected CSME managers' entry mode choices in the case of entering the North of England markets.

4.7.1.1 Low-Cost Advantage

The findings of this study indicated that choosing direct exporting entry mode via setting overseas sales branch was determined by low production cost factor. Five interviewed managers who adopted direct exporting entry mode by setting sales branch in the North of Englandcommented that they did not possess advanced technology and international business know-how, their primary firm-specific advantage is based on the low cost of labour-intensive production. **Manager P** claimed that:

> *Entering Western developed countries is different from entering Asian developing countries. Low cost production is the main firm-specific advantage we can explore in Western developed countries. Loosing this advantage means the end of our international business in the Western markets. We have never thought to manufacture our products in the Western countries due to the high materials and labour costs.*

Comments above demonstrate that low cost production is a unique ownership advantage which CSME managers often used to enter the Western developed markets. The Chinese price is a special resource which was utilised by these CSME managers in determining their entry mode choices in the North of England markets. The findings of this study shows that majority of CSME managers from manufacturing sector (except the Chinese food company due to its niche market strategy) considered to choose setting overseas sales office as their entry mode choice rather than wholly-owned subsidiary because of the high material and high labour costs in the UK. Additionally, 2 CSME managers from the services sector also confirmed this point. One of them explained that:

> *Computer web-site design is our core business. Honestly, we cannot compete with Western computer companies in many ways except low-cost and fast response to customer services. Sharing ownership with Western company makes us loose these advantages. Wholly-owned subsidiary, from our experience, is the most appropriate entry mode for us.*

By being probed to explore the reason why collaborating with Western foreign companies makes them lose low-cost advantages, the manager further confirmed that sharing ownership with Western companies meant high cost and less flexibility.

4.7.1.2 Flexibility

As another influencing factor, flexibility emerged as a low code underlying the theme of firm-specific factors. CSME managers asserted that as an ownership advantage, flexibility most likely affected

their entry mode choice. The findings of the research showed that CSMEs with greater capacity of

flexibility, especially service companies, were more interested in high risk and control entry mode,

such as wholly-owned subsidiary. Inversely, CSMEs that do not possess capacity of flexibility tended

to adopt low risk and control models, such as direct exporting. **Manager W** from the consultant

company asserted that:

> *Flexibility is one of our important competitive advantages. It enables us to adapt to the changes very quickly in the business decisions and customers services. For example, sometimes our staff started work in the very early morning or middle night due to the time difference between UK and China. In many cases, we need to control some of the business activities to allow our company to better adapt to changing circumstances. Joint venture entry mode certainly was not appropriate one for us.*

Manager Z from the web-design company echoed to Manager F's comments by saying that:

> *Our services cannot be produced in one country for export to another. Therefore, exporting is not a suitable entry mode for the service companies like us. As we adapted our business activities such as quick services in a very flexible way, to sustain this competitive advantage, we need to adopt the high control entry mode rather than joint venture forms.*

From what the above two managers disclosed, it was evident that flexibility was one of the critical

characteristics that distinguished CSMEs' services from its foreign competitors in the North of

England markets. Due to this high degree of flexibility competitive advantage, CSME managers from

the service sector preferred the high control entry mode wholly-owned subsidiary instead of

exporting mode.

4.7.1.3 Knowledge Know-How

During the data analysis, CSMEs' knowledge know-how also emerged as an influencing factor based on firm-specific advantages. According to CSME managers' narratives, knowledge know-how was an important ownership advantage that determined their entry mode choices, especially the service companies. Three CSME managers from service companies, web-design, Chinese consultant and the Chinese herb medicine company, used their special knowledge of Chinese culture and Chinese heritage to market their products in the North of England markets. **Manager W** confirmed that:

> *Reviewing many cases I did, it was fairly to say that our knowledge know-how in relation to Chinese culture made us survive in UK market. Some of our Chinese customers went to local consultant companies first, but finally came to us. If you ask me, why, my answer is simple as we know better than our foreign competitors from our customers' perspectivs. This know-how is like a tacit component that is difficult to be transferred*

These 3 cases implied that know-how turned as implicit knowledge which affected CSME managers' entry mode choices when entering the North of England markets. Agreeing with Manager W, Manager **N** explained that: *"Our business (traditional Chinese herb and medicine), as you know, is very different from others. Some of the knowledge could not be put into words and hardlyto be explained"*. Manager N's comments reflected that 'knowing what' is different from 'knowing how'. The manager from another service company asserted that: *"In many of the circumstances, we just know how to do it ... we know more than we could tell."* These managers confirmed that they wanted to protect some of their intangible assets. Consequently, the CSME managers from these companies preferred high control investment entry modes such as wholly-owned subsidiary that enables them to facilitate their tacit knowledge know-how without erosion of this competitive advantage.

4.7.2 Strategy-Specific Factors

According to the findings of this research, it was evident that CSME managers gave great concern of a number of strategic factors in their initial market entry mode choices. Four themes emerged regarding the strategy-specific factors during the data analysis: 1) market consolidation by exporting-oriented strategy 2) market expanding strategy, 3) niche market strategy and, 4) strategic freedom seeking. Derived from interviewed managers' narratives, it was discovered that different strategic objectives led to different entry mode choices: 1) CSME managers who adopted market consolidation by exporting-oriented strategy preferred to the low cost entry mode of setting overseas sales branch in the host country, 2) CSME managers who favoured market seeking strategy intended to use joint venture entry mode to enter the local British partner's sales networks, 3) niche market strategy and seeking strategic freedom were the 2 factors that led to high control entry mode choices.

4.7.2.1 Market Consolidation by Exporting-Oriented Strategy

In exploring why 5 CSME managers decided to set overseas sales subsidiary as their initial entry mode choices, participants revealed that securing their exporting business was one of the important objectives to consolidate their international markets in the host country. **Manager G** confirmed that high cost and high control entry modes were not attractive to them since they were more interested in consolidating their international markets by exporting-oriented strategy. This manager explained that:

> *Our exporting businesses had been very profitable by then (before they came to the UK) . We wanted to maximum our profits by continually carrying on the export-oriented strategy. Setting overseas sales office in the the North of England for us was to gain more direct marketing experience and consolidate our performances. Find a local business partner?—No! We did not want to have any coordination problems with Western partners, plus we made good money by exporting, why we wanted to share it with somebody else?*

From what Manager G commented, it was evident that these CSME managers strategically had no intention to change their exporting strategy since their international business relying on exporting was in the growth stage profitably. Instead of moving to next stage, what these CSME managers wanted was to consolidate their exporting growth in the host country markets. Adopting the overseas sales branch exporting entry mode enabled these CSME managers to 1) enhance their customer services, 2) gain first hand marketing experience, 3) and build up their own international expertise.

Furthermore, in light of the market objective of enhancing customer services, interviewed managers explored that they already had a number of British customers before they set their overseas sale offices in the UK. However, some poor performances threatened that these CSME managers could lose their British customers. According to CSME managers' experiences, communication had emerged as a key issue that affected CSMEs' international performance. **Manager M** has been working more than 10 years in a small Chinese jewellery manufacturing company. He recalled that they started their international businesses via a large Chinese trading company. Every year, paying commissions to the trading company made them lose profits. After the Chinese Government released the restriction of exporting, this jewellery firm immediately cut off their trading companies and tried to sell their products to foreign customers directly. Putting great efforts, they built up their business networks and started to export their jewellery to Western customers.

However, issues arose over time. Manager M commented that "*Internet and telephone creased a lot of communication problems. Minor communication mistakes cause big troubles, especially for new sample development.*" He stated that they tried to recruit people with rich international experiences and speak good English. Problematically, they could not entice them to stay longer. It is believed that bad communication is a big issue that damaged relationships between CSMEs and their foreign

customers. Manager M exemplified:

> We had ever lost an order that was worth a big money, it's a large single order
> for SMEs. One of our British customers designed 3 fashion necklaces for their
> Christmas season sales. After 3 weeks hard work, samples were completed
> and sent to our customer on time. However, soon after, we were told that the
> samples were rejected because of the incorrect design. Afterwards, we found
> that it was our girl who misunderstood it. Although the re-made samples took
> only seven days, it was still late.... the customer missed the opportunity to
> take catalogue photos for those delayed samples, and we finally lost the order.

Manager P from the plastic packing company reinforced manager M's comments by saying:

> Doing business with the foreign partners requires effective communication,
> especially for those partners from two different countries that are far away
> from each other physically, such as Western and Eastern partners. It is very
> important to get everything right at the first place, such as sample
> development. Otherwise, it creates a lot of problems. Setting up overseas
> sales branch can definitely reduce miscommunications.

Agreeing with Manager M and P, **Manager Q** asserted that "*I do believe that we could avoid many

mistake if we communicated with our customer face-to-face. This is an important factor that

encouraged our company setting the oversea sales branch in the UK*". Manager M's example and

Manger P and Q's comments disclosed that due to the far physical distance and high costs, it is

difficult for both Chinese and British SMEs visit each other very often. It is therefore that effective

communication seems extremely important to enhance CSMEs' international business performances

and to underpin their existing exporting businesses in the foreign countries. These practitioners

emphasised that enhancing communication with British customers by face-to-face was one important

strategic factor that drove them to set up a sales subsidiary in the North east of England.

Another CSME manager also confirmed that he favored setting overseas sales branch entry mode due to the strategic thinking of gaining direct market experience and building up their own international professional team. Accordingly, this interviewed owner manager illuminated that Chinese products currently are popular to Western customers mainly because of its incredible low prices. However, some interviewed CSME managers explored that CSMEs' competitive advantage relying on low product cost is facing great challenges from other developing countries such as Vietnam and India. From these CSME managers' experiences, the cost advantage of 'the China price' will be lost sooner or later. **Manager M** exemplified: *"Labour cost has already increased in China, particularly in the well developed provinces. 3years ago, Chinese Government increased the prices of the raw metal materials, our business were largely affected".*

CSME managers asserted that competitions from other developing countries are fierce, to become successful in the international markets, they must prepare themselves from long-term of view. These CSME managers highlighted that although setting overseas sales branch in England increased the administration cost, it enables CSME managers to have a relative control over the selected markets and gain comprehensive feedback about the performance of each individual product so that they could compete with their competitors from other East developing countries. According to **Manager P**'s narrative, having a local presence in England at the beginning surely placed them in a better position to acquire direct market knowledge and enhance their capabilities of serving their foreign customers effectively.

Manger M from the jewellery company recalled that during the first 2 years of setting up a sales branch in England, apart from consolidating their business via improving customer services, they attempted to approach new customers in the UK markets. The first large customer they approached is a British Jewellery whole seller which has more than 400 high street chain shops. After nearly

3months hard work, this Chinese Jewellery company had half way through to step into its sales

networks. However, they finally lost such a valuable customer. **Manager M** explained that:

> *Our marketing manager and I went to this firm's headquarter in London. The senor buyer was very interested in our low-price necklaces and rings, as well as the designs. First meeting was successful. After a few further meetings, this British company decided to buy more 20 items from us for a sale trial. However, for some supplying and financial payment conflicts between us, we were removed from their supplier list unfortunately.*

Critically, Manager M reflected that lacking of marketing and management knowledge of the UK was

the main reason why they did not get into this British firm's sales networks. Many CSME managers

emphasised that enhancing staff's international knowledge through learning by doing was an

important strategy for them when considering setting up an overseas sales office in England. These

practitioners confirmed that to improve customer service in a long-term commitment, directly

involving the foreign markets is necessary because as a proactive approach it can strategically protect

them from potential competitors that attempt to gain a foothold through foreign subsidiary. For all

reasons discussed above, CSME managers confirmed that they preferred to low cost exporting entry

mode by adopting consolidating strategy in the North of England.

4.7.2.2 Marketing Expanding Strategy

Amongst these investigated CSME managers, there was only one firm that successfully adopted joint

venture entry mode initially for certain reasons. In this case, the CSME manager had strong intention

to use local sales networks from their Western partner. This market expanding strategy led the CSME

manager's choice of joint venture entry mode. For most CSME managers, gaining market shares in

the Western developed countries is not an easy task to do. A few managers whose companies adopted direct exporting entry mode confirmed that negative images of Chinese product was a barrier that

prevented CSMEs from further market expanding in the Western countries. The **Manager F** from this

joint venture case reinforced this comments by saying that:

> *By choosing British partners in the UK, our initial intention was to*
> *expand our markets in the Western countries by overcoming the products*
> *image of 'made in China'. Currently many Western customers label*
> *'Chinese products = poor quality'. Personally, I think this is very wrong.*
> *This might be applicable for high technology products, but not for some*
> *common products like our textile products. However, this has become a*
> *big barrier for Chinese company to further expand their international*
> *markets in the Western countries, especially for CSMEs*

Based upon what he commented, this CSME manager tried to seek Western partners who could help

them to expand their market shares in the North of England markets. Additionally, this CSME

manager believed that manufacturing the product jointly with a Western partner could change poor

quality images of Chinese products. *'To choose this joint venture entry model"*, Manager F continued,

"We could leverage our products quality by working together with our British partner. By doing so,

we make profitable money from expanded markets". However, the interviewed manager from this

joint venture admitted that choosing this entry mode required certain resources such as well pre- and

post-developed relationship with foreign business partners. This successful case advises that joint

venture entry mode is a special method that can be adopted by CSME managers. It is difficult but

possible. As confirmed by this CSME manager, seeking market expanding is one of key strategic

factors led to their joint venture entry mode choice by sharing their British partner's local sales

networks via a flexible and smart way.

4.7.2.3 Niche Market Strategy and Strategic Freedom Seeking

Further regarding strategy-specific factors, it was identified that niche market strategy and strategic freedom seeking were 2 main elements that led to CSME managers' selections of wholly-owned subsidiary entry mode. Reviewing these cases, 3 CSME managers had a strong intention to adopt niche market strategy when first entering the North of England. The computer web-design company developed an effective niche market strategy by focusing on bilingual web designs (Chinese and English). Another consultant CSME offered services for both CSMEs entering the UK markets and British SMEs that are interested in the Chinese markets. **Manager W** expressed that:

> *From marketing investigation to settle down, many things have to be considered by CSMEs. It's not just about issues of employees working in the UK but also their families: the dependents' visa applications/accommodations/finding schools for their children...this probably is too much hassle for large consultant companies. We offered a wider range of services by providing both Chinese-English oral and written translation services. It was relatively low risk and achieved a steady rate of growth. Similarly, we provide same services to our British clients.*

Moreover, the Chinese Tufu manufacturing company was an extremely interesting case in this study. It is the only invested manufacturing company in which the manager chose wholly-owned manufacturing subsidiary in the North of England. According to Manager T's accounts, their entry strategy was niche market focus via selling highly differentiated products. The Tufu products manufactured by this company were very traditional Chinese styles (detail is to be discussed in the next section 'product-specific factor'). Strategically, they designed their Tufu products to be recognised mainly by Chinese nationalities in the UK markets. **Manager T** from this company confirmed that

> *The populations of Chinese people, in particular the Chinese students, has increased quickly in last 5 years in the UK. We targeted this market segment because traditional Tufu products are very popular for many home-made dishes in China. Two or three old Chinese supermarkets sell very basic Tufu products, options were very limited. Although the prices of the products are not as cheaper as in China, they are acceptable. Indeed, by this niche market strategy, we are operating on good margins.*

From their narratives, **Manager W** from the consultant company confirmed that the niche markets they targeted were the areas that large companies normally have no great interest. Building wholly-owned manufacturing subsidiary was the most suitable entry mode for them.

The findings of this research also indicated that CSME managers seeking strategic freedom were more likely to choose wholly-owned subsidiary entry mode. Underlying this circumstance, CSME managers explained that establishing wholly-owned subsidiary in the North of England, for them, were to escape management restrictions from Chinese Government and explore their entrepreneurial talents abroad maximally. One CSME manager commented that *"Even though you have some great (business) ideas, it was always difficult to get these ideas implemented due to various restrictions"*. Through building wholly-owned subsidiary, CSME managers could use this platform to practice their business ideas underlying their own business philosophy. Building upon this assumption, entry mode based upon high level of control is most suitable. As some CSME managers asserted that differences of business culture between Chinese and Western nations may create big barriers in achieving strategic decision harmony. Choosing joint venture entry mode could increase coordination problems and again constrain their pursuer of strategic freedom entrepreneurially.

Overall, from what was discussed above, it implied that strategy-specific factors played important roles in affecting CSME managers' entry mode choices when entering The North of England markets. However, it was acknowledged that the strategy-specific factor did not affect these CSME managers' entry mode choices as a sole element. Other elements, such as product-specific factors, also affected

CSME managers' entry mode choices.

4.7.3 Product-Specific Factors

After analysing the data, it was discovered that 2 factors based on production-specific factor had a considerable impact on CSME managers' entry mode choices when they entered the North of England markets. Accordingly, the findings of this research show that CSMEs that manufacture standard manufacture products were likely to favour low cost entry mode such as direct exporting mode via setting overseas sales offices. In contrast, highly differentiated products, including both service and manufacturing products, pushed CSME managers toward high control equity investment entry mode such as wholly-owned subsidiaries in the host country.

4.7.3.1 Standard Manufacture Products

Five manufacturing CSMEs that produce neither highly differentiated products nor technologically intensive products adopted the exporting entry mode in this study. According to these CSME managers' explanations, all products they produced did not require an array of post-purchase services. Manger Q from the ties company added that: "*our ties are standard manufacturing products. They do not require considerable adaptation before we marked them into the western markets. We might, sometimes, just change the pattern and colour*". This comment was confirmed by other interviewed managers. Manager G from computer accessory company reinforced it by saying: "*Our products can be made either in China or the UK as they are labour-intensive products instead of technological intensive products ....my point here is very simply, to save costs, we would rather to make them in China than manufacturing here (The UK)* ". Bringing these comments together, it was underpinned that labour-intensive standard products pushed CSME managers more likely choosing direct exporting entry mode rather than building a wholly owned manufacturing branch in the North East of England.

4.7.3.2 Highly Differentiated Manufactured Products

In the contrast, the findings of this research shows that CSMEs provided highly differentiated manufactured products preferred to wholly-owned subsidiary entry mode when entering the North of England markets. This finding is evident by the case of the Chinese food company. As discussed earlier, in fulfilling their niche market strategy, this Chinese company offered traditional Chinese Tufu products for Chinese customers in the North of England markets. The CSME manager described that: *"Our products were highly different from the Tufu sold in the British supermarkets. They were sold very well by focusing on the Chinese customers in the North East area due to its specified Chinese styles and these products are all fresh made"*. Due to these specific features of their products, this manager asserted that it is impossible to export these products from China to the UK. He confirmed that high product differentiation was one of the important factors that drove him choosing the wholly-owned manufacturing subsidiary in England. Moreover, the Chinese medicine and herb company that provided highly differentiated Chinese traditional Chinese herbs also adopted the wholly-owned subsidiary entry mode when entering the North of England markets.

4.7.3.3 Highly Differentiated Service Products

Additionally, high level control mode such as wholly-owned subsidiary is also favorable for CSMEs who provide service intensive products. It was discovered from the data process if CSMEs' products were service focused, especially the differentiated products, then managers from these CSMEs preferred to the wholly-owned subsidiary entry mode when entering the North of England markets.

Evidently, one Chinese consultant company adopted the wholly-owned subsidiary entry mode by providing different bilingual language service and marketing knowledge know-how from multi-cultural perspective. The owner **Manager W** from this consultant company confirmed that

> *Our main services are interactive Chinese-English language and knowledge know-how specificity. To bring our services to the UK markets, we must find a way to produce our services....exporting is impossible as we have no brand reputation at all. Directly selling our services in the host country probably is the most suitable way to enter foreign markets.*

The small Chinese computer web-design company had the similar experience with what manager W mentioned. Being aware of their bilingual-specific culture advantage, this company tailed their products through providing fast response and flexibility services. Some of the services often require high level of control and higher resource commitment (especially HR resources), as **Manager Z** explained: *"Some time we had to overcome time differences between China and UK for fast response and back-up support services. In this case, we need to arrange our work in a very flexible way"*. These special service products are highly differentiated. Wholly-owned subsidiary entry mode helped these CSMEs to ensure that adequate services were performed.

In summary, 3 influencing factors based on product-specific were identified in relation to CSME manager's choice of entry mode when entering The North of England markets. Amongst these CSMEs, there were no companies whose products actually belong to technologically intensive products. Other 3 kinds of products such as standard products, highly differentiated products and intensive services products led to 2 different entry mode choices: direct exporting via overseas sales office and wholly-owned subsidiary.

4.7.4 CSME Managers' Characteristics

According to the research findings of this study, it was discovered that CSME managers' characteristics played certain roles in their foreign market entry mode choices. Through the data analysis, 2 CSME managers' characteristics, including 1) personal successful and failed experience, 2) personal international experience including managers' personal educational level, emerged as influencing factors that affected CSME managers' entry mode choices when entering the North of England markets.

4.7.4.1 Personal Business Experience

The theme of personal business experience emerged in this research mainly referred to CSME managers' domestic working experience, such as ability of fast response to emergency situations, capability of negotiation etc. In particular, from CSME managers' accounts, it was disclosed that successful firm experience had a different impact on CSME managers' entry mode choices comparing with failed firm experience. It is evident that CSME managers who were more successful in the past were more confident of dealing with changes than those who had more failure records. The field data, furthermore, indicated that CSME managers with greater experiences in the past favoured high-control mode such as setting overseas solo venture, while those with less successful business experiences were more inclined to favour low-control mode, such as direct exporting. Interestingly, 4 CSME managers' who adopted the wholly-owned subsidiary entry mode had more successful stories to tell than the CSME managers from the companies that used other entry modes in the North of England markets.

Manager **N** from the Chinese Herbs company claimed that "*I have been doing medicine, especially*

Chinese Herb business, for more than 20 years. My experience made me quite successful in the past (in Beijing) . " Manager T from the wholly-owned food manufacture venture echoed that *"My special knowledge know-how of Tufu products gave me a lot of confidence of running my own small Tufu factory here (in the North East of England) . Plus I am a very hard work person. The experience I gained from the successful business activities in China, I believe, benefits my international business a lots. "* CSME managers who adopted wholly-owned subsidiary entry asserted that they were doing fairly good in China, and they were also desired to learn more and expected more successful business experience in the international markets. In contrast, not many successful stories had been told by those CSME managers who used the direct exporting entry mode.

4.7.4.2 Personal International Experience

According to the field data, CSME managers' personal international experience also emerged as an influencing factor in relation to CSME managers' entry mode choices. In this study, data attributed the fact that CSME managers with great knowledge of foreign markets and culture and English language proficiency tended to favor high or relative high control entry modes. One CSME manager asserted this by saying *"These experiences (knowledge of Western culture) make me feel more confident and comfortable since it allows me effectively either working with foreign partners or do-it-alone".* For example, some respondents confirmed that English language proficiency helped them to establish business contacts with foreign partners in the host country. Moreover, these CSME managers addressed that English language proficiency improved their communication skills that enabled them to have better understanding of foreign business practices. One CSME manager explained that:

This (English language proficiency) helped me to reduce uncertainties of my business activities in the foreign countries. Comparing with the Chinese Managers who do not speak English, I probably have better understanding of the complex of managerial environment of the foreign country than relying on the interpretations via third person who has different business experience from me.

Underlying the theme of international experience, it was identified that CSME managers with Western educational background differed their foreign entry mode choices comparing with those CSME managers who did not ever work or study in the Western foreign countries. Research data showed that 4 CSME managers who had studied in the Western developed countries such as Switzerland and the UK adopted the wholly-owned subsidiary entry mode. Deriving from their accounts, it was evident that these CSME managers with Western educational background were more open-minded and more interested in international business expansion as decision makers. One CSME managers affirmed that *"My multi-culture knowledge of both home country and host country enables me to have better understanding of the foreign culture and business practices. It provides me more confidence to manage the business activities in complex foreign business environments."* Thus, these managers are more willing to choose relatively high risk modes such as joint ventures and wholly-owned subsidiary entry modes.

4.7.5 Networks and Cultural Factors

As another interesting finding, this research discovered that the scope of CSME managers' networks in the host country affected their entry mode choices under the context of CSMEs entering the North of England. The more networks they have, the more likely they adopt high control entry modes. A number of CSME managers asserted that networks had becoming increasingly important for them to secure information and access to foreign markets knowledge that would help them to reduce relative uncertainties and risks. One of respondents addressed that:

> *Influenced by Confucian culture, Chinese managers generally believe that they might benefit from guanxi connections they developed in the foreign country. The more connections you have in the foreign country, the less insecure you feel. I personally made a lot of connections when I was studying in the UK, these networks become unique resources for me. Of course, I took this factor into account when I made the decision making of entering the the North of England markets.*

This manager further commented that his networks in the UK facilitated him to choose wholly-owned

subsidiary as the initial entry mode. Another CSME manager echoed that: *"If something badly*

happened, I know where to seek help. The networks in the host country not only bring more business

opportunities but made me feel relative safe. " Above comments illuminated that CSME managers'

entry mode choices were shaped by their already developed networks in the host country.

Of note, from CSME managers' accounts, national culture differences also emerged as a factor that

influenced CSME entry mode choices. After analysing the data, most interestingly, it was evident that

CSME managers tried to avoid the joint venture mode mainly because of the differences between

Chinese and British cultures. **Manager M** from the jewellery company asserted that:

> *I was not keen to look for British partners to form joint venture in the UK, not before, not now, not future! There are many culture dissimilarities between Western and eastern countries: different language, different management attitudes, different business decision making styles and different ways approaching customers...too much hassle! It is easy to miss the business chances when opportunities come.*

This research revealed that joint venture entry mode was less popular choice comparing with setting

overseas sales office and wholly-owned subsidiary in the cases of CSME managers' entry mode

choices. The large culture distances create a lot of barriers for successful collaborations of business

partners between CSMEs and British SMEs. Consequently, it is less likely that CSME managers choose joint venture entry mode unless there is a very strong relationship between the Chinese and British partner.

4.7.6 Discussion

So far, factors that affected CSME managers' entry mode choices in the North of England markets have been discussed. Evidently, 5 sets of influencing factors emerged from the data. Internally, these factors included firm-specific factors, strategy-specific factors, and product-specific factors. Externally, it included networks and cultural factors. Moreover, CSME managers' personal characteristics also played a role in CSME managers' entry mode choices in the case of entry the North of England. Based on the final developed hierarchy template, the detailed factors underlying each sub-category were summarised and presented in table 4.3.

On the basis of the empirical data, it is concluded that factors identified in table 4.3 led to 3 different market entry mode choices in the case of CSME managers' entering the North of England markets, including direct exporting entry mode (setting overseas sales office in the North East of England), joint venture entry mode and wholly-owned subsidiary entry mode.

It is found that some outcomes of this research are consistent with existing literature, but other findings have not been previously identified in the current research. to have a better understanding of CSME managers' entry mode choices in the context of entering the North of England markets, by recalling the theoretical frameworks presented in Chapter two, details of each set of factor and its influences on CSME managers' entry mode choices are to be discussed.

Table 4.3 Summary of influencing factors of entry mode

- **Firm-specific factors**
  1. Low-cost firm advantage
  2. Capability of flexibility
  3. Knowledge know-how

- **Strategy-specific factors**
  1. Market consolidation by exporting oriented strategy
     - o   Gaining direct market experience
     - o   Building up international professional team
     - o   Enhancing customer services by improving communication skills
  2. Market expanding strategy
  3. Niche market strategy
  4. Strategic freedom seeking

- **Product-specific factors**
  1. Manufactured products
     - o   Standard products
     - o   Highly differentiated products
  2. Service products

- **Decision makers' personal characteristics**
  1. Personal business experience
     - o   Successful experience
     - o   Failed experience
  2. Personal international experience
     - o   Knowledge of foreign markets
     - o   English language proficiency
     - o   Western education background

- **Networks and cultural factors**
  1. Networks
     - o   Connections in the host country
     - o   Chinese Guanxi and networks
  2. Cultural factors
     - o   Dissimilarities of Chinese and British culture
     - o   Different management attitudes

4.7.6.1 Ownership Advantages

Reflecting the existing literature, influencing factors based on firm-specific level have been well studies. According to the mainstream of the Western FDI theories, firm-specific factors involve a wide range of resources from tangible assets to intangible assets, such as nature resources, firm size, human resources and financial commitment, knowledge know-how and international experience etc... These assets could be a firm's important ownership advantages which are associated with their market entry mode choices (Capron and Hulland, 1999; Conner, 1991; Dunning, 1988; Eleledo and Sivakumar, 2003; Hunt, 2002; Anderson and Gatignon, 1986; Cannon, 1993). However, ownership advantages differ across countries and result in different choices of entry modes by different firms.

In Chapter Two of literature review, 3 influencing factors based on firms' specific: firm size, international experience and knowledge know-how were discussed. In this study, 3 different firm-specific factors were identified. They are *low-cost advantage, flexibility and knowledge know-how.* Comparatively, firm size in this case did not emerge as an influencing factor that had effectiveness in CSME managers' entry mode choices. This finding is against Erramilli and Rao (1993) who proposed that firm size is positively associated with high risk entry mode. It did not support Chung and Enderwick (2001) who suggested that there is a negative relationship between firm size and high control entry mode either. However, this research supports Nakos and Brouthers' (2002) comments that firm's size is irrelevant with SME entry mode choices. One of the possible explanations could be that firm size was not important in this case since sizes of all investigated companies were CSMEs. They all face similar resource constraints. Moreover, as internationalisation of CSMEs is just a new phenomenon, instead of following normal or regular procedures, CSME managers' entry mode choices may not be simply explained by the main FDI theories.

According to the existing literature, international experience is one firm-specific factor that affects firms' entry mode choices (Kim and Kogut, 1996; Mudambi, 1998; Evans, 2002; King and Tucci, 2002; Anderson and Gatignon; Reuber and Fisher, 1997). However, being different from previous studies, the factor of international experience emerged in this study refers to CSME managers' personal international experience rather than the firm's international experience. This could be

170

explained that SME managers, especially owner managers, normally are the key strategic decision makers, their experiences can be treated as the firm's international experiences. This factor as one of the owner managers' personal characteristics is to be discussed later.

Having commented in the literature, companies with know-how knowledge is more likely to use high control mode of wholly-owned subsidiary (Dunning, 1988; Hill et al, 1990; Kim and Hwang, 1992). Being consistent with existing literature, this research confirmed that special know-how knowledge encouraged CSME managers choosing wholly-owned subsidiary instead of joint ventures. This result also supported the resource-based theory (Capron and Hulland, 1999; Conner, 1991; Hunt, 2002; Eleledo and Sivakumar, 2003) in that there is a fit between firms' resources and external opportunities in their entry mode choices. This research illuminates that CSME managers considered their specific know-how knowledge as a unique resource in choosing their entry mode choices. They wanted to ensure that these resources can be best transfer into the host country without eroding the values (Aulakah and Kotabe, 1997; Madhok, 1998; Erramilli and Agarwal, 2002).

Having not been fully explored in existing literature, this research has revealed that cost advantage and flexibility emerged as 2 ownership advantages that were considered by CSME managers in their entry mode choices. According to Anderson and Gatingnon's (1986) TCA model, firms' entry mode choices are exclusively determined on a least-cost basis. In this study, CSME managers selected their entry mode choices on basis of the same assumption Anderson and Gatingnon (1986) proposed, but interpreted it in a different way. TCA model emphasises total transactional costs in firms' entry mode choices. CSME managers in this study concerned how they can still keep the low cost production ownership advantage in their entry mode choice. Most of the CSME managers from the

171

manufacturing sector chose exporting entry mode to maintain their low cost products advantages (Tufu manufacturers and joint venture were two special cases in this study).

By extending this low cost advantage into service sector, flexibility emerged as a factor influencing the entry mode choices. The findings of the research explored that CSMEs with greater capacity of flexibility were more interested in high control entry mode. Conversely, CSMEs with inflexibility tended to adopt low control model. As discussed earlier in this section, flexibility is a great resource for CSMEs to maintain their low cost products advantage. For example, the Chinese web design and consultant companies, both of them provided speeding up and complex services to customers based on their flexibility capacity. Notably, the existing literature built upon TCA model investigates influencing factors by examining organisational structure and marketing problems (Anderson and Weitz, 1986); environment factors (Hill, *et al*, 1990), information impacts, uncertainty and complexity (Jones and Hill, 1988). By expanding TCA mode, this research added 2 new factors based on consideration of transaction costs: low cost production and flexibility.

4.7.6.2 Strategy-specific Factors

Based on the results of this research, initially, CSME managers were driven strongly by strategic objectives to expand their business internationally. These strategic objectives as influencing factors had played important roles in their entry mode choices in the case of entering the North of England markets. Being different from the existing literature, global or multi-domestic strategy (Anderson and Gatignon, 1986; Hwang, 1988; Hill, Hwang and Kim, 1990) and market diversification strategy (Cannon, 1993) have not emerged as influencing factors in this qualitative research. The possible explanation is that above strategies are mainly adopted by MNEs. Because of many constraints,

CSME managers normally have no capability to use these strategies expanding their international business, especially when entering the Western developed countries. Combining Cannon's (1993) market consolidation strategy and Shi, Ho and Siu's (2001) exporting-oriented strategy, *this research indicates that CSME managers adopted the market consolidation by exporting oriented strategy. This strategy led to CSME managers' preferences of low cost entry mode.* The results did not support Cannon (1993) who have theorised that market concentration strategy leads to high control entry mode. Also, it was against Shi, Ho and Siu's (2001) exporting-oriented strategy that suggested that Hong Kong SMEs following an export-oriented strategy prefer wholly owned subsidiary entry mode with highest control.

The findings of this study explored that CSME managers preferred to joint venture model to expand market shares. This outcome supports Shi, Ho and Siu (2001) who found that Hong Kong SMEs preferred joint venture entry mode to expanding their market shares in mainland China. Differently, the joint venture entry mode discovered in this study required well developed personal or business relationships between two joint venture partners. This outcome can be explained by network theory (Malhotra *et al*, 2003; Coviello and McAuley, 1999). Being consistent with what different authors have stated in the literature, this research confirmed that, in the context of CSME managers entering The North of England markets, network relationships play an important role in their entry mode choices (Coviello and Munro, 1997). Well developed business relationships encourage SME managers adopt equity investment entry mode (Bell, 1995; Lindqvist, 1988; Johanson and Mattsson, 1988).

.

Surprisingly, 2 new emerging strategic factors, including niche market strategy and strategic freedom seeking, have not been well studied in existing literature in SME entry mode choices. Previous niche marketing research has mainly focused on firms' motivations and how to sustain and develop the niche (Brown and McDonald, 1994; Doole and Lowe, 2004). However, how niche market affects SME entry mode choices is left unchallenged. During the data process in this study, it was discovered that CSME managers who are interested in niche market strategy preferred high control entry mode such as wholly-owned subsidiary. Of note, in the case of the Chinese food company, the manager adopted niche market strategy by providing highly different traditional Chinese Tufu products to Chinese nationals in the UK. This unique feature had determined the manager to avoid using joint venture mode.

Strategic freedom seeking as an influencing factor has not been identified in previous research but emerged in the cases of CSME managers' entry mode choices in this study. The possible explanations could be derived by considering the business environment in which CSME managers are operating. Before the Chinese Government released open door policy, state-owned companies dominated Chinese economic development. SMEs in China were highly controlled by the Chinese Government. However, after the Chinese economic reform in 1978, Chinese private enterprises that are mainly SMEs have grown successfully and speedily. These CSMEs have become an important force in Chinese economic development. Affected by Western enterprises in China, many CSME managers realised the importance of strategic freedoms. Underlying this assumption, a wholly-owned subsidiary could provide these CSME managers a platform to explore their creative business ideas. *These 2 strategy-specific factors are new findings in the market entry mode literature. This is particularly valuable for shedding light on aspects of SME entry mode choices, especially for SME managers from transactional economic markets.*

4.7.6.3 Product-specific Factors

In Chapter Two, Root's (1998) product specification and its impact on a firm's entry mode choices are discussed. In comparing the differences between Root's (1998) theory and the results of this study, instead of the 4 influencing factors Root's (1998) claimed, 3 product-specific factors emerged in this research: 1) standard manufactured products, 2) differentiated manufactured products, 3) service products. The fourth product factor, technological intensive products, suggested by Root (1998), was not discovered in this study. The possible explanation for this is because most CSMEs have not owned highly advanced technologies in their product innovations and developments. Moreover, submitting to Root's (1998) claim that firms with service-intensive products cannot export entry mode, this study confirmed CSME managers from service companies preferred to adopt wholly-owned subsidiary entry mode rather than exporting.

Surprisingly, the findings of this study were completely against what Root (1998) claimed that highly differentiated products push companies to adopt exporting mode, and standard products lead to local production through contract manufacture or equity investment to keep its low cost advantages. Root (1998) explains that highly differentiated products can retain competitive advantage in host markets since they can absorb the high unit transaction cost. However, Root does not take the transaction specificity of the products into account. For example, traditional Chinese Tufu products in this study were featured as highly differentiated products, according to Root (1998), the Chinese Tufu company should adopt exporting entry mode. Indeed, these specific Chinese Tufu products cannot be exported due to its nature of the products (they must be kept in fresh). In this sense, *this research more clearly illuminated Root's claims by adding the insight that the nature feature of the internalized products relating to its transaction specificity has to be considered*. Moreover, this research also indicated that providers of standard products tended to enter The North of Englandmarket using direct exporting entry mode. Thus Root's (1998) claim that standard products normally led to local production through contract manufacture or equity investment to keep its low cost advantages is not supported because Root's (1998) conclusions are based on the firms from Western developed countries entering the developing countries. This draws attention that contextualisation should be considered by comparing developing and developed countries.

4.7.6.4 Decision Makers' Personal Characteristics

This study confirmed that entry mode choices by CSME managers in the North of England markets were strongly influenced by decision makers' personal characteristics. It was revealed that CSME managers' personal business experiences were related to equity entry mode choices. This finding partially supports Herrman and Datta (2003, 2006), but differences exist. In their empirical research, Herrman and Datta (2003, 2006) identified, in the large USA companies, CEOs' business experience has positive impact on firms' entry mode choices. However, they did not further investigate the different influences between successful experience and failed experience. *More specifically, this research further expanded their work by discovering that successful business experience was positively related to high control entry mode. However, CSME managers with less successful business experiences tended to choose low-cost non-equity entry modes such as exporting.*

Reflecting the existing literature discussed in Chapter Two, it is argued that the age of the top management team are negatively associated with a high-risk decision making (Wroon and Pahl, 1971). This argument is further extended into the entry mode choices by Datta and Herrmann (2006) who suggested that young CEOs in US large companies tended to select equity entry modes.

176

Nevertheless, no interviewed CSME managers in this study confirmed that age was actually associated with CSME managers' entry mode choices.

A number of empirical studies indicate that CEOs' personal international experiences are associated with their entry mode choices. These experiences often includes CEO's knowledge of foreign markets (Herrman and Datta, 2006), their language proficiency of the host country (Leonidou *et al*, 1998; Suarez-Ortega and Alamo-Vera, 2005). However, most prior studies largely focus upon MNEs and neglect SMEs. The findings of this research confirmed that CSME managers' knowledge of foreign markets and English language proficiency both affected their entry mode choices. The more knowledge of foreign markets and higher level of English language proficiency these CSME managers have, the more likely they choose high control equity entry modes. This result linked to CSME managers' education. The findings of this research show that CSME managers who were ever educated in the Western developed countries tended to use high control entry mode. This is because CSME managers with Western education experiences are supposed to have more knowledge of the foreign markets, and their English language proficiency helps them to deal with foreign customers more efficiently than the CSME managers who have not been either working or studying in the western developed countries. As a new finding, *the education factor identified in this research is particularly valuable for shedding light on aspects of individual education background and the management decision making.*

4.7.6.5 Networks and Social-Culture Influences

In Chapter Two, network theory and social cultural factor in line with firms' entry mode choices have been reviewed. Submitting to different authors (Malhotra *et al*, 2003; Johanson and Mattsson, 1988;

177

Carter and Jones-Evans, 2006), this study confirmed that CSME managers regarded their connections and Guanxi networks in host country as important factors in deciding their entry mode choices. These networks helped CSME managers to gain access to resources and markets in the host country (Malhotra *et al,* 2003; Johanson and Mattsson, 1988). Specifically, the Guanxi networks discovered in this study referred to the various connections such as business and personal relationships rather than only ethically linked personal connections in the host countries (Sim and Pandian, 2003). Not surprisingly, influenced by Chinese 'Guanxi' business culture (Luo, 2001; Tsang, 2002), CSME managers generally believe that obtaining large scope of networks with either business partners or local Government in the host country can lower their investment risks and reduce business uncertainties. These CSME managers felt that the networks could enable them to exploit their ownership advantages more easily in the host country (Hakanson, 1998; Meyer and Skak, 2002). This study also shows that well developed network relationships encourage CSME managers using equity entry mode such as joint venture. This result supports Bell (1995) and (Lindqvist, 1988) and Johanson and Mattsson (1988).

According to the existing literature, social-cultural differences between home and host countries have a great influence on firms' entry mode choices. According to different authors stated (e.g. Dunning and Bansal, 1997; Johanson and Valhne, 1975; Kogut and Singh, 1988, 1999; Hill et al, 1990), 2 different results exist among current theories. One argument demonstrates that the cultural difference is inversely related to the degree of control of a foreign market (Anderson and Gatignon, 1986; Root, 1987; Kogut and Singh, 1988; Erramilli and Rao, 1993). Other international researchers' empirical studies show that the culture distance is positively related to high control entry mode (Delios, 1997, Padmanabhan and Cho, 1996). However, being different from previous studies, the findings of this research did not support either of them. Interestingly, it was confirmed that due to large national cultural differences between Chinese and British, including different management attitudes such as collective decision making versus individual decision making, most CSME managers admitted that they were more likely to choose either *setting sales office* (manufacturing industry) or wholly-owned subsidiary (service industry). In other words, CSME managers tried to avoid using joint venture mode to reduce conflicts and management problems between 2 partners in their entry mode choices. *As a new finding in this study, joint venture mode is only selected when possible or necessary by CSME managers. This is evident that among all the invested CSMEs, only one company selected joint venture entry mode. In order to avoid culture clashes, these CSME managers would either use exporting mode to reduce risks or using wholly-owned subsidiary as high control mode to minimize the management conflict between Chinese and business partners.*

In summary, 5 groups of influencing factors were identified from CSME managers' accounts. Each set of factors has been explicitly discussed in relation to their entry mode choices. Through analysis of each factor, some new findings have been emerged in this study which draws the attention that the contextualisation has to be taken into account in the research of SMEs' entry mode choices. Otherwise, research outcomes might be ambiguous.

4.8 CSME Managers' Entry Mode Decision-Making Process

Previous discussions have explored relevant issues regarding CSME managers' entry mode choices which include motivations of entering the North East of England, factors and their influences on firms' choices of entry mode. From a practical standpoint, it is valuable to discover in which process these CSME managers made their market entry mode choices. This section sets out to explore CSME managers' entry decision-making by focusing on 3 main areas in light of their entry mode choices: the raised decision making issues, adopted decision making strategy, and finally the key decision-making process.

4.8.1 Raised Problems

During the semi-structured interviews, many CSME managers recalled problems and issues that they encountered in making their entry mode choices when entering the North of England. From a dark side, these CSME managers shared their negative experiences with the researcher. From these CSME managers' accounts, 2 main issues emerged externally in this study. One was difficulties of information acquiring, and another one was continuing government support in the home country.

4.8.1.1 Acquiring Information of the Host Country

The findings of this research showed that the difficulty of acquiring information of the host country turned up as a barrier that affected the quality of CSME managers' entry mode decisions under the circumstance of entering the North of England markets. It was highlighted by some participants that non-system and limited information of the host country they accessed in China prevented them from choosing optimal entry modes. One CSME manager commented that:

> *For some political reasons - I don't want (to) make further comments on that- we encountered some difficulties in acquiring relevant information about UK at initial stage. For example, gaining information via internet is probably the method that cost least (comparing with other approaches). However, we could not log on some of the websites for SOME REASONS. Moreover, some of the information provided by official websites was limited and not appropriate, they were not updated.*

Manager G from the computer company reinforced this problem from financial perspective. He further explained that:

> *Of course we can seek professional assistants, but the problem is that large consultant companies with great international experience charge expensively, we cannot afford that. Alternatively, to save cost, we can go to some CSME consultant companies. However, some of them were lack of international experience as well, just like us...*

Because of these constraints, some CSME managers stated that they had to rely on the information provided by local government and their business partners in the host country by free of charge. However, it was difficult for them to triangulate how reliable the information was. *"Seeking professional services is the best way but expensive"*, one of CSME managers addressed. Manager G illuminated this issue by providing an example. He recalled that the information they collected at the first stage was not as helpful as they expected. Then the manager decided to buy professional services. Recommended by the local government, they hired a British consultant company by paying 6 thousand pounds as the agreed price. Expectedly, the information this British consultant company provided was extremely valuable and they felt that it was necessary to carry out further investigations. However, financial constraints became a problem for them. Manager G commented that: *"As agreed from the very beginning, the British consultant company carried out certain market investigations for us. If we want to go further, we have to pay extra money, but we were really struggling to budget it."* Other CSME managers also revealed their experienced problems in seeking valuable and accurate information in the process of deciding their entry mode choice.

4.8.1.2 Government Continuing Supports

A few number of CSME managers explored that weak Chinese Government continuing support also emerged as an issue that prevented CSME mangers from making optimal entry mode choices.

Participants revealed 3 main issues in light of government continuing support: information providing, training and financial support. Some CSME Managers expressed their comments regarding these issues by saying that:

> *Chinese government released some favourable policies to encourage CSMEs going international without doubt. However, the continuing supports were not enough. For example, it was difficult for us to find appropriate government SMEs institutions that can truly provide us valuable information*
>
> （**Manager P**）

> *Lacking of management skills, especially the international management knowledge, certainly affects decision makers' capabilities in processing information. Consequently, it would provide uncomfortable decision making environment for managers in their entry mode choices. Chinese Government should provide more international management training for CSMEs.*
>
> （**Manager M**）

> *For some obvious reasons, most of the CSMEs are lacking of financial supports. Realising this, 'do-it-together' with Government is a better way than 'do-it-alone' for CSMEs in raising capital. However, in my opinion, Chinese Government did not do well to assist CSMEs in their access to capital supports.*
>
> （**Manager Q**）

From above CSME managers' accounts, it is implied that the Chinese Government played an important role in CSMEs' internationalisation. Although the Chinese Government strongly encourages CSME managers to think about 'going abroad', *continuing* support from the Chinese Government did not fully match CSME managers' requirements. Overall, it can be concluded from above discussions, the decision making environment in home country may have either positive or negative impact on CSME managers' entry mode choices because decision-making environment in home country may create more complexities for decision makers. This environment is determined by external factors such as continuing government support.

4.8.2 Strategy Adopted in CSME Managers' Entry Mode Choices

According to the empirical data of this study, it was evident that CSME managers prioritised different groups of influencing factors in their entry mode decision-making process. Some managers emphasised that it was difficult for them to look thoroughly at the large amount and high quality of accurate information due to expensive cost and time constraints. From a strategic perspective, CSME managers' experiences revealed that they adopted a combination of cybernetic strategy and rational strategy in their entry mode choices (see discussion in section 4.8.4).

One of the interviewed CSME managers asserted that: *"We had neither enough time nor resources to collect exhaustive information, instead, only certain areas were actually considered when we decided our entry modes."* This comment was echoed by **Manager P** from the plastic company who asserted that:

> *Because of these constraints (time and financial issues) we can only investigate certain important aspects such as marketing and cultural differences. Unrealistically, we could spend plenty of time and money doing large mounts of research and collecting a vast amount of information as large companies (using rational analytical strategy)*

On the other hand, a number of CSME managers stressed that entering foreign market was definitely different from business expanding in home country, the decision-making environment was far more complex and dynamic. To create more winning chances in international markets, these CSME managers were more formal and rational in making their international strategies comparing with their business decisions in home country. From these CSME managers' narratives, it was discovered that in some of the specific areas, they did use formal analysis process in their entry mode choices. For example, 2 CSME managers confirmed that they made great efforts in their marketing research before

183

they decided which entry mode they were going to adopt in entering the North of England markets, such as market structures in the UK, products analysis etc.

In terms of strategy adopted by CSME managers in their entry mode choices, the findings of this research indicated that CSME managers tended to be more rational and elaborative in their entry mode choices comparing with their domestic decision-making. Moreover, as they stated, these CSME managers also were sometimes flexible in deciding what kind information was essential, and which information they were not enable to access due to time and financial and other constraints.

4.8.3 Decision Making Process

During the semi-structured interviews, CSME managers explored the decision-making process they focused in their entry mode choices when entering the North of England markets. According to the interpreted data, most of the CSME managers followed 3 consequent stages: gathering information, examining relevant influencing factors, deciding the right entry modes.

4.8.3.1 Information Gathering

The findings of this research revealed that information gathering stage was conducted by CSME managers as the first step of entry decision process. The assumption of doing this was mainly because of the unfamiliarity of the host country. Manager N explored that: "*Entering England markets was our first foreign investment in Western developed countries, lack of the experience and information really bothered me. Getting relevant information is extremely important.*" A number of CSME managers stressed the same comments with Manager N. From their accounts, there was so much uncertainty and unpredictability in the entry mode decision process. Gathering information helped them to make optimal entry mode decision. These CSME managers used various channels, such as Government agents in the host country, business partners, websites, professional consultant (not many CSME managers can afford), managers' personal contacts in the host countries etc. Some of the CSME managers spent one or 2 months visiting the UK to search for the first hand market information. The **Manager T** from the food company explained that:

> *At the beginning, we were JUST interested in doing business in UK, but we had no clear business idea till the first time when we visited the UK. During the visit, we found that many Chinese students and scholars living in the North East of England, this information helped us to identify our niche markets. After further investigation and analysis, we started our business here (in the North East of England) . In my experience, information must be collected before any decisions have been made, especially the accurate, reliable and valid information.*

From Manager T's narratives, it was interpreted that the uncertainty of internationalisation was truly a concern of CSME managers in deciding their entry modes when entering the North of England. Most of them confirmed that entering the Western foreign markets was a big decision for them. In this sense, these CSME managers tended to be rational because of the less-accountable environment in the international markets. However, at the same time, these CSME managers made their personal judgements by prioritising different groups of information in their market entry mode choices.

4.8.3.2 Data Process and Analysis

After collecting the information, then CSME managers claimed that they moved to data processing and analysis stage. In this stage, key influencing factors discussed earlier in this chapter were carefully analysed. One CSME manager confirmed that: *"I then carefully evaluated the business environment mainly on focus of the marketing structure including customer demands and prices, Government supports, cultural differences between Chinese and British etc."* Of note, a number of CSME managers stressed that data processing and analysis stage was very dynamic and contingent. Sometimes, decision makers' interpretations of the collected data varied from one manager to another. So in this sense, results of this stage may lead to different entry mode choices. Most interestingly, one interviewed CSME manager explored that

> *We had never so systemically spent that much time making a business decision before. Plus, we did not have the experience and (were)unfamiliar with the mode of entry decision comparing with the managers from multinational firms. To choose an optimal entry mode, we had to think carefully in making our decision.*

From these CSME managers' accounts, 2 patterns were discovered. First, it was evident that CSME managers tended to be more rational in their entry mode choices compared with their domestic decision-making. In the case of this study, these CSME managers tried to conducted data analysis in a rational manner at some stages during their entry decision-making process. Meanwhile, these CSME managers' personal decision-making attitude and personal characteristics (as discussed earlier in this chapter) had certain influences on their entry mode choices. For example, different experiences and educational backgrounds may affect their interpretations of collected information, and further influence their entry mode choices. In this sense, the data process and analysis by CSME managers might not be as elaborate as they planned.

4.8.3.3 The Choice of Entry Mode

From some CSME managers' narratives, the last stage of the decision-making process was to identify the choice of entry mode. This stage was described by CSME managers as *"the most subjective and dynamic stage.*" The findings of this study showed that decision- making at this stage was contingent

upon CSME managers' personal characteristic. In addition to CSME managers' knowledge, ability of

English language and Western education backgrounds etc., their personal decision-making styles and

preferences also played roles in the choice of entry mode. For example, according to CSME managers,

the time they would like to devote to the analysis and evaluation, the ability to focus their attentions

etc. may affect their final entry decisions.

One CSME manager explained how he made his entry mode choice by following this entry mode

decision-making process. Most interestingly, he addressed his final entry mode decision by saying

that:

> *What I did was that I had a few options in light of entry mode choices at beginning in my mind such as direct exporting, joint venture and Wholly-owned subsidiary, strategic alliance. To move down to the next level, I decided the 'optimal entry mode' by analysing and evaluating a set of factors and made my choices of 'the best entry mode'. However, the best entry mode sometimes could not be turned into 'the final entry mode' in a real-life situation. For example, I initially wanted to look for a joint venture partner in UK, but we cannot satisfy the potential British partner's needs (financial condition in mainly). Then we had to adopt exporting entry mode as our 'final entry mode'.*

Other 2 managers had similar comments with the above manager's opinion. They both confirmed that

they had their ideal entry mode determined after the analysis was conducted. However, to achieve it,

they had to work hard to overcoming some constraints, such as seeking government support in home

countries, negotiating the percentage of shared equity with potential joint venture partners. One of

them explained that: *"As our efforts made no results, we had to choose the other possible entry mode*

as our 'final entry mode' instead." Another manager echoed that: *"The 'best' one was not always*

workable, so in this sense, we had to give up the best and choose the second best." According to these

CSME managers' experiences, clearly, the decision of the final entry mode in this decision-making process is very dynamic.

4.8.4 Discussion

So far the findings of CSME managers' decision-making problems, strategic approaches and the key process in relation to their entry mode choices have been explicitly presented and analysed. In order to facilitate the further discussion on CSME managers' choices of entry mode for this research, relevant theories reviewed in Chapter Two will be discussed explicitly.

4.8.4.1 Combination of Rational and Cybernetic strategy

In light of managers' international decision-making, 2 strategies could be possibly adopted: rational strategy (Mintzberg, Ahlstrand and Lampel, 1998) and cybernetic strategy (Lindzey and Aronson, 1985; Kumar and Subramaniam, 1997). According to existing literature, rational strategy is more suitable for MNEs because formalised rational decision strategy requires various analysis tools and entails very complex procedure, and involves sufficient resources (Johnson, Scholes and Whittington, 2006; Porter, 1996). SMEs, in the contrast, more prefer cybernetic strategy suggested by Kumar and Subramaniam's (1997). Building upon the data analysis and findings presented earlier, *this research illuminates that CSME managers adopted a combination of the cybernetic strategy and rational strategy approach in their entry mode choices. It extended the existing literature that suggests that SME managers normally take short cuts and inadequate evaluations in their international decision making* (Buckley, 1998). The case of CSME managers' decision making of entry mode choices indicated that sometimes SME managers make their evaluations in a rational manner in their international decision making, such as entry mode choices.

Building upon the cybernetic decision making strategy originally from Simon's (1955) and Steinbruner (1974), Kumar and Subramaniam's (1997) assumed that SMEs tend to use less formal strategic process such as cybernetic decision model in their entry mode choices. So far, no empirical studies were conducted yet to support Kumar and Subramaniam's (1997) theoretical mode in existing literature. The findings of this research identified empirical evidences and filled this gap. On the one hand, CSME managers in general are unable (or would not be willing) to afford financial budgets due to the expensive cost. Consequently, it is not reliable for them to make comprehensive analysis rationally. Instead, only a certain critical set of factors on the basis of the limited information were considered by these CSME managers in determining their entry mode choices. On the other hand, this research indicated that entering foreign market is different from business expanding in domestic. The decision making in this scenario is more dynamic and complex (Aharoni, 1966; Ghauri and Holstius, 1996; Griffin and Pustay, 2005; Johnson, Scholes and Whittington, 2006). Rational strategy is requires in some levels because CSME managers were more careful in their international decision making. This result did not follow the lead of Buckley (1998) who stated that SMEs normally take short cuts and inadequate evaluations in their international decision making. Putting the 2 aspects together, it is concluded that CSME managers adopted the combination of rational and cybernetic strategy in their entry mode choices when entering the North of England markets. This result corroborated with Beach and Mitchell (1978) and Payne (1982) who suggested that the strategy selection should be the results of compromise between to make a correct decision and desire to minimise efforts.

4.8.4.2 Key Entry Decision Process

Building upon process-oriented models in line with firms' foreign market entry mode choices, this research more explicitly paints a picture of how CSME managers made their entry mode choices. According to Root (1998), MNEs often start with examining all entry modes at the same level and then decide the feasible entry modes based on the outcomes of the internal and external analysis. Finally, the right entry mode is identified. Nevertheless, the findings of this study did not completely support Root's decision making model since CSME managers did not examine all entry modes at the first stage. In fact, in their three-stage decision making process, different entry modes were only considered in the last stage.

Comparing with Kumar and Subramaniam's (1997) 5-step contingency model, the first 3 stages of problem recognition, evaluating time and resources and selection of decision strategy, had not identified by CSME managers in their entry mode decision-making process. Evidently, CSME managers did not begin with entry problems recognition that proposed as the first stage by Kumar and Subramaniam (1997) in their contingency model. Instead, they started with external information gathering mainly focusing upon markets and cultural investigation in England. Moreover, in their entry decision-making process, these CSME managers consciously considered what resources they have, but did not actually evaluate time they would spend. Meanwhile, they did not clearly know what strategy they were going to adopt. Just like some of them addressed "*We just followed the steps in our mind*". The process-oriented model developed in this research is similar with Kumar and Subramaniam's (1997) contingency model in step 4 'data collection' and step 5 'decision choices of entry mode', but *it clearly brought more details than contingency mode and provided more practical insights for CSME managers in line with their decision- making process of entry mode choices.*

The third process-oriented decision-making process of entry mode choices discussed in Chapter Two is Pan and Tse's (2000) hierarchical mode. They suggested that managers first sort all entry modes into equity-based and non-equity-based. Within equity-based modes, wholly owned subsidiary and equity joint venture are selected. For non-equity-based modes, the choice is between contract agreement and exporting. However, the results of this study were not consistent with this hierarchical mode. Distinguishing from Pan and Tse's (2000) hierarchical mode, the outcomes of this research explored that, instead of dividing equity and non-equity entry mode, 3 different levels of entry modes were explored. They were *possible entry modes, optimal entry mode and final entry mode*. Within the possible entry modes, only 3 modes, including exporting, joint venture and wholly-owned subsidiary, were first reviewed by CSME managers. The possible explanation is that most of the CSME managers were lacking knowledge of international entry modes (this was discovered in the pilot study in this research as mentioned in the methodology chapter). According to the pilot study, from low risks to high risks entry modes, exporting, joint venture and wholly-owned subsidiary were the 3 modes that CSME managers are most familiar.

4.8.4.3 Raise Problems in Entry Mode Choices

From CSME managers' accounts, 2 decision making issues in light of CSME managers' entry mode choices emerged in this study: the difficulties of acquiring accurate and valuable information and weak spots of the continuing support of the Chinese Government. This draws attention to the role of governments in SMEs international business expansion. The existing literature usually focused upon the factors and its influences on firms' entry mode choices. Nevertheless, the problems that SMEs face in their entry mode choices have not been well studied in current research. Issues discovered in this study might not be problems for MNEs, but they certainly influence the quality of SMEs' strategic entry mode decisions and their international business performances. These findings are particularly valuable for SME policy makers from a practical perspective.

4.9 Chapter Summary

In summary, drawing primarily on the interview data, this chapter has discussed how CSME managers conducted their entry mode choices in the context of entering the North of England markets. To explore CSME managers' individual experience in relation to their entry mode choices, the author interpreted the interview data by focusing upon 4 aspects: motives of outward investments, actual entry modes CSME managers employed when entering the North of England markets, key influencing factors of entry mode choices, and key entry decision making possess. Moreover, this study also offered a vision of how existing FDI theories are extended in the context of CSME managers' outward investment decisions when entering the Western developed country.

Overall, the findings of this study in line with the entry mode choices by CSME managers offered a good understanding of SME managers' entry mode choices. Particularly, the findings offered additional insights on the mainstream FDI theories by exploring CSME managers' entry decision-making from Eastern developing countries in the scenario of entering the Western developed countries. Theoretically, regarding SMEs' entry mode choices, this research identified a few sets of new influencing factors that have not been well studied in existing literature. Most importantly, this research more clearly illuminated the detailed process related to CSME managers' foreign entry mode choices by integrating some of the single theories, which only examine one or two particular influencing factors, into the process-oriented model. This is particularly valuable for shedding light on the aspects of SME managers' entry mode choices from practical point of view. This research implied that there is no standard decision making procedure that can be applied to all cases. SME decision makers should carefully consider different circumstances and scenarios when deciding their

entry mode choices.

CHAPTER FIVE

CONCLUSIONS AND IMPLICATIONS

5.1 Introduction

This chapter provides a conclusion to the whole research effort. In Chapter Two, mainstream literatures in line with firms' internationalisation, with particular interest in the choices of entry mode were reviewed. However, some pieces are missing in the context of CSMEs entering Western developed countries. Through Chapters Three and Four it becomes clear how the missing pieces have been explored and what new insights have been discovered.

To make concluding remarks based on the key findings of the study, this chapter is to return to the beginning of the research and briefly summarise how the findings of this research make the whole picture clear. Firstly, the research objectives of this study outlined in Chapter One are revisited. The second section of this chapter makes concluding remarks based on the findings and discussions of this research. Following this, theoretical contributions and implications of this study to SMEs' internationalisation are highlighted, specifically in the context of Asian SMEs from developing countries entering developed countries. This is followed by looking into the trustworthiness and relevance of this research. Finally, the limitations of this study and some suggestions for further research on Asian SME managers' choices of entry mode are recommended.

5.2 Conclusions of the Research Issues

As identified at the beginning of Chapter One, the general purpose of this research was to extend the understanding of foreign market entry strategies of SMEs from developing countries in the context of entering Western developed countries, with particular interest in CSME managers' individual experiences. To answer the research question 'How do Chinese SME managers make their strategic market entry choices when entering the UK?', several research objectives have been set out to guide this study: To identify the motives of CSME managers' foreign investments in Western developed countries; to explore key influencing factors and their impact on CSME managers' entry mode choices and to disclose the key decision making process associated with the choice of entry mode adopted by CSME managers. To achieve these research aims and objectives the patterns of CSME managers' entry mode choices were empirically investigated based upon their individual experiences of entering The North of England markets. Clearing order to clarify, the specific findings of this research are elaborated on and concluded below.

5.2.1 Motives for Entering a Developed Country

There are many different reasons why MNEs and SMEs expand their businesses internationally. A variety of external and internal drivers affect firms' motives for entering foreign markets. Motives for internationalisation, based on SMEs from Western developed countries, are presented in Chapter Two. Clearly, the author argued that motives of SME managers' foreign investments from developing to developed countries have not been properly investigated. To fill this gap, through analysing and interpreting interview data based on CSME managers' individual entry decision making experiences, the findings based on the empirical results reveal that 4 groups of motives of CSME managers entering the North of England markets have emerged. Among these motives, most of the factors are similar to the motives discovered in past research on Western SMEs. However, some of them did not appear in the case of CSME managers' foreign investment in the North of England markets. Most interestingly, two motives (marked * in table 5.1) are typical and originated in relation to CSME

managers' intentions of entering Western developed countries.

Table 5.1 Motives of CSME managers entering the North of England

Motives (high-code)	Motives (low-code)	Notes

Push factors
On home country basis
 	
(China)
	• Release of Government control: Central & local
	• Government supports and encouragement
	
	  o 'Going global' policy by the Chinese Government
	  o Release of favourable outward investment policy for CSME(e.g. foreign currency exchange)
	
	• Fierce competition in home country
	
	  o Competitions from abroad: MNEs & SMEs
	  o Competitions from domestic: MNEs & SMEs
	  o Immature market environment (vicious competitions in Chinese markets)
		Typical important from CSME Managers' accounts

Pull factors
On host country basis
 	
(the UK)
	• Government agency's comprehensive supports
	(One North East one-stop' services)
	
	• Encouragement from networks in the host country
	
	  o Personal contacts in the host country
	  o Supports from existing business customers in the host country
	  o Encouragement from potential business customers (e.g. exhibitors met through international trade fairs)	

Entrepreneurial factors	• SME owner manager's personal preferences of internationalisation • SME manager's strong intention of gaining entrepreneurial freedom (e.g. lack of management manpower in China) *	The one marked* is originated for CSME
Strategic factors	• Gathering information from host country • Seeking niche markets in host country • Building firm's own international & managerial expertise for long-term commitment *	The one marked* is originated for CSMEs

As table 5.1 indicates, the Chinese Government plays an important role in stimulating CSME

managers' determinations of 'going international'. Although China is following a unique path to

adopt market-oriented economic policies, many Chinese companies' business activities are still under the Communist Party's watchful eye. The Chinese Government's support is crucial for CSME managers to decide whether to go abroad or not. Moreover, fierce competition in China emerged as another force which pushed CSME managers to look for opportunities overseas. As one of the deciding factors, local Government support in the host country was crucial in determining CSME managers' foreign investment in a particular country. It is also evident that the network perspective has immense value to the understanding of CSME managers' motivation for internationalisation. It seems that CSME managers prefer to go to a foreign country where there are some people they know well.

However, whatever the 'push factors' or 'pull factors', they alone may not be sufficient to persuade CSME managers to invest in Western developed countries. A company may lose markets in its home country, but might still decide against moving to international markets. In fact, CSME managers' personal preferences of internationalisation became a considerable incentive in this study. Most interestingly, seeking strategic freedom to act entrepreneurially in Western developed countries has not been previously recognised in the research of SME motivations of internationalisation. This finding suggests that one reason why CSME managers look for opportunities to invest in Western developed countries is to escape the managerial and Government controls of the Communist Party in China. For some CSME managers with clear strategic objectives, moving into Western developed markets was in order to search niche markets and absorb information in the host countries. Others strategically wanted to build up their own international management team for long-term commitment and prepare them for further international investments.

In summary, some classic motives of internationalisation discovered in previous research, such as to secure raw materials and seek low-cost labour and materials in the host country, did not appear as indicators in the case of CSME managers entering the North of England markets. This implied that mainstream theoretical literature, which is largely and exclusively derived from Western MNEs and SMEs, needs to be modified before applying to Asian SMEs such as CSMEs.

5.2.2 Key Influencing Factors and Entry Modes

As discussed in Chapter Two, intensive research has been carried out to investigate what factors affect the choice of entry mode based on Western MNEs. Building upon CSME managers' experiences of entry mode choices when entering the North of England, the findings of this study add new insights from different angles. A summary of the key influencing factors and their impact on CSME managers' entry mode choices is presented in figure 5.1, highlighting 5 sets of influencing factors and their influences on CSME managers' choices of entry mode. Some of the factors were similar to, and supported by, existing literature. However, these factors marked * in figure 5.1 were typical and original in relation to CSME managers' entry mode choices.

The underlying 5 sets of influencing factors presented in figure 5.1, some of the elements identified in this study, have been previously studied in light of the choice of entry mode on the basis of Western MNEs and SMEs. Most valuably, a set of previously unrecognised factors; decision makers' characteristics, emerged as a group of influencing factors in this study. Those factors include CSME managers' personal business and international experiences, educational background - especially their knowledge of Western countries. Empirical research in relation to SME managers' personal characteristics in the past mainly focused on the relationship between SME managers' personality and the firm's performance. The direct impact of their personalities on the choices of entry mode has not been explored properly. This is particularly valuable for shedding light on aspects of SME managers' decision making surrounding entry mode choices.

Figure 5.1 Summary of Key influencing factors and entry mode choices

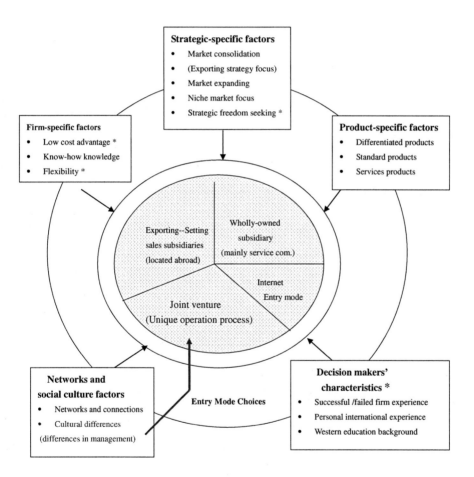

Source: Summarised from field data

199

The factors indicated in figure 5.1 have led to 4 main different entry mode choices by CSME managers. They are direct exporting, joint venture and wholly-owned manufacturing subsidiaries. Internet entry mode was triggered unexpectedly. By adopting a direct exporting entry mode, CSME managers preferred to locate their overseas sales office in the host country. The wholly-owned subsidiary entry mode was the most favourable choice for CSME managers from service companies. The joint venture mode used by the CSME managers in this study is operationally different from the traditional joint ventures (see details in Chapter Four). In addition, another novel result regarding CSME managers' joint venture entry mode choices is that, interestingly, cultural differences between the Chinese and British made joint venture entry less favourable for CSME managers compared with other entry modes. It was discovered that large cultural differences prevented CSME managers from using joint venture entry mode unless well-developed personal and business relationships existed. Otherwise they would choose either low control mode (for most manufacturing SMEs) or high control mode (for most service companies). In essence, CSME managers avoided choosing a joint venture entry mode from a cultural perspective, because of the difficulties of managing multi-culture differences which may prove uneconomical and limit a CSMEs' flexibility.

In summary, the finding of this study implies that SME managers may use specific resources to employ a wide range of market entry modes rather than just exporting if they can innovatively internalise these specific resources in the host country. Moreover, with the emergence of internet entry mode, this study advises that in spite of a lack of management experience and financial constraints, SME managers still can consider employing different entry modes simultaneously and prepare themselves for rapid expansion in foreign markets.

5.2.3 The Key Decision Making Process in Entry Mode Choices

Most of the existing literature review failed to paint a complete picture by exclusively examining the relationship between the factors and their impact on the choice of entry mode. To provide more practical insights for practitioners, this research discovered how CSME managers actually made their entry mode choice when entering the North of England markets. Building upon the experiences of the CSME managers' entry decision making process, a more work-based model was developed by integrating different resources (see figure 5.2).

As shown in figure 5.2, this process-oriented model combined different components together in 3 stages: Information gathering, data processing including factor analysis and decision on entry mode choice. In deciding what kind information was to be collected, a cybernetic strategy was adopted by CSME managers in the first instance since time, energy and financial constraints prevented them from being deliberate and rational. Once the necessary data had been collected, the CSME managers moved to the next stage: data process and analysis. In analysing influencing factors, CSME managers were more rational compared to the information gathering stage. Interestingly, in the last stage, a contingent approach might be adopted in making the final choices of entry mode. CSME managers first made their selection between possible entry modes and rejected entry modes. Afterwards, they chose the best entry mode they desired. If the 'best' entry mode was not feasible, due to financial constraints for example, as a back-up measure, these CSME managers would choose the 'second best' as their final entry mode. The findings are particularly valuable for illuminating the issue of how the final entry mode is actually chosen by SME managers from a practical point of view.

Figure 5.2 The Key Decision Process of Entry Mode Choices

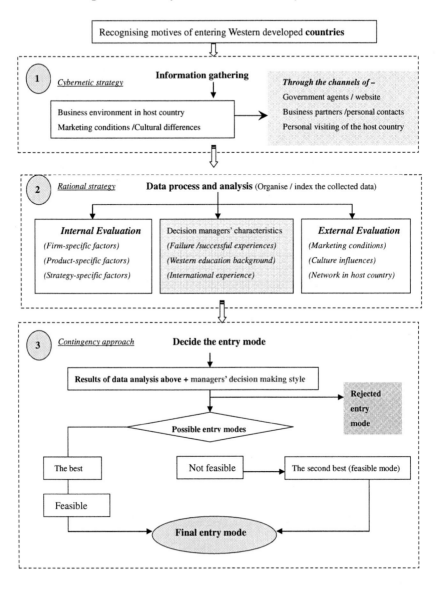

In conclusion, to answer the research question posed at the beginning of this study: **'How Do Chinese**

SME Managers Make Their Strategic Market Entry Choices When Entering the UK?', the researcher has achieved some preliminary conclusions by analysing the data gathered from 10 CSME managers in association with their market entry mode choices. Four sets of motives of CSME managers entering the North of Englandand 5 groups of influencing factors were discovered in this study. These motives and factors led to 3 entry mode choices directly and the internet entry mode unexpectedly. These findings suggest that Asian SME managers' entry mode choices, especially in the context of entering Western developed countries, could be very flexible and dynamic. The different strategic approaches adopted by CSME managers in this research imply that SME managers are more rational in their international decision making compared with their domestic business. So far, how the research question was answered and how the research objectives were achieved has been explored. Theoretical contributions and implications of this study are presented below (the unique practical contributions will be offered separately in Chapter Six).

5.3 Theoretical Contributions and Implications

The choice of entry mode is an important issue in a firm's internationalisation. In comparing the literature and empirical results throughout this research some unique contributions and implications have been made to existing theory by filling the research gaps identified in the literature review chapter on SME basis. Details of these contributions and implications are to be presented in this section.

The purpose of this study is to make an in-depth investigation of CSME managers' entry mode choices by extending Western-based existing foreign investment theories into the SME sector. By achieving this main purpose, this study makes several contributions to international business management theories:

- Unlike previous research, which is generally confined to the activities of large multinational enterprises from Western developed countries, this study has offered some new insights that have extended mainstream foreign investment theory and provided a different understanding of Asian SMEs' strategic market entry choices, particularly in entering Western developed countries.

- Moreover, the existing literature has concentrated much on the factors and their influence on the choices of entry mode by separating them from the whole decision making process. This study has extended the choices of entry mode by gaining a more insightful understanding of how CSME managers actually make their entry mode choices. Through exploring the decision making problems and strategic approaches adopted by CSME managers at different levels, this study, from a qualitative perspective, filled the gap by developing a comprehensive framework in relation to SMEs' entry mode choices.

- Furthermore, this study identifies the roles of SME decision makers' characteristics and their impact on entry mode choices which have been largely neglected in previous studies. The empirical results of this study have revealed that CSME managers' personal preferences and educational backgrounds are important to their strategic entry mode choices. It is particularly valuable to discover that CSME managers' educational experiences in Western developed countries affects their strategic market entry choices. Overall, based on the findings of this research, a complicated but clearer picture has been provided for SME entry mode choice, particularly in the context of CSME managers entering Western developed countries.

From a theory-building standpoint, the results of the study imply that many FDI theories built upon MNEs from Western developed countries must be extended before becoming more effective as general theories. More to the point, international management theories should be developed more concretely to avoid theoretical and empirical conflicts. Evidently, CSME managers interviewed in this study did exhibit unique characteristics of motives and entry mode choices in their internationalisation path. They varied from Western MNEs from developed countries. As noted, the Chinese Government and institutions in this study play an important role in CSMEs' internationalisation. This finding implies that extra attention has to be paid from a contextual perspective in internationalisation theory-building. For instance, research in SMEs' internationalisation should be conducted by separating developing and developed countries. Furthermore, this study also implies that cross-boundary cognitive disciplines may be used to explain SME managers' complex strategic decision making rather than focusing on parent disciplines exclusively. As this study has presented, CSME managers' entry mode decision making involves not only the international marketing and management disciplines but also personality characteristics and behaviour attitude.

5.4 Evaluations of the Research

Once researchers complete their investigation, they must judge the merit of their work. All studies, regardless of whether qualitative or quantitative, should be evaluated (Strauss and Corbin, 1998). However, qualitative research has long been criticised of lacking structure; too subjective and difficult to replicate (Bryman, 2004). As a result, evaluation of qualitative research has become a core issue for qualitative researchers, especially for international business due to cultural and institutional contexts (Clyne, 1987, Sullivan and Weaver, 2000, Anderson and Skates, 2004). Notions of qualitative research evaluation are to build confidence in the 'truth' of the findings and convince researchers themselves and audiences that their findings are "worth paying attention to, worth taking account of" (Lincoln and Guba, 1985: 290). To find out whether the results of the qualitative research have covered the research phenomena researchers claim to cover, appropriate evaluation frameworks and criteria have to be adopted (Hammersley, 1992, LeCompte and Goetz, 1982). The purpose of this section is to provide an account of how this qualitative research ensured its rigour by adopting relevant evaluation frameworks and criteria.

5.4.1 Evaluation Framework and Criteria

Measurement criteria for quantitative research have been well established (Saunders et al, 2006, Bryman, 2004). However, evaluation methods used in quantitative research, such as reliability and validity, have always been challenged by qualitative researchers since they cannot be simply applied to evaluate qualitative studies. Alternative criteria of evaluating qualitative research have to be judged and developed (Hammersley, 1992, LeCompte and Goetz, 1982, Johnson and Duberley, 2003, Mason, 2002, Strauss and Corbin, 1998, Lincoln and Guba, 1985).

'What criteria can be used to assess the quality of qualitative research' has long been a pivotal issue in social research. Anderson and Skates (2004: 475) point out: "there is no single way of validating one's qualitative research findings." In fact, there are sets of frameworks and procedures that can be used to evaluate the rigours of qualitative research. Reviewing the existing evaluation frameworks developed by leading qualitative researchers, Johnson and Duberley (2003) developed a contingent criteriology by considering 4 schools of philosophical thought: Positivism, neo-empiricism, critical theory and postmodernism. By adopting Johnson's framework more detailed epistemic reflections of this research will be explored in the research reflection section in Chapter Six.

Alternatively, Strauss and Corbin (1998) developed their criteria relatively for qualitative research.

They argued that judgments have to be made by evaluating: 1) validity, reliability and credibility of the data, 2) the theory itself, 3) the adequacy of the research process where the theory generated, and conclusions are made about the empirical grounding of the research. As a third framework, Lincoln and Guba (1985) proposed two primary criteria for assessing qualitative research: *Trustworthiness* and Authenticity. By trustworthiness, 4 criteria can be taken into account in evaluating qualitative research: Credibility, Transferability, Dependability and Confirmability. Criteria of authenticity are mainly used to judge action research (Lincoln and Guba, 1985). Examining the above frameworks, it is apparent that credibility, reliability of data and adequacy of the research process in Strauss and Corbin's (1998) framework is consistent with Lincoln and Guba's (1985) evaluation criteria of trustworthiness. Considering the features of this research, *Trustworthiness* is believed to be appropriate criteria in making judgments of this research.

Moreover, Hammersley's (1992) *relevance* criterion is also to be used to evaluate this research. By relevance, Hammersley (1992) argues that the importance of a topic within its substantive field and contributions to the literature on that field have to be taken into account in evaluating the qualitative research. In particular, he suggests that practitioners' concerns might be an aspect of relevance. Hammersley's relevance criterion touches on the key consideration of this research that mainly focused on the practical contribution rather than the more academic contribution with which most PhD theses are concerned.

Examining different evaluative criteria, Strauss and Corbin (1998) argue that the criteria are meant as guidelines. Qualitative criteria must be modified to fit the circumstances of the research. Considering the reasons discussed above, the evaluation frameworks and criteria for this qualitative research will concentrate on Lincoln and Guba's (1985) trustworthiness and Hammersley's (1992) relevance. Very importantly, Johnson and Duberley (2003: 81) state that no matter what frameworks or criteria are used in assessing qualitative research, it is crucial "to use the appropriate evaluation criteria in a reflexive manner." The process of evaluation of this research is to be conducted in a reflective manner.

5.4.2 Trustworthiness

Trustworthiness, to Lincoln and Guba (1985:290), is to disclose 'how can an inquirer persuade his or her audiences (including self) that the findings of an inquiry are worth paying attention to, worth taking account of?" To assess trustworthiness, Lincoln and Guba (1985) developed 4 criteria that include credibility, transferability, dependability and confirmability.

5.4.2.1 Credibility

Credibility concerns the feasibility of the account that the research provides. In other words, it determines the acceptability to others (Lincoln and Guba, 1985). Establishing credibility is to ensure that the researcher has "carried out a good practice.... the investigator has correctly understood that social world" (Bryman, 2004: 275). In judging the quality of this research, a few reasons can be considered to convince readers and the author that this research has its own merits. First of all, the choice of the research topic gives valuable credibility for this research. Rather than choosing the research question through literature routes, this topic is developed on the basis of the author's own professional and personal international business experiences. This can be judged as a valuable indictor of a potentially successful research, especially from a practical standpoint. Moreover, the adequacy of the research process can be also used to judge the fairness and rigour of this research. In retrospect, the original research samples were selected with unique features. Before the final research

samples were determined, I consulted the manager from the Asia department at One North East who

was in charge of Asian foreign investments in the North East of England. Based on his

recommendations, I assessed my personal relationship with these potential sampled CSME managers

(I used to work for a CSME as a marketing assistant manager in England) to ensure the access and

trust of targeted participants.

Following this, appropriate research methods were adopted in collecting data. After the

semi-structured interviews were conducted, in addition to the interview transcripts, I made field notes

and a reflexive research summary report after each individual interview. Assessing the strengths and

weaknesses of an interview enabled me to conduct better subsequent interviews. Meanwhile, to

ensure the true value of the data, some interview transcripts were sent to the participants for data

reviewing and clarifying. During the data collection, I kept these questions in mind: Am I collecting

the right data? What else do I need to know? How can I ensure the data are valid? These questions

helped me to ensure credibility of data collection during the research process.

Regarding the data analysis, King's (2004) template technique was employed in this study. By

adopting this method, the researcher defines the relationships between themes through a hierarchical

structure (King, 2004). In some senses, this data analysis method follows a specified procedure which

is more relative rigour than other subjective data analysis methods. The key consideration in creating

the template was that *when I finish the final template.* To ensure the collected data was comprehensive,

I decided that I would continue to conduct interviews until there were no new themes emerging in the

process of data collection. Furthermore, building upon the core categories the researcher developed, I developed my arguments by considering how I could use theoretical insights to understand and explore my data, and what role my data played in my arguments. Another lens I used to maintain credibility was to understand and review this study through my own culture lens. Rather than being biased, I claim that I adequately used my Chinese cultural background to produce high-quality research outcomes by understanding CSME managers' 'talking' and 'feelings' in deciding their entry mode choices.

In summary, to convince others and myself that this study is a good qualitative research, I reflected the research process from formulating the topic to data collection and data analysis above. It is noted that it is not possible for researchers to inform readers how the analysis was exactly and accurately carried out. However, certain types of information such as those above would provide the audience with evidence that this research is 'worth paying attention to' and 'taking account of.'

5.4.2.2 Transferability

Transferability addresses the issue of how research findings are applicable to other contexts (Lincoln and Guba, 1985). In determining the transferability of this research, I adopted the 'thick description' (Geertz, 1993, Patton, 1990) strategy by providing detailed descriptions of the research process in the research methodology and methods chapter. Building upon the descriptive data, similarities and differences can be observed by others and transfer some of the findings of this study into certain research contexts through appropriate adjustments. Clearly the findings of this research were based upon CSME managers' individual experiences. It is specific and contextually oriented. The conclusions of this study cannot make broad generalizations. However, they can be transferred into a small-scale. For example, some of the insights provided by this research may help SME managers from other Asian developing countries to make their generation by considering the certain circumstance.

5.4.2.3 Dependability

Dependability is about the issue of whether the research is applied consistently (Lincoln and Guba, 1985). It requires researchers to maintain the consistence of the findings if the research is carried out again. To achieve dependability, researchers are advised to adopt an 'auditing' trail in which the external auditors can not only follow the investigator's research decisions trail, but also arrive at the same (almost impossible), or at least not contradictory conclusions (Lincoln and Guba, 1985). However, the fundamental problem here is *who are going to be the 'auditors'?* For this research, I made a claim of social constructionism as my epistemology stance. Making this claim means I believe that my own culture shapes the way in which I view the world. Thus, understanding Chinese culture has important implications for this research, such as how I interviewed CSME managers, how I interpreted the data and how I constructed the knowledge of CSME managers' entry mode choices from my cultural lens. The auditors' knowledge of Chinese culture is essential in evaluating the dependability of this research. To return to the point of an auditing trail mentioned above, although all research records such as interview transcripts, fieldwork notes, research summary reports etc. for this study have been maintained in an accessible manner, I still doubt that divergent interpretations of this phenomenon (CSME managers' entry mode choices) might exist amongst those auditors with different cultural backgrounds from my own. Its dependability may not be seen as a very effective evaluation criterion fitting into this research.

5.4.2.4 Confirmability

Confirmability is concerned with how the researcher can be shown to 'have acted in good faith, in other words, it should be apparent that he or she has not overtly allowed personal values or theoretical inclinations manifestly to sway the conduct of the research and findings derived from it" (Bryman, 2004:276). This is the question that has sparked much debate about how the relationship between the researcher and the researched is to be maintained (Lincoln and Guba, 1985). To avoid my personal values overtly influencing the conduct of the research during the data collection, I tried as much as possible to adopt openness, a willingness to listen and to 'give a voice' to participants. In interpreting the interview data I acted as a factist (Alasuutari, 1995) in exploring CSME managers' views and experiences honestly. However, due to the nature of my role as a Chinese person who used to work for both MNEs and SMEs as a manager in the USA, the UK and China, my 12 years of business and management experience made it impossible for me to be completely removed from this research. My interpretations of the data and re-presentation of CSME managers' accounts would not be completely confirmable to other researchers. In addition, my ontology and epistemological assumptions concern CSME managers' individual experience, consequently confirmability is not seen as an issue for this research.

So far, evaluations of this research have been explicitly reflected by adopting Lincoln and Guba's (1985) trustworthiness criteria. In detail, why credibility and transferability were deemed appropriate for this research and why dependability and confirmability did not very effectively fit into this research was discussed. In the next section I will move on to another evaluation criterion which is important to this project from a practical perspective.

212

5.4.3 Relevance

The last evaluation criterion relating to this qualitative research is **Relevance** as suggested by Hammersley (1992, 2002). In his works, Hammersley strongly argues that there is distinction between practical research and scientific research. Practical research aims to create knowledge of practice for practitioners. He suggests that practitioners (either people who are participants of this research or who are extremely interested in the research questions, and the implications of the findings) should be taken into account as one aspect of relevance. Hammersley (2002) continuously argues that researchers and practitioners might have different interests. As practitioners, they are most interested in how the research findings can help them to understand and address problems. The point Hammersley (2002) raised here is exactly what I focused on and pursued throughout this research.

Adopting from Hammersley (1992, 2002), I viewed practitioners' assessments of the findings as one important evaluation for this qualitative research. I believed that practitioners with practical knowledge and experiences can make very valuable judgments from a practical perspective. Primarily, the findings of this research have made valuable contributions to both CSME managers and Government policy makers in relation to the entry mode decision making. To test its relevance to practice, I conducted 5 mini interviews (of 20 minutes duration on average), which is called *post-research*. In August 2006, during a business trip in China, a government officer introduced me to 2 CSME managers who intend to expand their business in the UK. Taking this great opportunity, I discussed my research findings with them and gained very positive feedback. During this trip I also interviewed a provincial president of the SME Bureau who commented this research 'very valuable for CSME policy makers.' In addition to this, another 2 managers in England, who attended the first round interviews of this research, were invited to give their feedback on the findings of this research.

These 2 CSME managers highlighted this research positively from practitioners' points of view. Overall, the value of relevance to practitioners gave me greater confidence in this research.

In summary, all identified evaluation criteria for this research have been discussed and examined in a reflective manner. In essence, researchers should recognise what is crucial and what criteria should be used to judge the merit of the qualitative work. Although there is no single way to evaluate qualitative research findings, 2 key principles have to be applied. Primarily, reality of the research process has to be ensured. Moreover, sufficient and heuristic information has to be offered to readers and researchers for judging the quality of the research. Building upon the evaluations, some of the limitations of this research are highlighted in the next section to provide a platform for future research.

5.5 Limitations and Suggestions for Future Research

This study has tried to increase knowledge of SME managers' strategic market entry choices with focus on CSME managers from developing countries. It is noted that this research suffers from a number of limitations as every study does (Taylor-Powell and Renner, 2003). One of the obvious limitations is that the outcomes of this study are not generalisable. The findings of this research have enhanced SME managers' and international researchers' understanding of the phenomena of SME managers' strategic market entry choices. However, it is very specific context oriented. Readers may only make their own generalisation by considering certain circumstances.

Moreover, foreign investment by CSMEs in England is a relatively new phenomenon. No research has been conducted by sampling CSMEs thus far. To gain a more general insight at an early stage, the interpretations of this research were based on the sampled companies from both manufacturing and service sectors. This could be a primary limitation for this research because some international researchers such as Sharma and Johanson (1987) and Erramilli and Rao (1993), have suggested that research results generated from manufacturing firms may not be generalisable to service firms. Another limitation which the author recognised is that this research sets out to explain CSME managers' strategic market entry choices when entering the North of England markets. The findings of this research are derived only on the basis of English markets. This may affect the result of a firm's decision making with regard to location. Consequently it will limit managers' and international business scholars' understanding of Dunning's OIL mode (1980, 1985).

However, the above limitations in turn provide a platform and opportunity for future research.

- First of all, as discussed above, this research did not separate manufacturing and service sectors when sampling investigated CSMEs. In the future research, international researchers may consider investigating this issue in a given industry or sector to gain a comprehensive understanding of Asian SME managers' strategic market entry choices.

- Another research opportunity arising from this study is that the future research should extend this investigation into CSMEs entering other Western developed countries in different geographic areas to provide more precise descriptions of SME managers' entry mode choices, especially by separating the European and Latin American markets due to their cultural differences.

- In addition, according to the findings of this research, CSME managers' personal characteristics such as education experiences in Western developed countries played important roles in their strategic market entry choices when entering the UK. It is suggested that further research could be conducted to explore SME managers' strategic market entry choices across disciplines. For example, international researchers from human resource management areas could also stimulate possible theoretical extensions regarding SME managers' entry mode choices from an interdisciplinary perspective. Overall, given the limitations discussed earlier, more empirical studies on Asian SME managers' entry mode choices are needed.

In spite of some limitations, this study still provides important valuable insights to SMEs' internationalisation. It is among the first to capture strategic market entry mode choices in the context of Asian SMEs from Eastern developing countries entering Western developed countries. This study makes a large contribution by extending current mainstream FDI theory of international marketing management disciplines.

5.6 Chapter Summary

This chapter has summarised and tied the whole project together by reviewing how research aims and objectives have been achieved through summarising the research findings. In addition, research contributions to the understanding of CSME managers' entry mode choices are identified followed by suggested implications from a theoretical standpoint. Overall, traditional entry-mode investigations have tended to concentrate on MNEs from Western developed countries. This study represented an important step towards a better understanding of how Asian SME managers, especially CSME managers, make their strategic decisions in line with their entry mode choices. This qualitative research shows that SME managers' foreign market entry mode choices are more complicated than most previous research suggested. One challenge facing international researchers is that future research on this topic should be studied from an interdisciplinary perspective. Most importantly, this chapter has evaluated the whole research by engaging in methodological reflexivity to assess how trustworthiness of this research has been established.

In conclusion, it is believed that no individual study can be entirely conclusive on such a complex area as international business management. From both theoretical and practical perspectives, this study has extended the understanding of the impact of different factors on the firms' entry mode choices, with particular interest in CSME managers' strategic market entry decisions when entering Western developed countries. The comprehensive entry decision making framework developed in this research could assist CSME managers to prioritise certain identical factors instead of considering various potential factors. This could also help CSME managers to better focus their time and resources in deciding on an appropriate foreign entry mode. In the last chapter, more details of practical contributions and applications of this research will be offered.

CHAPTER SIX

CONTRIBUTIONS TO PRACTICE AND REFLECTIONS

6.1 Introduction

As an ending to this intellectual journey, 2 important issues to this research are explored in this chapter: Contributions to practice and research reflections. The chapter begins by disclosing what original contributions have been made to business and management practice by the study. In detail, it presents the practical contributions and implications to both CSME managers and policy makers of both home and host countries in the SME sector. Following this, I reflect on my intellectual journey and research process through my epistemic reflexivity and methodological reflexivity. Furthermore, my role as a researcher throughout this research is evaluated and judged.

6.2 Contributions and Implications to Practice

In the introduction to this thesis, I stated that one of the important objectives of this research is to make contributions to practice rather than only focusing on advancing theory. Theoretical contributions and implications have already been provided in Chapter Five. The empirical findings and original contributions of this research to business and management practice are discussed in this section from a practical perspective.

6.2.1 Formulating the Research Question from a Practical Level

Reflecting on how this research topic was initially formulated will help the audience to understand the contributions of this research to practice. The research problems of PhD research are often derived from existing theories. Most importantly, PhD students strive to generate theoretical understandings in certain areas by filling the gaps of existing theories and research (Rudestam and Newton, 1992). In comparison, this research topic was formulated based on my personal and professional experience of the purpose of contributing to business and management practice.

I have more than 12 years of international working experience, working for several US SMEs in Philadelphia, New Jersey and two British SMEs in England. These SMEs have been involved in international business with Chinese companies for many years. Particularly, I used to be a marketing assistant manager for a CSME located in the North of England. Through the business and social networks of CSMEs in England, I had the opportunity to understand CSME international activities. From my observations, managers in these CSMEs utilised different entry modes when initially entering the UK. Some CSME managers procured footholds by being successful in he North of England markets, but others did not. Building upon my working experiences and through talking with some CSME managers, the varieties of entry mode choices by CSME managers caught my attention and aroused my research motives. I believe that studying entry mode choices in the context of CSMEs entering Western developed markets could help CSME managers make their entry decisions more effectively and efficiently. As this research idea was generated from my professional experience, results of this research are more valuable from the practical standpoint. Reviewing the findings of this research, the outcomes of this study benefit practitioners in many ways at operational levels.

6.2.2 Contributions to Business and Management Practice

Building upon the data collected, the findings of this research offer comprehensive views of how CSME managers actually made their entry mode choices from a practical perspective. This study made a number of original contributions to business and management practice for SME managers from the private sector.

Entry decision is a very complex task. A large number of influencing factors have been hypothesised to explain the choice of entry mode in previous studies. For example, Root (1986) lists 27 factors in relation to large firms' entry mode choices. However in practice, it is not necessary or possible for SME managers to analyse all factors due to time and resource constraints. This research explored 5 sets of influencing factors that are closely linked to CSME managers' entry mode choices. Identifying these factors provides great insights to enable CSME managers to prioritise the different groups of factors when making their entry mode choices. Practically, it guides CSME managers to make their entry mode decisions effectively when faced with limited time and resources.

Unlike previous studies, instead of focusing upon the relationship between influencing factors and entry mode choices alone, this study explored CSME managers' entry mode choices systemically to provide them with more practical guidance. Building upon the findings of this research, a practice-based framework has been developed for practitioners (see figure 6.1). The framework presented in figure 6.1, working complementally with figures 5.1 and 5.2, can be used as a comprehensive practical tool to guide CSME managers assessing and making the optimal entry mode decision. Moreover, with the recognition of a combination of rational and cybernetic decision making strategies at different stages, this study offers CSME managers a valuable insight as to how to relocate their resources and devote their time on their entry mode decision making effectively and efficiently.

Figure 6.1 Factors and their impact on entry mode choices

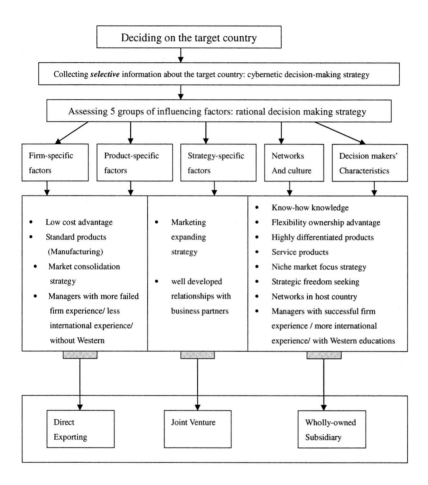

On an operational level, the framework developed in this study provides CSME managers an extensive understanding of entry mode choices and helps them address the totality of the multidimensional and complex entry mode decision. As one of the CSME managers comments in my post-research interviews: "It offers us guidance to considering our entry decision making process systemically. From your findings, we learned how other CSME managers made their entry decision.

Their experiences will benefit our future international entry decisions." More to the point, another participant in the post-research interview expressed that he would definitely consider applying the 'modified joint venture' entry mode to his future international entry considerations. These practitioners' voices have offered valuable evidence in order to judge the practical contributions of this research.

6.2.3 Contributions to Policy Makers

In addition to the contributions to SME management and business practices, this research also has made practical contributions to government foreign investment policy makers in the SME sector. The successes and issues raised by CSME managers regarding government involvement from both home and host countries in this study offer a guide of how to stimulate and support SMEs' internationalisation and help the government and authorities to identify what specific supports SME managers need from the government side.

From the home country's perspective, the findings of this research demonstrate that although the Chinese government has realised the importance of CSMEs' internationalisation, there still exists some restrictions and problems. This finding provides a guide to Chinese SME policy makers and helps them to realise that the Chinese government support of SMEs should not just remain superficial, more services and support at operational levels are required, such as specific government agents providing sufficient information in particular countries and offering more international business training for CSME managers etc.

From the host country's side, this study makes a practical contribution to SME policy makers in the UK. It provides insights of how to effectively attract and manage foreign SME investors for local government and regional development agents in the UK, specifically in the North of England. The outcomes of this study explore that more specific services and support should be tailored to consider the features of SMEs from developing countries. For example, most Asian SMEs normally lack advanced technology and management knowledge, and strategically, extra care has to be taken into account in developing SME policies by the government in the UK. To create a favourable investment environment for Asian SMEs, it is necessary to hire a bi-linguist to work for regional development agents in the host country.

6.2.4 Implications

The results of this research have several implications for SME practitioners, especially CSME managers. This study illustrates CSME managers' entry mode decision making depends not only on the firm's specific and external factors but also on the decision maker's personal characteristics. This implies that SME managers must recognise that the foreign investment decision process is very complex involving attitudes, opinions, experience and social relationships both in and outside the organisation. To choose the optimal entry mode, SME decision makers should consider how their personal strengths or bias affect their final entry mode choices.

Moreover, this study implies that no matter how wise SME managers are, it is impossible for them to obtain all the information they ideally require due to a ranges of constraints. Consequently, SME decision makers should combine different decision making strategies to better scrutinise the key issues underlying their entry mode choices at different stages. In addition, the findings of 4 entry modes CSME managers adopted in this study indicates that high control entry mode can be used in the case of SMEs from Eastern developing countries entering Western developed countries. It highlights that, in spite of limited resources, SME decision makers should not limit their entry mode choices by only focusing upon the exporting entry mode. To make optimal entry mode choices, SME managers need to consider how to use their capabilities and resources flexibly and innovatively.

Overall, from a practical point of view, this context specific research has made important contributions to SME practitioners (especially for CSME managers) and SME policy makers for both Chinese and British governments. This study provides an opportunity for SME managers and government policy makers, as well as international business researchers, to acquire an in-depth understanding of SMEs' internationalization.

6.3 Research Reflections

There is a growing recognition that qualitative research should be scrutinised through self-critical reflections. Revealing the relationship between the researcher and the object researched can help researchers to have a better understanding of the social context in which the research occurred and people engaged (Johnson and Duberley, 2000, May, 2002). In Chapter Five, I began to reflect upon the research process involved in this research to evaluate its trustworthiness. In this section, by adopting a reflexivity approach (Johnson and Duberley, 2000, 2003), I will reveal how my social location, beliefs, values and feelings affected this research and how other participants involved in this project impacted upon the research outcomes of this study.

6.3.1 Epistemic Reflexivity

To get qualitative researchers involved in critical self-scrutiny is a major challenge but the most effective way to understand good qualitative research (Manson, 2002). Epistemic reflexivity refers to the systematic attempts to relate research outcomes to knowledge. It explores the ways in which the researcher's involvement influences a particular study, such as the researcher's own social and historical biography, experiences and paradigms (Johnson and Duberley, 2000, Nightingale and Cromby, 1999). Through epistemic reflexivity, the researcher aims to make "the analysis of analysis" (Johnson and Duberley, 2000) and the "interpretation of interpretations" (Alvesson and Skoldberg, 2000). To provide more transparent evidence to explore the relationship between myself as a researcher and the object researched in this study, I try to undertake self-reflexivity in a critical manner. However, revealing the self is not an easy task as it involves exposing the subjective and individual experience behind the work to respondents and research audiences.

Reflecting on the intellectual journey of this research, my social constructionism paradigm employed throughout has been guiding me on constituting the knowledge for this study. In earlier sections, I explored how my personal beliefs and initial assumptions shaped this research topic and structured the research activities by reflecting on 'who I am' and 'where I am from.' On acknowledging the proposition of constructionism philosophy, I claim that meaning (or truth) does not exist without a mind. All meaningful reality is socially constructed (Crotty, 1998). Accordingly, I strongly believe that social phenomena and their meanings are *continually* being accomplished by social actors. In other words, knowledge should be justified accompanying the changes of social contexts. As meaningful realities are socially constructed, people are inevitably viewing phenomena through lenses bestowed upon them by their own culture (Crotty, 1998).

In retrospect, my initial assumption relating to the research problem is that CSME decision makers presumably act differently compared with managers from other countries in their entry mode choices, particularly those who are from Western countries. I agree with Crotty (1998) that culture is liberating, but culture is also limiting. It sets us free but at the same time it sets boundaries. The theories and concepts created on the basis of Western cultures must be moderated. Reflecting upon the outcomes of this research and my personal experience, this research firmly consolidates my social constructionism paradigm. Consequently, the cross-culture comparisons of this study make me aware that the same phenomena may have different interpretations at different times and in different places (different contexts). Critical perspectives should be emphasised in constituting knowledge in cross-culture research.

Moreover, I have been struggling with how I identify the role my multi-culture background played and how I judge its impact on this research. As a native Chinese, I spent 26 years of my life studying and working in China and it is apparent that some Chinese cultures have already firmly embedded in my mind. However, I also lived and worked in the Western countries for many years (in America for 7 years and in the UK for more than 6 years). Western cultures also inevitably have some impact on my thinking and behaviour. At the beginning of the research, my mixed Chinese-Western culture background made me aware of how this situation was going to impact upon my research; is it to be positive or negative? Reflecting upon the interviews, after interviewees giving their answer for a certain question, participant C said to me "you know what I mean by this?" Differently, Participant G went as far as "you've been living abroad for too many years. You may not completely understand the situation." Obviously, through respondents' lenses, I have been labelled and treated differently by participants. For manager C, I was labelled as a 'pure' Chinese who understands what they understood. However, for participant G, I was treated only *partially* as Chinese because they believe that my thoughts inside are somehow different from them. From my observations, there are two types of respondents that acted differently during the interviews. Participants with the same feelings as manager C were more conscious of my position than with other 'powerful' people and tried to avoid saying anything negative even though I promised that their responses would be strictly confidential (Eckhardt, 2004). Differently, interviewees who agreed with manager G seemed more open as they only treated me as a Chinese, mostly because of my appearance, not my mind and thoughts.

Another lesson I learned from this research is that an interviewer's social position is important for making Chinese respondents open up during interviews. During the interview, one respondent asked me very sensitive questions "Do you still have a lot of connections with other Chinese companies in this region?" As I mentioned earlier, I used to work as a marketing assistant manager for a CSME in the North of England, this past social role of mine became intimidating in some way for this respondent. Reflecting upon this intellective journey, from my observations and personal experience, my mixed culture background and past social position played a positive role in this study, as I have a better understanding of these participants due to my specific multi-cultural background and different social roles.

Another great challenge of this research for me was how to ensure that 'my voice' did not dominate over 'respondents' voices' in data analysis and writing the thesis. Although most of the interviewed CSME managers treated me as 'a Chinese academic researcher' working at a university in the UK, my multi-culture background and past working experiences made me very uncomfortable when I first started to interpret the interview data. In producing the data analysis, I had always been sensitive to the questions: Whose interpretation? Whose truths? It is apparent that my mixed cultural backgrounds and international working experiences made it impossible to divorce myself from the process of this research. In retrospect, although I have endeavoured to ensure that respondents' voices are heard; their truths were presented, my interpretation of their interpretations were realistically conducted, it is almost certain that I interpreted the findings somehow through the lens of my own cultural values and beliefs. It is therefore the case that I am still not comfortable with my successes at this point. In addition to this, I also struggled with how I produced the final written report. My main concern at this stage is how I can honour my commitments about confidentiality and privacy for this research.

So far, I have discussed my engagements in epistemic reflexivity (Johnson and Duberley, 2003). The reflections on my own social role and how it affected the form and results of this research show that the self as a researcher can never truly be removed from the research. The discussions above provide research audiences with an honest account of how I dealt with my experiences and beliefs while confronting difficult situations throughout this study.

6.3.2 Reflections on Methodology

In Chapter Two, I described how data was collected and analysed during the research process. This section will make further reflections on the research methodology by re-examining the design of the research methodology and methods. In addition to that, how my 'research behaviours' were monitored throughout this research is to be discussed.

In reviewing previous studies, as most of them were conducted by surveys, researchers often limited influencing factors which were pre-hypothesised from a positivism perspective. However by doing surveys participants had little opportunity to reflect on influencing factors comprehensively (factors have been already predefined by researchers) involved in their entry mode choices by completing the questionnaires. Considering the SME cases, it is wondered whether all SME managers understood the questions when completing the questionnaires. As mentioned in the methodology chapter, this research took great consideration of interviewees' understanding of theoretical concepts and specific terminologies related to foreign market entry mode choice. The reasoning behind this was that respondents' understanding of the research questions directly influences the outcomes of this research as they are the 'meaning makers.'

It is widely accepted that most managers from SMEs lack of theoretical knowledge compared with professional managers of large organisations. The question of "are my questions meaningful to interviewees?" has concerned me throughout the whole research journey. Although conducting the pilot study increased my confidence and ability to produce good quality research, the *interaction of asking questions and getting meaningful answers* still was a challenge for me during the research process. To ensure the spokespersons' voices were heard accurately, I tried to pass all interview transcripts back to the participants, but this was not always feasible as some participants informed that they were too busy to read the long transcripts. Similarly, I tried to invite these absent participants to discuss the outcomes of this research at my post-research stage.

Reflecting upon the research process, another important lesson I learned was that building the reflexive process for each of the interviews was essential for good quality research as doing this enables the researcher to justify semi-structured interview questions effectively. This is particularly important for a new researcher. After each interview, I produced a research summary report including general interview information: Who, where, when, interview duration etc, and also reflected both the researcher's (me) and respondents' *behaviours* during the interview. First, I checked the notes I took during the interview, and reflected on participants' attitudes and reactions. In this reflection process, I paid attention to their interest and involvement in the interview, and tried to reflect whether there were particular questions I asked that offended or embarrassed the interviewee. If so, I would consider ethical issues and adjust my questions for the next interview. I undertook critical self-scrutiny and reflected on my actions and role in the research process after each interview. As a part of the reflexive process, I reflected on the interview by asking myself the questions "Have I collected the data I want? Did I use the right strategies or approaches for my data collection? Did anything unexpected happen during the interview?" In reflecting upon and answering these questions, I listed all the important points on which I wanted to improve during the next interview. As a new researcher, I found this interview reflexive process extremely useful for producing good interviews.

In brief, building upon the epistemic reflexivity and methodology reflexivity, I conclude that offering a more transparent account of what has happened in the research process contributes more credit to the trustworthiness of the research findings. Most importantly, in my experience, reflexivity should not be carried out only after the research is completed, reflections during the research process are even more valuable. Alternatively, the post-research reflexivity offers a different way of understanding researchers' and participants' experiences, it cannot change what happened. The latter one enables researchers to conduct their research in more effective ways, and improve the quality of the research. The reflexivity I carried out after each interview enabled me to dramatically improve subsequent interviews. By providing the above reflections on this research, it is evident that I have made every effort to produce research of the highest quality throughout this social research process.

6.5 Chapter Summary

This chapter has outlined the practical contributions of this research to both practitioners and policy makers. In particular, it provides great insight for CSME managers in their foreign market entry mode choices under the context of entering Western developed countries. Moreover, this concluding chapter has also highlighted my epistemic reflexivity and methodology reflexivity. In doing this, I disclosed myself as a qualitative researcher in a critical manner. It offered me the opportunity to reflect upon my research behaviour during the research process.

Going through this learning journey has made me realise that leaning is endless. As a researcher, my research travel experience taught me that qualitative research is confusing sometimes, just as life is confusing. In retrospective, I admit that the journey was hard and the whole process was painful, but it provided a great opportunity for me to listen to business practitioners' experiences. Having the chance to talk to practitioners enabled me to understand my research area from the practical perspective. It is valuable and worthwhile. To end this research story, I want to say that pleasure is sweeter after pain. Without doubt, this research journey has opened a whole new world for me as a social researcher. This learning journey has taught me that it is important to become a life-long learner. My professional learning journey should never end for the rest of my life. I do treasure the experience I gained from this research journey.

REFERENCES

Acs, Z. and Audretsch, D. (1990) *Innovation and Small Firms.* Cambridge: MIT Press.

Agarwal, S. and Ramaswami, S. R. (1992) 'Choice of foreign market entry mode: impact of ownership, location and internalisation factors', *Journal of International Business Studies*, 23(1), pp. 1-27.

Agarwal, S. (1994) 'Social-Cultural Distance and the Choice of Joint Ventures: A Contingency Perspective', *Journal of International Marketing*, 2(2), pp. 63-80.

Aharoni, Y. (1966) 'The Foreign Investment Decision Process' in Buckley, P. and Ghauri, P. N. (ed.) *The Internationalization of the Firm: A reader.* 2nd edn. London: International Thomson Business Press.

Alasuutari, P. (1995) *Researching Culture: Qualitative Method and Cultural Studies.* London: Sage.

Ali, A. J. and Camp, R. C. (1993) 'The Relevance of Firm Size and International Business Experience to Market Entry Strategies', *Journal of Global Marketing*, 6(4), pp. 91-111.

Almor, T. (2001) 'Towards a Contingency View of Market Entry Strategies: Contextual and Strategic Factors', *Journal of Euro-marketing*, 10(1), pp.5-25.

Alon, I. (2004) 'International Market Selection for a Small Enterprise: A Case Study in International Entrepreneurship', *SAM Advanced Management Journal*, Winter, pp. 25-32.

Alvesson, M. and SKoldberg, K. (2000) *Reflexive Methodology: New Vistas for Qualitative Research.* London: Sage.

Ambler, T. and Wang, X. (2003) 'Measures of marketing Success: A comparison Between China and the United Kingdom', *Asia Pacific Journal of Management*, 20(2), pp. 267-282.

Anderson, A. R. *et al.* (2003) 'The Increasing Role of Small Business in the Chinese Economy', *Journal of Small Business Management*, 41(3), pp. 310-316.

Anderson, V., Boocock, G. and Graham, S. (2001) 'An Investigation into the Learning Needs of Managers in Internationalising Small and Medium-Sized Enterprises', *Journal of Small Business and Enterprise Development*, 8(3), pp. 215-232.

Anderson, E. and Gatignon, H. (1986) 'Modes of foreign entry: A transaction cost analysis and proposition', *Journal of international Business Studies*, 17(3): pp.1-26.

Anderson, E. and Weitz, B. A. (1986) 'Make-or-Buy Decision: Vertical Integration and Marketing Productivity'. *Sloan Management Review*, 27, pp. 3-19.

Anderson, O. (1997) 'Interntionalisation and Market Entry Mode: A review of Theories and Conceptual Frameworks', *Management International Business Studies,* 17(2), pp.1-26.

Anderson, K. (1998) 'Social Constructionism and Belief Causation'. Available at: http://www.stanford.edu (Accessed: 4 December, 2005).

Anderson, T. and Svensson, R. (1994) 'Entry Modes for Direct Investment Determined by the Composition of Firm Specific Skills', *Scandinavian Journal of Economics,* 96(40), pp. 551-560.

Andersen, P. H. and Skaates, M. A. (2004) 'Ensuring Validity in Qualitative International Business Research' in Marschan-Piekkari, R. and Welch, C. (ed.) *Handbook of Qualitative Research Methods for International Business.* Cheltenham: Edward Elgar.

Annual Report of China Foreign Trade Committee, 2000.

Antti, H., Graham, H. and Rik, D. (1998) *The Internationalization of SMEs: The Interstratos Project.* London: Routledge.

Athanassiou, N. and Night, D. (2000) 'Internationalization, Tacit Knowledge and the Top Management Teams of MNCs', *Journal of International Business Studies,* 31(3), pp.471-487.

Australian Department of Foreign Affairs (DFAT, 1995).

Axelsson, B. and Johanson, J. (1992) 'Foreign Market Entry' in Axelsson, B. and Easton, G. (ed.) *In Industrial Networks: A New View of Reality.* London: Routledge.

Baird, I. S., Lyles, M. A. and Orris, J. B. (1994) 'The Choice of International Strategies by Small Businesses'. *Journal of Small Business Management.* January, pp. 48-59.

Baran, R., Pan, Y. and Kaynak, E. (1996) 'Research on International Joint Ventures in East Asia: A Critical Review and Future Directions', *Journal of Euro marketing,* 4(3-4), pp. 7-21.

Beamer, L. (1998) 'Bridging Business Cultures', *The China Business Review,* May-June, pp.54-58.

Bedward, D. (1999) *Quantitative Methods: a business perspective.* Butterworth Heinemann.

Bell, J. (1995) 'The Internationalization of Small Computer Software Firms', *European Journal of Marketing,* 29(8), pp.60-75.

Bell, J. (1999) *Doing Your Research Project.* 3rd edn. Buckingham: Open University Press.

Bell, J., Crick, D. and Young, S. (2004), 'Small Firm Internationalization and Business Strategy: An Exploratory Study of Knowledge Intensive and Traditional Manufacturing Firms in the UK', *International Small Business Journal,* 22(1), pp.23-54.

233

Benito, G. R. G. and Welch, L. S. (1994) 'Foreign Market Servicing: Beyond Choice of Entry Mode', *Journal of International Marketing*, 2(2), pp. 7-27.

Bennett, R. (1999) *International Business*. 2nd edn. Harlow: prentice Hall.

Black, J. A. and Champion, D. J. (1976) *Methods and Issues in Social Research*. New York: John Wiley & Sons, Inc.

Bilkey, W. J. and Tesar, G. (1977) 'The Export Behaviour of Smaller Sizes Wisconsin Manufacturing Firms', *Journal of International Business Studies*, 8, pp. 33-46.

Birkinshaw, J. and Hood, N. (1998) 'Multinational Subsidiary Evolution: Capability and Character Change in Foreign-Owned Subsidiary', *Academy of Management Review*, 23(4), pp. 773-795.

Bonaccorsi, A. (1992) 'On the Relationship between Firm Size and Export Intensity', *Journal of International Business Studies*, 23(4), pp. 605-636.

Bradley, F. (2000) 'Does the Firms Technology and Marketing Profile Affect Foreign Market Entry?' *Journal of International Marketing*, 8(4), pp.12-36.

Brouthers, K. D. (2002) 'Institutional, Cultural and Transaction Cost Influences on Entry Mode Choice and Performance', *Journal of International Business Studies*, 33(2), pp. 203—221.

Brouthers, K. D. and Brouthers, L. E. (2001) 'Explaining the National Culture Distance Paradox', *Journal of International Business Studies*, 32(1), pp. 177—189.

Brouthers, L. E., Brouthers, K. D. and Werner, S. (1999) 'Is Dunning's Eclectic Framework Descriptive or Normative?' *Journal of International Business Studies*, 30(4), pp. 831-844.

Brouthers, L. E., Brouthers, K. D. and Werner, S. (2000) 'Perceived Environmental Uncertainty, Entry Mode Choice and Satisfaction with EC-MNC Performance', *British Journal of Management*, 11(3), pp.183-195.

Brouthers, K. D., Brouthers, L. E. and Werner, S. (1999) 'Dunning's Eclectic Theory and the Smaller Firm: The Impact of Ownership and Locational Advantages on the Choice of Entry-modes in the Computer Software Industry', *Journal of International Business Research*, 5(4), pp. 377-396.

Boter, H. and Holmquist, C. (1994) *Internationalization of Small and Medium-Sized Industries in Manufacturing*. Sweden: Umea Business School.

Brockhaus, R. H. (1980) 'Risk Taking Propensity of Entrepreneurs', *Academic of Management Journal*, 23(3), pp.509-520.

Brown, J. R., Dev, C. S. and Zhou, Z. (2003) 'Broadening the Foreign Market Entry Mode Decision: Separating Ownership and Control', *Journal of International Business Studies*, 34(5), pp.473-488.

Brush, C. (1995), *International Entrepreneurship: The Effect of Firm Age on Motives for Internationalization.* New York: Garland Publishing.

Bryman, A. (2001) *Social Research Methods.* Oxford University Press

Bryman, A. (2004) *Social Research Methods.* 2nd edn. Oxford University Press

Bryman, A. and Bell, E. (2003) *Business Research Methods.* Oxford: Oxford University Press.

Buckley, P. J. (1998) 'Models of Multinational Enterprise', *Journal of International Business Studies,* 29(1), pp. 21-44.

Buckley, P. J. and Casson. M. (1998) 'Analysing foreign market entry strategies: extending the internalisation approach', *Journal of International Business Studies,* 29(3), pp. 539-561.

Buckley, P. J. and Casson. M. (1976) *The Future of Multinational Enterprise.* London: McMillan.

Buckley, P. J. and Ghauri, P. N. (1999) *The Internationalization of the Firm: A Reader* (2nd ed.). London: International Thomson Business Press.

Burdis, C. and Peck, F. (1999) 'East Asian Investment and Reinvestment in the 1990s': Implications for Regional Development' in Garrahan, P. and Richie, J. (ed.) *East Asian Investment in Britain: Studies in Asian Pacific Business.* London: Frank Cass.

Burgel, O. and Murray, G. C. (2000) 'The International Market Entry Choices of Start-Up Companies in High-Technology Industries', *Journal of International Marketing,* 6(2), pp. 33-62.
Burns, P. and Dewhurst, J. (1986) *Small Business in Europe.* London: Macmillan.

Burrell, G., and Morgan, G. (1979). *Sociological Paradigms and Organizational Analysis,* New Hampshire: Heinemann.

Burton, F. N. and Schlegelmilch, B. B. (1987) 'Profit Analysis of Non-Exporters versus Exporters Grouped by Export Involvement', *Management International Review,* 27(1), pp. 38-49.

Calof, J. L. and Beamish, P. W. (1995) 'Adopting to Foreign Market: Explaining Internationalization', *International Business Review,* 4(2), pp. 115-131.

Cannon, M. (1993) 'Towards a Composite Theory of Foreign Market Entry Mode Choice: the Role of Marketing Strategy Variables', *Journal of Strategic Marketing,* 1, pp. 41-54.

Capron, L. and Hulland, J. (1999) 'Redeployment of Brands, Sales Forces and General Market Management Expense Following Horizontal Acquisitions: A Resource-Based View', *Journal of marketing,* 63(2), pp. 41-54.

Carpenter, M. and Fredrickson, J. W. (2001) 'Top Management Teams, Global Strategic Posture, and the Moderating Role of Uncertainty', *Academic of Management Journal,* 44, pp. 477-492.

Carr, D. (1986) *Narrative Methods for Organizational & Communication Research.* Australia: Sage.

Carrier, C. (1994) 'Intrapreneurship in Large Firms and SMEs: A Comparative Study'. *International Small Business Journal,* 12(3), pp. 54-61.

Carstairs, R. T. and Welch, L. S. (1982) 'Licensing and the Internationalization of Smaller Companies: Some Australian Evidence', *Management International Review,* 22(3), pp. 33-44.

Carter, S. and Jones-Evans, D. (2006) *Enterprise and Small Business: Principles, Practice and Policy.* 2nd edn. Harlow: Prentice Hall.

Cateora, P. R., Graham, J. L. and Ghauri, P. N. (2000) *International Marketing.* London: McGraw-Hill.

Caves, R. E. and Mehra, S. K (1986) 'Entry of Foreign Multinationals into US Manufacturing Industries' in Porter, M. E. (ed.) *Competition in Global Industries.* Boston: HBS Press.

Cavusgil, S. T. (1984) 'Differences among Exporting Firms based on Their Degree of Internationalization', *Journal of Business Research,* 12, pp.195-208.

Cavusgil, S. T. and Nevin, J. R. (1984) 'Internal Determinants of Export Marketing Behaviour: An Empirical Investigation', *Journal of Business Research,* 18, pp. 104-119.

Chalmers, A. F. (1999) *What is This Thing Called Science* (3rd edn), Open University Press.

Chan, K, W. and Hwang, P. (1992) 'Global Strategy and Multinationals' Entry Mode Choice', *Journal of International Business Studies,* 23(1), pp. 29-53.

Chang, S. and Rosenzweig, P. M. (1998) 'Industry and Regional Patterns in Sequential Foreign Market Entry', *Journal of Management Studies,* 35(6), pp.797-822.

Chen, M. (1994) 'Guanxi and the Chinese Art of Network Building', *New Asia Review,* Summer, pp. 40-43.

Chen, H. (1999) 'International Performance of Multinationals: A Hybrid Model', *Journal of World Business,* 34(2), pp. 157-170.

Chen, T. (2006) 'Liability of Foreignness and Entry Mode Choice: Taiwanese Firms in Europe', *Journal of Business Research,* 59, pp.288-294.

Chetty, S. K. and Holm, D. B. (2000) 'Internationalisation of Small to Medium-Sized Manufacturing firms: A Network Approach', *International Business Review,* 9, pp.77-93.

Chetty, S. (1999) 'Dimensions of Internationalisation of Manufacturing Firms in the Apparel Industry', *European Journal of Marketing,* 33(1/2), pp. 121-142.

Child, J., Faulkner, D. and Pitkethly, R. (2000) 'Foreign Direct Investment in the UK 1985—1994: The Impact on Domestic Management Practice', *Journal of Management Studies,* 37(1), pp. 141-164.

Child. J. and Lu, Y. (1996) *Management Issues in China: Volume II: International Enterprises.* London: Routledge.

Child, J. and Tse, D. K. (2001) 'China's transition and its implications for international business', *Journal of International Business Studies,* 32(1), pp. 5-21.

Child, J. and Rodrigues, S. B. (2005) 'The Internationalization of Chinese Firms: A Case for Theoretical Extension?' *Management and Organization Review,* 1(3), pp.381-410.

China Foreign Economic Trade White Book (2002).

China National Foreign Trade Yearbook (1998/1999).

Choo, S. and Mazzarol, T. (2001) 'An Impact on Performance of Foreign Market Entry Choice by Small and Medium-Sized Enterprises', *Journal of Enterprising Culture,* 9(3), pp. 291-312.

Chung, H. F. L. and Enderwick, P. (2001) 'An Investigation of Market Entry Strategy Selection: Exporting vs Foreign Direct Investment', *Asia Pacific Journal of Management,* 18 (4), pp.443-460.

Clyne, M. (1987) 'Discourse Structures and Discourse Expectations: Implications for Anglo-German Academic Communication in English' in Smith, L. E. (ed.) *Discourse Across Cultures.* Hemel Hempstead: Prentice-Hall.

Conner, K. R. (1991) 'A Historical Comparison of Resource-Based Theory and Five Schools of Thought within Industrial Organization Economics: Do you have a new Theory of the Firm?' *Journal of Management,* 17, pp. 121-154.

Conte-Helm, M. (1999) 'The Road from Nissan to Samsung: A historical Overview of East Asian Investment in a UK Region' in Garrahan, P. and Richie, J. (ed.) *East Asian Investment in Britain: Studies in Asian Pacific Business* .London: Frank Cass.

Cooper, D. R. and Schindler, D. A. (2001) *Business Research Methods.* 7th edn. London: MvGraw-Hill.

Coviello, N. E. and Martin, K. A. (1997) 'Internationalization of Service SMEs; An Integrated Perspective from the Engineering Consulting Sector', *Journal of International Marketing,* 7(4), pp. 42-66.

Coviello, N. E. and Munro, H. (1997) 'Network Relationship and the Internationalization Process of Small Software Firms', *International Business Review,* 6(6), pp. 361-386.

Coviello, N. E. and Munro, H. (1995) 'Growing the Entrepreneurial Firm: Network for International Market Development', *European Journal of Marketing,* 29(7), pp. 49-61.

Coviello, N. E. and McAauley, A. (1999) 'Internationalization and the Smaller Firm: A Review of Contemporary Empirical Research', *Management International Review,* 39(3), pp.223-234.

Crabtree, B. F. and Miller, W. L. (1999) *Doing Qualitative Research.* 2nd edn. Thousand Oaks: Sage.

Creswell, J. W. (1994) *Research Design: Qualitative and Quantitative Approaches.* London: Sage Publications.
Crotty, M. (1998) *The Foundations of Social Research: Meaning and Perspective in the Research process,* London: Sage.

Daniels, J. D. and Cannice, M. V. (2004) 'Interview Studies in International Business Research' in Marschan-Piekkari, R. and Welch, C. (ed.) *Handbook of Qualitative Research methods for International Business.* Cheltenham: Edward Elgar.

Davidson, W. H. (1982) *Global Strategic Management.* New York: John Wiley and Sons.

Davis, P. S. (2000) 'Model of International Entry: An Isomorphism Perspective', *Journal of International Business Studies,* 31(2), pp. 239-258.

Davis, W. (1999) 'Foreign Manufacturing Firms in the UK: Effects on Employment, Output and Supplier Linkages', *European Business Review,* 99(6), p. 393-398.

Dawson, L. M. (1985) 'Marketing to Less Developed Countries', *Journal of Small Business Management,* 23(4), pp.13-19.

Decker, R. and Zhao, X. (2004) 'SME Choice of Foreign Market Entry Mode: A Normative Approach', *International Journal of Business Economics,* 3(3), pp.181-200.

Delios, A. and Ensign, P. (2000) 'A Subnational Analysis of Japanese Direct Investment in Canada', *Canadian Journal of Administrative Sciences,* 17(1), pp. 38-51.

Delios, A. and Makino, S. (2003) 'Timing of Entry and the Foreign Subsidiary Performance of Japanese Firms', *Journal of International Marketing,* 11(3), pp. 83-105.

Delmar, F. (1996) *Entrepreneurial Behavior and Business Performance.* Stockholm: Stockholm School of Economics.

Denzi, N. K. and Lincoln, Y. S. (2003) *Colleting and Interpreting Qualitative Materials.* 2nd edn. Thousand Oaks: Sage.

Denekamp, J. G. (1995) 'Intangible Assets, Internationalization and Foreign Direct Investment in Manufacturing', *Journal of International Business Studies,* 26(3), pp.493-504.

238

Dey, I. (1993) *Qualitative Data Analysis,* London: Routledge.

Doherty, A. M. (2000) 'Factors influencing International retailers' Market Entry Mode Strategy', *Journal of Marketing Management,* 16(1-3), pp. 223-245.

Doole, I. and Lowe, R. (2001) *International Marketing Strategy: Analysis, Development and Implementation.* 3rd edn. Australia: Thomson.

Donckels, R. and Aerts, R. (1998) 'Internationalization and Ownership: Family versus Non-Family Enterprises' in Haahti, A., Hall, G. and Donckels, R. (ed.) *The Internationalization of SMEs.* London: Routledge.

Dunning, J. H. (1980) 'Toward an Eclectic Theory of International production: some empirical tests', *Journal of International Business Studies,* 11(Spring/Summer), pp.9-31.

Dunning, J. H. (1981) *International Production and the Multinational Enterprise.* London: Allen & Unwin.

Dunning, J. H. (1985) 'US and Japanese Manufacturing Affiliates in the UK: Some Similarities and Contrast', *Journal of International Business Studies,* 90 (October).

Dunning, J. H. (1988) 'The Eclectic Paradigm of International Production: A Restatement and Some Possible Extensions', *Journal of International Business Studies,* 19(1), pp. 1-31.

Dunning, J. H. (1989) 'Japanese Participation in British Industry (Book Review)'. *Journal of International Business Studies,* 20(3), pp. 572-575.

Dunning, J. H. (1995) 'Location and the MNE: A Neglected Factor?' *Journal of Business Studies,* 29(1), pp. 45-65.

Dunning, J. H. (1997) *Alliance Capitalism and Global Capitalism.* London: Routledge.

Dunning, J. H. (1998) 'Location and the Multinational Enterprise: A Neglected Factor', *Journal of International Business Studies,* 29(1), pp.45-66.

Dunning, J. H. (2000) 'The eclectic Paradigm as an Envelope for Economic and Business Activity', *International Business Review,* 9(1), pp1029.

Dunning, J. H. (2001) 'The Key Literature on IB Activities: 1960-2000' in Rugman, A. C. and Brewer, T. L. (ed.) *Oxford Handbook of International Business.* Oxford: Oxford University Press.

Dunning, J. H. (2002) 'A Professional Autobiography Fifty Years Researching and Teaching International Business', *Journal of International Business Studies,* 33(4), pp.817--835.

Dunning, J. H. & Bansal, S. (1997) 'The Cultural Sensitivity of the Eclectic Paradigm'. *Multinational Business Review.* 5(1), pp.1-16.

Dunning, J. H. and Pearce, R. D. (1985) *The World Largest Industrial Enterprises.* Farnborough: Gower.

Duran, W. (1953) *The Pleasures of Philosophy.* New York: Simon and Schuster.

Easterby-Smith, M., Thorpe, R. and Lowe, A. (2002) *Management Research: An Introduction.* 2nd edn. London: Sage Publications.

Easterby-Smith, M., and Malina, D. (1999) 'Cross-Culture Collaborative Research: Toward Reflexivity', *Academy of Management Journal,* 42(1), pp.76-86.

EcKhardt, G. M. (2004) 'The Role of Culture in Conducting Trustworthy and Credible Qualitative Business Research in China' in Piekkari-Marschan, R. and Welch, C. (ed.) *Handbook of Qualitative Research Methods for International Business.* Cheltenham: Edward Elgar.

Edwards, R. W. and Buckley, P. J. (1998) 'Choice of Location and Mode: The Case of Australian Investors in the UK', *International Business Review,* 7(5), pp. 503-520.

Ekeledo, I. and Sivakumar, K. (1998) 'Foreign Market Entry Mode Choice of Service Firms: A Contingency Perspective', *Journal of the Academy of Marketing Science,* 26(4), pp.274-292.

Ekeledo, I. and Sivakumar, K. (2003) 'International Market Entry Mode Strategies of Manufacturing Firms and Service Firms: A Resource-Based Perspective', *International Marketing Review,* 21(1), pp. 68-101.

Emerson, R. M. (1981) 'Social Exchange Theory' in Roseberg, M. and Turner, R. (ed.) *Social Psychology: Sociological Perspectives.* New York: Basic Books.

Erdener, C. and Shapiro, D. M. (2005) 'The Internationalization of Chinese Family Enterprises and Dunning's Eclectic MNE Paradigm', *Management and Organization Review,* 1(3), pp. 411-436.

Erramilli, M. K., Agarwal, S. and Dev, C. S. (2002) 'The Choice Between Non-Equity Entry Modes: An Organisational Capability Perspective', *Journal of International Business Studies,* 33(2), pp. 223—242.

Erramilli, M. K. and Rao, C. P. (1990) 'Choice of Foreign Market Entry Modes by Service Firms: Role of Market Knowledge'. *MIR: Management International Review,* 30(2), pp.135-150.

Erramilli, M. K. and Rao, C. P. (1993) 'Service Firms' International Entry-Mode Choice: A Modified Transaction-Cost Analysis Approach', *Journal of Marketing,* 57(July), pp. 19-38

Erramilli, M. K. and D'Souza, D. E. (1993) 'Venturing into Foreign Markets: The Case of the Small Service Firm', *Entrepreneurship: Theory and Practice,* 17(4), pp.29-41.

Erramilli, M. K. (1991) 'The Experience Factor in Foreign Market Entry Behavior of Service Firms', *Journal of International Business Studies*, 22(3), pp.479-501.

Erramilli, M. K. (1990) 'Entry Mode Choice in Service Industries', *International Marketing Review*, 7(5/6), pp. 50-62.

Etemad, H. (2004) *International Entrepreneurship in Small and Medium Size Enterprises: Orientation, Environment and Strategy.* Cheltenham, UK: Edward Elgar.

European Fifth Annual Report for SMEs (1997).

Evan, W. M. (1993) *Organization Theory: Research and Design.* New York: McMillan.

Evans, J. (2002) 'International Determinants of Foreign Market Entry Strategy'. Manchester Metropolitan University Business School.

Fagenson, E. A. (1993) 'Personal Value Systems of Men and Women Entrepreneurs versus Managers', *Journal of Business Venture,* 8, pp. 409-430.

Fisher, T. F. and Ranasinghe, M. (2000) 'Culture and foreign companies' choice of entry mode: the case of the Singapore building and construction industry', *Construction* Management and Economics, 19, pp.343-353.

Flick, U. (2002) An Introduction to Qualitative Research. London: SAGE Publications.

Fontana, A. and Frey, J. (2003) 'The Interview: From Structured Questions to Negotiated Text' in Denzin, N. K. and Lincoln, Y. (ed.) Collecting and Interpreting Qualitative Materials. 2nd edn. Thousand Oaks: Sage.

Fraser, W. and Stonehouse, G. (2000) 'The Impact of Globalization on the Role of Small-and-Medium-Sized Enterprises in Industry Supply Chains'.

Fujita, M. (1998) The Transactional Activities of Small and Medium-Sized Enterprises. Boston: Kluwer Academic Publishers.

Gaba, V. and Pan, Y. (2002) 'Timing of Entry in International Market: An Empirical Study of U.S Fortune 500 Firms in China', Journal of International Business Studies, 33(1), pp. 39-55.

Gannon, M. (1993) 'Towards a Composite Theory of Foreign Market Entry Mode Choice: The Role of Marketing Strategy Variables', Journal of Strategic Marketing, 1(1), pp.41-54.

Garrahan, P. and Ritchie, J. (1999) East Asian Investment in Britain: Studies in Asian Pacific Business .London: Frank Cass.

Gatignon, H. and Anderson, E. (1988) 'The Multinational Corporation's Degree of Control over Foreign Subsidiaries: An Empirical Test of a Transaction Cost Explanation', Journal of Law, Economics and Organisation, 4(fall), pp.305-336.

Geertz, C. (1973) Thick Description: Toward an Interpretive Theory of Culture. New York" Basic Books.

Gelinas, R. and Bigras, Y. (2004) 'The Characteristics and Features of SMEs', Journal of Small Business, 42(3), pp.263-278.

Gemes-Casseres, B. (1990) 'Firm Ownership Preferences and Host Government Restrictions: An Integrated approach', Journal of International Business Studies, 85(3), pp.489-514.

Gergen, K. L. (1985) 'The Social Constructionist Movement in Modern Psychology', American Psychology, 40, pp.266-275.

Gergen, K. L. and Gergen, M. (2003) 'The Social Construction of the Real and The Good: Introduction' in Gergen, K, J. and Gergen, M. (ed.) Social Construction: A Reader. London: Sage.

Gerhard, A. (2000) 'Why Small Enterprises Invest Abroad: The Case of Four Australian with U.S. Operations', Journal of Small Business Management, July.

Ghauri, P. (2004) 'Designing and Conducting Case Studies in International Business Research' in Marschan-Piekkari, R. and Welch, C. (ed.) Handbook of Qualitative Research methods for International Business. Cheltenham: Edward Elgar.

Ghauri, P. and Gronhaug, K. (2005) Research Methods in Business Studies: A practical Guide. Harlow England: Prentice Hall.

Ghauri, P. and Holstius, K. (1996) 'The Role of Matching in the Foreign Market Entry Process in the Baltic State', European Journal of Marketing, 30(2), pp.75-88.

Ghemawat, P. (1991) Commitment: the Dynamic of Strategy. Free Press.

Gidens, A. (1997) 'Positivism and its critics', in Giddens, A. (ed.) Studies in Social and Political Theory, Hutchinson.

Gill, J. and Johnson, P. (1997) Research Methods for Managers. 2nd edn. London: Paul Chapman Publishing Ltd..

Goodnow, J. D. and Hansz, J. E. (1972) 'Environmental Determinants of Overseas Market Entry Strategies', Journal of International Business Studies, 3(1), p.33—50.

Gorg, H. (2000) 'Analysing Foreign Market Entry', Journal of Economic Studies, 27(3), pp. 165-181.

Greenwood, J. (1994) 'Action Research and Action Researchers: Some Introductory Consideration', Contemporary Nurse, 3(2), pp.84-92.

Griffin, R. W. and Pustay, M. W. (2005) International Business. 4th edn. Harlow: Prentice Hall.

Hakim, C. (1988) 'Women at Work: Recent Research on Women's Employment'. Work, Employment and Society, 2(1), pp. 103-113.

Hall, G. (1995) Surviving and Prospering in the Small Firm Sector. London: Routledge.

Hall, G. and Naude, P. (1998) 'Strategic Management of British SMEs: Changes in Attitide 1991-1994' in Haahti, A., Hall, G. and Donckels, R. (ed.) The Internationalization of SMEs. London: Routledge.

Hamilton, G. G. (1996) 'Competition and Organization: A Re-Examination of Chinese Business Practices', Journal of Asian Business, 12, pp. 7-20.

Hammersley, M. (1992) What's Wrong with Ethnography? London: Routledge.

Hara, G. and Kanai, T. (1994) 'Entrepreneurial Networks Across Oceans to Promote International Strategic Alliance for Small Business', Journal of Business Venturing, 9, pp.489-507.

Harmill, J. (1997) 'The Internet and International Marketing', International Marketing Review, 14(5).

Harrigan, K. R. (1983) Strategy for Vertical Integration. Heath and Company.

Harrigan, K. R. (1985) Strategies for Joint Ventures. Lexington: MA: D. C. Heath.

Harvie, C. and Lee, B. C. (2005) 'The Role of Small and Medium-Sized Enterprises in Achievingj and Sustaining Growth and Performance', Studies of Small and Medium Sizes Enterprises in East Asia Series. 3, pp.3-27.

Hedlund, G. and Kverneland, A. (1984) Investing in Japan – The Experience of Swedish Firms. Sweden: Institute of International Business.

Hennart, J. and Park, Y. (1993) 'Greenfield vs. Acquisition: The Strategy of Japanese Investors in United States', Management Science, 39(9), pp. 1054-1070.

Herrman, P. and Datta, D. K. (2002) 'CEO Successor Characteristics and the Choice of Foreign Market Entry Mode: An Empirical Study', Journal of International Business Studies, 33(3), pp. 551-569.

Herrman, P. and Datta, D. K. (2006) 'CEO Experience: Effects on the Choice of FDI Entry Mode', Journal of Management Studies, 43(4), pp. 755-778.

Hill, C. W., Hwang, W. and Kim, W. C. (1990) 'An eclectic theory of the choice of international entry mode', *Strategy Management Journal*, 11 (2), pp. 117-28.

Hoesel, R. V. (1999) *New Multinational Enterprises from Korea and Taiwan.* London: Routledge.

Hofstede, G. (1980) *Culture's Consequences: International Differences in Work-related Values.* Beverly Hills: Sage Publications.

Hofstede, G. (1986) 'Cultural Difference in Teaching and Learning', *International Journal of Intercultural Relations,* 10, pp. 301-320.

Hofstede, G. (1994) 'Defining Culture and its Four Dimensions', *European Forum for Management Development.*

Hofstede, G. (1998) 'The Business of International Business in Culture' in Buckley, P. J. and Ghauri, P.N. (ed.) *The Internationalization of the Firm: A reader.* London; Thomson Publishing Company.

Holliday, A. (2002) *Doing and Writing Qualitative Research.* London: Sage Publications.

Hollis, M. (1994) *The Philosophy of Social Science: An Introduction.* Cambridge University Press.

Holger, G. (2000) 'Analysing Foreign Market Entry: the Choice between Greenfield Investment and Acquisitions', *Journal of Economic Studies,* 27(3), pp. 165-181.

Holstein, J. A. and Gubrium, J. F. 1995) *The Active Interview.* Thousand Oaks: Sage.

Hood, N., Young, S. and Lal, D. (1994) 'Strategic Evolution within Japanese Manufacturing Plants in Europe: UK Evidence', *International Business Review,* 3(2), pp. 97-122.

Huang, P. J. (1988) 'Multinationals Strategy Choice of Institutional Mode: A Decision Mode for Market Entry'. Doctoral Thesis, Graduate School of Management Michigan State University.

Huang, L. (2000) 'Choice of Market Entry Mode in Emerging Markets: Influences on Entry Strategy in China', *Journal of Global Marketing,* 14(1/2), pp.83-109.

Hughes, J. A. and Sharrock, W. W. (1997) *The Philosophy of Social Research.* 3rd Edn. Longman.

Hunt, S. D. (2002) *Foundations of Marketing Theory.* New York: M. E. Sharpe.

Hymer, S. (1960) 'The International Operation of National Firms: A Case of Direct Investment'. Unpublished Doctoral Thesis, MIT.

Hymer, S. (1976) *The International Operations of National Firms: A Study of Direct Investment.* Massachusetts: MIT Press.

Isobe, T., Makino, S. and Montgomery, D.V. (2000) 'Resource Commitment, Entry Timing, and Market Performance of Foreign Direct Investments in Emerging Economies: the Case of Japanese International Joint Ventures in China'. *Academy of Management Journal,* 43(3), pp. 468-484.

Johanson, J. and Vahlne, J. E. (1992) 'Management of Foreign Market Entry', *Scandinavian International Business Review, ,* 1(3), pp. 9-27.

Johanson, J. and Mattsson, L. G. (1988) ' Internationalization in Industrial System – A Network Approach' in Hood, N. and Vahlne, J. E. (ed.) *Strategies in Global Competition.* London: Groom Helm.

Johanson, J. and Vahlne, J. E. (1990) 'The Mechanism of International', *International Marketing Review,* 7(4), pp. 11-24.

Johanson, J. and Vahlne, J. E. (1977) 'The international process of the firm-a Mode of knowledge development and increasing foreign market commitments'. *Journal of International Business Studies,* 7(4), pp. 23-32.

Johanson, J. and Wiedersheim-Paul, F. (1995) 'The Internationalization of the Firm: Four Swedish Cases', *Journal of Management Studies,* October, pp. 305-322.

Johanson, P. and Duberley, J. (2003) 'Reflexivity in Management Research', *Journal of Management Studies,* 40(5), pp.1279-1301.

Johanson, P. and Duberley, J. (2000) *Understanding Management Research: An Introduction to Epistemology.* London: Sage.

Johnson, G., Scholes, K. and Whittington, R. (2006) *Exploring Corporate Strategy.* 7edn. London: Prentice Hall.
Johnson, J. M. (2001) 'In-depth Interviewing' in Holstein, J. A. and Gubrium, J. F. (ed.) *Handbook of Interview Research: Context & Method.* Thousand Oaks: Sage.

Johnson, B. R. (1990) 'Toward a Multidimentional Model of Entrepreneuriship: The Case of Achievement Motivation and the Entrepreneur', *Entrepreneurship Theory and Practice,* 14(3), pp. 39-54.

Jones, G. R. and Hill, C. W. L. (1988) 'Transaction Cost Analysis of Strategy-Structure Choice', *Strategic Management Journal,* 9, pp. 159-172.

Jones, M. V. (1999) 'The internationalisation of Small High-Technology Firms', *Journal of International Marketing,* 7(4), pp.15-41.

Kamel, S.M. and Bryton, J. (2002) *A Comparison of Small and Medium Sized Enterprises in Europe and in the USA.* London: Routledge.

Karagozoglu, N. and Lindell, M. (1998) 'Internationalisation of Small and Medium-sized Technology-Based firms: An Exploratory Study', *Journal of Small Business Management*, 36(1), pp.44-59.

Katsikeas, C. S. and Piercy, N. F. (1996) 'Determinants of Export Performance in a European Context', *European Journal of Marketing*, 30(6), pp.6-35.

Kedia, B. and Chockar, J. (1986) 'Factors Inhibiting Exporting Performance of the Firm – An Empirical Investigation', *Management International Review*, 26(4), PP. 33-43.

Khan, R. and Cannell, C. F. (1957) *The Dynamics of Interviewing.* New York: John Wiley.

Kindleberger, C. P. (1969) *American Business Abroad.* New Haven.

Kill, C. W. and Hwang, P. (1992) 'Global Strategy and Multinational Entry Mode Choice', *Journal of International Business Studies*, 23, pp.29-53.

Kim, D, J. and Kogut, B. (1996) 'Technological Platforms and Diversification', *Organization Science*, 7(3), pp. 283-301.

King, A. and Tucci, C. L. (2002) 'Incumbent Entry into New Market Niches: The Role of Experience and Managecial Choice in the Creation of Dynamic Capabilities', *Management Science*, 48(2), pp. 171-186.

King, N. (2004) 'Using Templates in the Thematic Analysis of Text' in Cassell, C. and Symon, G. (ed.) *Essential Guide to Qualitative Methods in organizational Research.* London: Sage.

Koch, A. J. (2001a) 'Factors influencing market and entry mode selection: developing The MEMS model', *Marketing Intelligence and Planning*, 19(5), pp.351-361

Koch, A. J. (2001b) 'Selecting Overseas Markets and Entry Modes: Two Decision Processes or One?' *Marketing Intelligence and Planning*, 19(5), pp. 65—75.

Kogut, B. (1988) 'Joint Ventures: Theoretical and Empirical Perspectives', *Strategic Management Journal*, 9, pp.319-312.

Kogut, B. and Singh, H. (1988) 'The Effect of National Culture on the Choice of Entry Mode', *Journal of International Business Studies*, 19(3), pp. 411-432.

Kogut, B. and Zander, U. (1993) 'Knowledge of the Firm and the Evolutionary Theory of the Multinational Corporation', *Journal of International Business Studies*, 24(4), pp. 625-645.

Kojima, K. (1978) *Direct Foreign Investment.* London: Croom Helm.

Kown, Y. and Konopa, L. J. (1993) 'Impact of Host County Market Characteristics in the Choice of Foreign Market Entry Mode', *International Marketing Review*, 10(2), pp.60-66.

Krueger, R. and Casey, M. (2000) *Focus Groups: A Practival Guide for Applied Research.* 3rd edn. Thousand Oaks: Sage.

Kulkarni, S. P. (2001) 'The Influence of Type of Uncertainty on the Mode of International Entry', *American Business Review,* 19(1), pp.94-101.

Kumar, R. (1999) *Research Methodology.* 2nd Edn. London: Sage Publications.

Kumar, V. and Subramaniam, V. (1997) 'A Contingency Framework for the Mode Entry Decision', *Journal of World Business,* 32(1), pp. 53-72.

Lalls, S. *et al* (1983) *The New Multinationals: The Spread of Third World Enterprises.* John Wiley & Sons.

Lampert, S. I. and Jaffe, E. D. (1996) 'Country of Origin Effects on International Market Entry', *Journal of Global Marketing,* 10(2), pp. 27-52.

Lecraw, D. J. (1984) 'Bargaining power, ownership, and profitability of transactional Corporations in developing countries'. *Journal of International Business Studies,* 15(Spring/Summer), pp.27-43.

LeCompte, N. and Goetz, J. (1982) 'Problems of Reality in Ethnographic Research', *Review of Educational Research,* 52, pp.31-60.

Lee, J. and Chen, J. (2003) 'Internationalization, Local Adaptation, and Subsidiary's Entrepreneurship: An Exploratory Study on Taiwanese Manufacturing Firms in Indonesia and Malaysia', *Asia Pacific Journal of Management,* 20(1), pp.27-50.

Lee, H. Y. (1986) 'The Implications of Reform for Ideology, State and Society in China', *Journal of International Affairs,* 39(2), pp. 77-90.

Lincoln, Y. S. and Guba, E. G. (1985) *Naturalistic Inquiry.* London: Sage.

Lindqvist, M. (1988) ' International of Small Technology-Based Firms: Three Illustrative Case studies on Swedish Firms', *Stockholm School of Economics Research Paper,* 88/15.

Lindzey, G. (1985) *The Handbook of Social Psychology.* New York: Random House.

Liu, X. H., Buck, T., and Shu, C. (2005) 'Chinese Economic Development, the Next Stage: Outward FDI?' *International Business Review,* 14, pp. 97-115.

Lu, J. W. and Beamish, P. (2001) 'The Internationalization and Performance of SMEs', *Strategic Management Journal.* 22, pp. 565-586.

Lu, Y. (1996) *Management Decision-Making in Chinese Enterprises.* New York: ST. Martin's Press.

Luckman, T. (1967) *Thee Social Construction of Reality.* New York: Anchor books.

Luo, Y. (1997) 'Guanxi and Performance of Foreign-Invested Enterprises in China: An Empirical Inquiry', *Management International Review,* 37(1), pp. 51-70.

Luo, Y. (2001) 'Determinants of Entry in an Emerging Economy: A Multilevel Approach', *Journal of Management Studies,* 38(3), pp.443-444.

Luo, Y. (2002) *Multinational Enterprises in Emerging Markets.* Denmark: Copenhagen Business School Press.

Luostarinen, R. (1979) *International of the Firms.* Helsinki.

Lynch, R. (2006) *Corporate Strategy.* 4th edn. Harlow: Prentice Hall.

Madhok, A. (1997) 'Cost, Value and Foreign Market Entry Mode: The Transaction and the Firm', *Strategic Management Journal,* 18, pp. 39-61.

Maffat, L. and Wood, P. A. (1995) 'Internationalization by Business Services: A Methodological Critique of Foreign-Market Entry-mode Choice', *Environment and Planning.* 27, pp.683-697.
Makino, N. and Kent. E. (2000) 'National Culture, Transaction Costs, and the Choice Between Joint Venture and Wholly Owned Subsidiary', *Journal of International Business Studies,* 31(4), pp. 705-713.

Malhotra, N. K., Ulgado, F. M. And Agarwal, J. (2003) 'Internationalization and Entry Mode: A Multi-theoretical Framework and Research Propositions', *Journal of International Marketing,* 11(4), p. 1-31.

Manson, J. (2002) *Quality Researching.* 2nd edn. London: Sage.

Marshall, G (1994) *The Concise Oxford Dictionary of Sociology.* Oxford: Oxford University Press.

Marshall, C. and Rossman, G. B. (1995), *Design Qualitative Research,* 2nd edn. London: Sage.

Marshall, C. and Rossman, G. B. (1999) *Designing Qualitative Research.* 3rd edn. London: Sage.

May, T. (2002) *Qualitative Research in Action.* London: Sage.

Maynard, M. (1994) *Methods, Practice and Epistemology: the debate about feminism and research.* Taylor & Francis.

McClelland, D. C. (1987) 'Characteristics of Successful Entrepreneurs', *Journal of Creative Behavior,* 2(3), pp.19-33.

Melin, L. (1992) 'Internationalization as a Strategy Process', *Strategic Management Journal,* 13, pp. 99-118.

Meyer, K. E. (2001) 'Institutions, Transaction Costs, and Entry Mode Choice in Eastern Europe', *Journal of International Business Studies,* 32(2), pp. 357-367.

Meyer, K. E. and Estrin, S. (2001) 'Brownfield Entry in Emerging Markets', *Journal of International Business Studies,* 32(3), pp. 575-584.

Meyer, K. and Skak, A. (2002) 'Networks, Serendipity and SME Entry into Eastern Europe', *European Management Journal,* 20(2), pp.179-188.

Millinton, A. L. and Bayliss, B. T. (1990) 'The Process of Internationalization: UK companies in the EC', *Management International Review.* 30(2), pp. 151-161.

Miles, M. B. and Huberman, A, M. (1994) *Qualitative Data Analysis: An expanded sourcebook.* Thousand Oaks: Sage.

Min, H. and Melachrinoudis, E. (1996) 'Dynamic Location and Entry Mode Selection of Multinational Manufacturing Facilities Under Uncertainty: A Chance-constrained Goal Programming Approach', *International Transactions in Operational Research,* 3(1), pp. 65-76.

Mitra, D. and Golder, P. (2002) 'Whose Culture Matters? Near-Market Knowledge and Its Impact on Foreign Market Entry Timing', *Journal of Marketing Research,* 39(3), pp. 350-365.

Morgan, G. and Smircich, L. (1980) 'The Case for Qualitative Research', *Academy of Management Review,* 5(4), pp.491-500.

Morris, C. (2000) *Quantitative Approaches in Business Studies.* 5th edn. Prentice Hall.

Morrison, A., Bouquet, C. and Beck, J. (2004) 'The Next Global Wave', *Long Range Planning.* 37(1), pp.11-27.

Morsink, R. L. A. (1998) *Foreign Direct Investment and Corporate networking: A Framework for Spatial Analysis of Investment Conditions.* Cheltenham: Edward Elgar.

Mudambi, R. and Mudambi, S. M. (2002) 'Diversification and Market Entry Choices in the Context of Foreign Direct Investment', *International Business Review,* 11(1), pp. 35-55.

Murray, M. (2003) 'Narrative Psychology' in Smith, J. A. (ed.) *Qualitative Psychology.* London: Sage.

Nadin, S. and Cassell, C. (2004) 'Using Data Matrices' in Cassell, C. and Symon, G. (ed.) *Essential Guide to Qualitative Methods in Organizational Research.* London: Sage.

Nakos, G., Brouthers, K. D. and Moussetis, R. (2002) 'Entry Mode Choice of SMEs in Central and Eastern Europe', *Entrepreneurship: Theory & Practice.* 27 (1), pp. 47-63.

Nakos, G., Brouthers, K. D. (2002) 'Entry Mode Choice of SMEs in Central and Eastern Europe'.

Nolan, P. (2001) *China and the Global Economy.* Basingstoke: Palgrave.

Nordstrom, K. A. and Vahlne, J. E. (1992) 'Is the Globe Shrinking? Psychical Distance and the Establishment of Swedish Sales Subsidiary', *International Trade and Finance Associations' Annual Conference.*

Okeshott, L. (1998) *Essential Quantitative Methods for Business, Management and Finance.* Macmillan Business.

O'Gorman, C. and McTiernan, L. (2000) 'Factors Influencing the Internationalisation Choices of Small and Medium—Sized Enterprises: The Case of the Irish Hotel Industry', *Enterprise & Innovation Management Studies,* 1(2), pp.141—151.

O'Grady, S. and Lane, H. W. (1996) 'The Psychic Distance Paradox', *Journal of International Business Studies,* Second Quarter, pp. 309-333.

Ohmae, K. (1985) *Triad Power: The Coming Shape of Global Competition.* New York: The Free Press.

Padmanabhan, P. and Cho, K. R. (1996) 'Ownership Strategy for a Foreign Affiliate: An Empirical Investigation of Japanese Firms', *Marketing Intelligence and Planning,* 19(3), pp.153-161.

Palenzuela, V. A. and Bobillo, A. M. (1999) 'Transaction Costs and Bargaining Power: Entry Mode Choice in Foreign Markets', *Multinational Business Review,* 7(1), pp.62-75.

Pan, Y. and Tse, D. K. (2000) 'The Hierarchical Model of Market Entry Modes', *Journal of International Business Studies,* 31(4), pp.535-554.

Pan, Y. (1995) 'Entering China through Equity Joint Ventures', *Journal of Asian Business,* 10(2), pp. 97-108.

Patton, M. Q. (1990) *Qualitative Evaluation and Research Methods.* Newbury Park: Sage.

Papadopoulos, N. (1988) 'Inventory, Taconomy and Assessment of Methods for International Market Selection', *International Marketing Review,* Autumn, pp.38-51.

Pearson, M. M. (1991) *Joint Ventures in the People's Republic of China.* NJ: Princeton University Press.

Phillips, E. M. and Pugh, D. S. (1992) *How to Get a PhD.* 2nd edn. Milton Keynes: Open University Press.

Pleitner, H. J., Brunner, J. And Habersaat, M. (1998) 'Forms and Extent of Success Factors: the Case of Switzerland' in Haahti, A., Hall, G. and Donckels, R. (ed.) *The Internationalization of SMEs*. London: Routledge.

Porter, M. P. (1996) 'What is Strategy?' *Harvard Business Review*, November/December, pp. 61-78.

Pratten, C. (1991) *The Competitiveness of Small Firms*. Cambridge: Cambridge University Press.

Quelch, J. A. and Klein, l. R. (1996) 'The Internet and International Marketing', *Sloan Management Review*, Spring, pp. 60-75.

Redding, S. G. (1990) *Spirit of Chinese Capitalism*. Berlin: De Gruyter.

Reftery, J., Mcgeorge, D. and Walters, M. (1997) 'Breaking up Methodological Monopolies: A Multi-paradigm Approach to Construction Management Research', *Construction Management and Economics* 15(3), pp. 291-297.

Reid, S. (1984) 'Information Acquisition and Export Entry Decision in Small Firms', *Journal of Business Research*, 12, pp.141-157.

Reid, S. (1981) 'The Decision-Maker and Export Entry and Expansion', *Journal of International Business Studies*, Fall, pp. 101-112.

Reuber, A. R. and Fischer, E. (1997) 'The Influence of the Management Team's International Experience on the International Behaviours of SMEs', *Journal of International Business Studies*, 28(4), pp. 807-825.

Riesman, C. (2004) 'Analysis of Personal Narratives' in Lewis-Beck, M. S., Bryman, A. and Liao, T. F. (ed.) *The Sage Encyclopedia of Social Science Research Method*. London: Sage.

Rivoli, P. and Salorio, E. (1996) 'Foreign Direct Investment and Investment Under Uncertainty', *Journal of International Business Studies*, 27(2), pp.335-357.

Robles, F. (1994) 'International Market Entry Strategies and Performance of United States Catalog Firms', *Journal of Direct Marketing*, 8(1), pp.59-70.

Robson, C. (1993) *Real World Research: a Resource for Social Scientists and Practitioner-Researcher*. Oxford: Blackwell.

Robson, C. (2002), *Real World Research: A Research for Social Scientists and Practitioner – Researchers*, 2nd edn. Oxford: Blackwell.

Robson, S and Foster, A. (1989) *Qualitative Research in Action*. Edward Arnold.

Roger, H., Ghauri, P. and George, K. (2005) 'The Impact of Market Orientation on the Internationalization of Retailing Firms: Tesco in Eastern Europe', *International Review of Retail Distribution and Consumer Research.* 15(1), pp.53-74.

Root, F. R. (1987) *Entry Strategies for International Markets.* Lexington: MA.
Root, F. R. (1994) *Entry Strategies for International Markets.* San Francisco, Jossey-Bass Publishers.

Root, F. R. & Ahmed, A. A. (1978) 'The Influence of Policy Instruments on Manufacturing Direct Foreign Investment in Developing Countries', *Journal of International Business Studies,* 9(3), pp. 81-93.

Root, F. R. and Ahmed, A. A. (1979) 'Empirical Determinants of Manufacturing Direct Foreign Investment in Developing Countries', *Economic Development & Cultural Change,* 27(4), pp. 751-777.

Rudestam, K. E. and Newton, R. R. (1992) *Surviving Your Dissertation: A Comprehensive Guide to Content and Process.* Newbury Park: Sage.

Rugman, A. M. and Collinson, S. (2006) *International Business.* 4th edn. Harlow: Prentice Hall.

Ryan, A. (1984) *The Philosophy of the Social Sciences.* 3rd edn. Macmillan Publisher LTD.

Ryan, G. W. and Bernard, H. R. (2003) 'Data Management and Analysis Methods' in Denzin, N. K. and Lincoln, Y. S. (ed.) *Collecting and Interpreting Qualitative Materials.* 2nd edn. Thousand Oaks: Sage.

Sarantakos, S. (1998) *Social Research.* 2nd edn. Macmillan Press LTD.

Saunders, M., Lewis, P. and Rhornhill, A. (2000) *Research Methods for Business Students* 2nd edn. Prentice Hall.

Saunders, M., Lewis, P. and Rhornhill, A. (2003) *Research Methods for Business Students* 3nd edn. Prentice Hall.

Saunders, M., Lewis, P. and Rhornhill, A. (2006) *Research Methods for Business Students* 3nd edn. Prentice Hall.

Schwandt, T. A. (2000) 'Constructivist, Interpretivist Approaches to Human Inquiry' in Denzin, N. K. and Lincoln, (ed.) Y. S. *Handbook of Qualitative Research.* Thousand Oaks: Sage.

Sekaran, U. (2000) *Research Methods for Business: A Skill-Building Approach.* 3rd edn. John Wiley & Sons, Inc..

Sexton, D. L. and Bowman-Upton, N. (1990) 'Female and Male Entrepreneurs: Psychological Characteristics and Their Role in Gender Discrimination', *Journal of Business Venturing,* 5(1), pp. 29-36.

Shama, A. (1995) 'Entry Strategies of U.S. Firms to the New Independent State, Baltic States, and Eastern European', *California Management Review,* 37(3), pp.90-109.

Shan, W. (1990) 'An Empirical Analysis of Organizational Strategies by Entrepreneurial High-Technology Firms', *Strategic Management Journal,* 11, pp. 129-139.

Sharma, D. D. (1988) 'Overseas Market Entry Strategy: the Technical Consultancy Firms'. *Journal of Global Marketing,* 2(2), pp. 89-110.

Sharma, D. D. and Johanson, J. (1987) 'Technical Consultancy in Internationalization', *International Marketing Review,* Winner, pp. 20-29.

Shi, Y., Ho, P. and Siu, W. (2001) 'Market Entry Mode Selection: The Experience of Small Hong Kong Firms Investing in China', *Asia Pacific Business Review,* 8(1), pp.19-41.

Sideri, S. (1995) 'The Economic Relations of China and Asian Pacific with Europe', *Development Policy Review,* 13, pp.219-246.

Silverman, D. (1993) *Interpreting Qualitative Data: Methods for Analysing Talk, Text and Interaction,* 2nd edn. London: Sage Publications.

Sim, A. B. and Pandian, J. R. (2003) 'Emerging Asian MNEs and Their Internationalization Strategies-case study Evidence on Taiwanese and Singaporean Firms', *Asia Pacific Journal of Management,* 20(1), pp.51-72.

Simon, H. A. (1955) 'A Behaviour Model of Rational Choice', *Quarterly Journal of Economics,* 69, pp. 99-118.

Simpson, C. L. and Kujawa, D. (1974) 'The Export Decision Process: An Empirical Inquiry', *Journal of International Business Studies,* 5(1), pp. 107-117.

Singh, B. & Kogut, B. (1989) 'Industry and Competitive Effects on the Choice of Entry Mode', *Academy of Management Proceedings.* 8, pp. 116-120.

Sivakumar, K. (2002) 'Simultaneous determination of entry timing and involvement Level', *Journal of International Marketing Review.* 19(1), pp. 21-38.

Stone, I. (1999) *East Asian FDI and UK Periphery* in Garrahan, P. and Richie, J. (ed.) *East Asian Investment in Britain: Studies in Asian Pacific Business* .London: Frank Cass.

Steinbruner, J. D. (1974) *The Cybernetic Theory of Decision.* Princeton: Princeton University Press.

Stonehouse, G. *et al.* (2000) *Global and Transactional Business: Strategy and Management.* Chichester: John Wiley & Sons. LTD.

Strauss, A. and Corbin, J. C. (1998) *Basic of Qualitative Research: Techniques and Procedures for Developing Grounded theory.* 2nd edn. Thousand Oaks: Sage.

Suarez-Ortega, S. M. and Alamo-Vera, F. R. (2005) 'SMEs' Internationalization: Firms and Managerial Factors', *International Journal of Entrepreneurship Behaviour and Research,* 11(4), pp.258-279.

Sullivan, D, P, and Weaver, Gt. R. (2000) 'Cultural Cognition in International Business Research', *Management International Review,* 40(3), pp.269-297.

Sun, H. (1999) 'Entry Modes of Multinational Corporations into China's Market: A Social-Economic Analysis', *International Journal of Social Economics,* 26(5), pp. 642-660.

Taylor, C. R. and Zhou, S. (1998) 'A Transaction Cost Perspective on Foreign Market Entry Strategies', *Thunderbird International Business Review,* 40(4), pp.389-412.

Taylor, C. R., Zhou, S. and Gregory, E. (2000) 'Foreign Market Entry Strategies of Japanese MNCs', *International Marketing Review,* 17(2-3).

Tse, D. K., Pan, Y. and Au, K. Y. (1997) 'How MNCs Choose Entry Modes and Form Alliances: The China experience', *Journal of International Business Studies,* 2894).

Thomas, A. S., Litschert, R. J. and Ramaswamy, K. (1991) 'The Performance Impact of Strategy-manager Coalignment: An Empirical Examination', *Strategic Management Journal,* 12, pp. 509-522.

The North East Chamber of Commerce data base (2002).

Ting, W. (1985) *Business and Technological Dynamic in Newly Industrializing Asia.* Westport: Quorum Books.

Trompenaars, F. (1993) *Riding the Waves of Culture: Understanding Cultural Diversity in Business.* London: Nicholas Brealey Publishing'.

Trochim, W. M, K. (1997) 'The Research Methods Knowledge base. Available at http://trochim.human.cornell.edu (Assessed: 15 June, 2004).

Turner, L. (1973) *Multinational Companies and the Third World.* London: Allen Lane.

Tjosvold, D. and Weicker, D. (1993) 'Cooperative and Competitive Networking by Entrepreneurs: A Critical Incident Study', *Journal of Small Business Management,* 31(1), pp.11-21.

Ulgado, F. M., Yu, C. and Negandhi, A. R. (1994) 'Multinational Enterprise from Asia Developing Countries: Management and Organizational Characteristics', *International Business Review,* 3(2), pp. 123-133.

UNCTAD (1997) *Sharing Asia's Dynamism: Asian Direct Investment in the European Union.* United Nationals publications.

UNCTAD, (2004) *World Investment Report 2004: The Shift towards Services.* New York and Geneva: United Nations. United Nations publication,

Vernon, R. (1966) 'International Investment and International Trade in the Product Cycle', *Quarterly Journal of Economics,* 80, pp. 190-207.

Vernon, R. and Wells, L. T. (1976) *Managing in the International Economy.* NJ: Prentice-Hall.

Vernon, R. (1979) 'The Product Cycle Hypoprojectin a New International Environment', *Oxford Bulletin of Economics and Statistics.* 41, pp. 255-267.

Vernon, R. (1983) 'Organizational and Institutional Responses to International Risk' in Herring, R. J. (ed.) *Managing International Risk.* Cambridge: Cambridge University Press.

Warren, C. A. B. (2001) 'Qualitative Interview' in Holstein, J. A. and Gubrium, J. F. (ed.) *Handbook of Interview Research: Context & Method.* Thousand Oaks: Sage.

Welch, L. S. and Luostarinen, R. (1988), 'Internationalisation: Evolution of a Concept', *Journal of General Management,* 14(2), pp.34-55.

Wells, L. T. (1977) 'The Internationalization of Firms from the Developing Countries' in Agmon, T. and Kindleberger, C. P. (ed.) *Multinational for Small Countries.* Cambridge: MIT Press.

Wells, L. T. (1978) ''Foreign Investment from the Third World: The Experience of Chinese Firms from Hong Kong', *Columbia Journal of World Business,* Spring, pp.39-49.

Wells, L. T. (1983) *Third World Multinationals: The Rise of Foreign Investment from Developing Countries.* Cambridge: MIT Press.

Wells, L. T. (1984) 'Multinationals from Asian Developing Countries' in Moxon, R. W., Roehl, T. and Truitt, J. F. (ed.) *Research in International Business and Finance.* Greenwich: JAI Press.

Wells, L. T. (1998) 'Multinationals and the Developing Countries', *Journal of International Business Studies,* 29(1), pp. 101-114.

Wengraf, T. (2001) *Qualitative Research Interview.* London: Sage Publication.

Wernerfelt, B. (1984) 'A Resource-Based View of the Firm', *Strategic Management Journal.* 5, pp.171-180.

Wheeler, C. and Jones, M. (1996) 'Market Entry Modes and Channel of Distribution in the UK Machine Tool Industry', *European Journal of Marketing,* 30(4), pp.40-57.

Whitelock, J. (2002) 'Theories of Internationalisation and Their Impact on Market Entry', *The Journal of International Marketing Review,* 19(4), pp. 342-347.

Whitelock, J. (1995) 'Influence of Competitors and Source of Information in Market Entry and Choice of Entry Mode', *European Journal of Marketing,* 29(5), pp. 75-76.

Whitelock, J. and Munday, P. (1993) 'Inward-Outward Connections in Internationalization', *Journal of International Marketing,* 1(4), pp. 19-30.

Wild, J., Wild, K. L. and Han, J. C. Y. (2000) *International Business: An Integrated Approach.* New Jersey: Prentice Hall.

Williams, D. (1999) 'Foreign Manufacturing Firms in the UK: Effects on Employment, Output and Supplier Linkages', *European Business Review,* 99(6), pp.393-398.

Williamson, O. E. (1985) *The Economic Institutions of Capitalism.* New York: The Free Press.

Williamson, O. E. and Ouchi, W. G. (1981) 'The Markets and Hierarchies and Visible Hand Perspectives' In V. A. and Joyce, W. (ed.) *Perspectives on Organization Design and Behavior.* New York: Wiley.

Wolcott, H. F. (2001) *Writing up Qualitative Research.* 2nd Edn. Thousand Oaks: Sage Publications.

Wolff, J. A. and Pett, T. L. (2000) 'Internationalization of Small Firms: An Examination of Export Competitive Patterns', *Journal of Small Business Management,* 38(2), pp.34-47.

Woodcock, C. P., Beamish, P. W. and Makino, S. (1994) 'Ownership-Based Entry Mode Strategies and International Performance', *Journal of International Business Studies,* 25(2), pp. 253-273.

Xiang, Y. (2001) *Go Abroad: New Hope for Chinese Firms.* Availableat http://Souhu.com/foreign. (Accessed: 14 November, 2004).

Xiao, Q. (2000) Foreign Trade: *How Chinese Firms Enter International Markets Successfully.* Available at http://Souhu.com/foreign. (Accessed: 14 November, 2004).

Yan, A. and Gray, B. (1994) 'Bargaining Power, Management, Control, and Performance in United States-China Joint Ventures: A Comparative Case Study', *Academy of Management Journal,* 37(6), p. 1478—1517

Yeung, H. W. C. (1994) 'Transactional Corporation from Asian Developing Countries: Their Characteristics and Competitive Edge', *Journal of Asian Business,* 10(4), pp.17-58.

Yeung, H. W. C. (1997) 'Cooperative Strategies and Chinese Business Networks' in Yeung, H. W. (ed.) *Transnational Corporations and Business Networks: Hong Kong Firms in the ASEAN Region.* London: Routledge.

Young, S., Hood, N. and Hamill, J. (1988) *Foreign Multinationals and the British Economy*. London: Croom Helm.

Young, S. *et al.* (1989) *International Market Entry and Development: Strategies and Management.* Englewood Cliffs: Prentice Hall.

Zacharakis, A. L. (1997) 'Entrepreneurial Entry into Foreign Market: A Transaction Cost Perspective', *Entrepreneurship Theory and Practice,* 21(3), pp.23-39.

Zhao and Decker, (2004) 'Choice of Foreign Market Entry Mode: cognitions from Empirical and Theoretical Studies', Available at http://Bieson.Ub.uni-bielefeld. (Assessed: 14 November, 2005).

Zhuo, D., Li, S. and Tse, D. K. (2002) 'The Impact of FDI on the Productivity of Domestic Firms: the Case of China', *International Business Review*, 11, pp. 465-484.

Zikmund, W. G. (2000) *Business Research Methods.* 6th edn. The Dryden Press.

Zimmerer, T. W. and Scarborough, N. M. (2002) *Essential of Entrepreneurship and Small Business Management,* 3rd edn. New Jersey: Pearson Education International.

Zweig, D. (2002) *Internationalizing China: Domestic Interests and Global Linkage.* Cornell: Cornell University Press.

Appendix I

Types of Entry Modes -- Focus Group Interview

In order to give fully understanding of the SME managers' strategic market entry mode choices, your knowledge of terminologies of entry modes developed in the existing literature are examined. Please complete the following mini questionnaire that takes only maximum 3 minutes. Thanks for your assistance.

How are you familiar with the following entry modes? -- (Please check where appropriate)

	Never heard	Heard	Familiar	Very Familiar
1. Indirect Export	☐	☐	☐	☐
2. Direct export	☐	☐	☐	☐
3. Licensing	☐	☐	☐	☐
4. Franchising	☐	☐	☐	☐
5. Piggyback	☐	☐	☐	☐
6. Turnkey agreement	☐	☐	☐	☐
7. Joint venture	☐	☐	☐	☐
8. Local assembly	☐	☐	☐	☐
9. Merge and acquisition	☐	☐	☐	☐
10. Sole manufacturing subsidiary	☐	☐	☐	☐

Interview Guide

1. Tell me about your business, including your parent company and your foreign venture (s).

2. Apart from the UK, does (did) your parent company ever invest in other Western developed countries, If so, where are (were) they?

3. Why are you interested in investing in Western developed countries rather than developing countries?

4. Tell me how you decided to become a foreign investor in The North of England markets.

5. How long has your business been operating in The North of England markets?

6. What market entry mode(s) did you choose when initially entering these markets? Was there anything special regarding the entry mode you chose?

7. Are you satisfied with the entry mode you chose when you initially entered The North of England markets? Why or why not?

8. Will you choose the same entry mode you used in the UK when considering to entry other Eastern developing countries? Why or why not?

9. Was your strategic entry decision made individually by the owner manager or by a management team collectively?

10. What competitive advantages do you think your company has? How did these advantages affect your market entry mode choices?

11. Were there any particular strategic goals when entering this market? If so, how did that affect your entry mode choices?

12. Tell me about the decision maker's personal profile (may be yourself). How do you describe the decision maker's personality?

13. What is the nature of your products? Did that affect your entry mode choices when entering the North East of England?

14. How do you describe cultural differences between British and Chinese?

15. Have these cultural differences been taken into account in your market entry mode choices? Why and how?

16. Have you had any personal connections or business relationships with somebody (or some organisations) in the UK before your entry? If so, did these relationships affect your entry mode choices? Why and how?

17. Do you consider that firm-size is 'a constraint' or 'an advantage' when you decided to enter The North of England markets? Why?

18. What was the process like when you decide your entry mode choices?

19. What was the most difficult thing you encountered when you were making your entry mode selection? What other problems have you had in deciding your initial entry mode choices?

20. Are there any further comments or suggestions which you want to give to other Chinese SME managers who are going to invest the Western developed countries?